Yannis Ritsos: Collected Studies

M000207054

PETER BIEN is Emeritus Professor of English and Comparative Literature at Dartmouth College. Author of over twenty books of translations and criticism on modern Greek literature, he is the translator into English of Myrivilis's *Life in the Tomb*, Kazantzakis's *The Last Temptation, Saint Francis*, and *Report to Greco*. His two-volume study, *Kazantzakis: Politics of the Spirit*, has been published by Princeton University Press and also in Greek by the University Presses of Crete. He has recently completed an edition of Kazantzakis's "Selected Letters" to be published in 2011 by Princeton University Press. Peter Bien is former president of the Modern Greek Studies Association and former editor of the *Journal of Modern Greek Studies*.

To Gazi,
hoping that this will
help him to know Ritsos
a little better than
before.

Peter Bien
Nov. 11, 2017

Other Books by Peter Bien

Peter Bien

YANNIS RITSOS:
COLLECTED STUDIES & TRANSLATIONS

Red Dragonfly Press — Northfield, Minnesota — 2011

ISBN 978-1-890193-44-7

Library of Congress Control Number: 2011931023

Original Greek texts reprinted by permission of Kedros
   from the fifteen volume collected poems of Yannis Ritsos

Cover painting by Jean-Germain Drouais, 'Philoctetes,' 1786-1788,
   Oil on canvas, 233 x 173.5 cm, Chartres, Musée des beaux-arts
   courtesy of Wikimedia Commons

Back cover painting by El Greco, 'The Burial of the Count of Orgaz,'
   courtesy of Wikimedia Commons

Designed and typeset by Scott King at Red Dragonfly Press
   text in Minion Pro, a digital type designed by Robert Slimbach
   display in RTF Cadmus, a digital type designed by Jim Rimmer

Printed in the United States of America
   on 30% recycled stock
   by BookMobile, a wind-powered company

Published by Red Dragonfly Press
   press-in-residence at the Anderson Center
   P. O. Box 406
   Red Wing, MN 55066

For more information and additional titles visit our website
   www.reddragonflypress.org

Contents

PART ONE

STUDIES

1. Introduction to *Yannis Ritsos: Selected Poems*

SPEAKERS OF ENGLISH HAVE APPRECIATED the Irish literary revival almost since its inception, but have been much slower to recognize an equally extraordinary florescence in Greece. One reason, obviously, is that Modern Greek is not only a foreign language but a "minor" one; nevertheless, more people keep learning Greek, and more translations keep appearing. Cavafy, Seferis and Kazantzakis are now widely known; Myrivilis, Palamas, Sikelianos, Elytis, not to mention younger figures such as Vassilikos, have also received some attention. How extraordinary, then, that Yannis Ritsos, who for decades has been acknowledged inside Greece as one of the undeniably major figures of her literary revival, and who has been increasingly recognized on the Continent, should be so new to the English-speaking world. And how nice to meet a fresh voice which is also a fully mature one, a "new" poet with an entire career behind him!

A few of Ritsos's poems have of course appeared recently in English and American periodicals, and a small collection, *Gestures and Other Poems 1968-1970*, was published by Cape Goliard in 1971. But the present volume is the first attempt to offer, in English translation, a general and representative selection of Ritsos's work which aspires to give a sense of this poet in his totality. When we realize the extent of Ritsos's writing (the three-volume *Ποιήματα 1930-1960*, runs to 1,500 pages and is itself only a selection) we can appreciate the translator's difficulty in choosing what to include. Anyone familiar with Ritsos will know at once that the present volume does not span the poet's full career chronologically. Indeed, the earliest work offered here dates from 1957, whereas Ritsos's writings go back to 1930. This means, as well, that several of the most famous poems, works that established Ritsos's reputation in Greece, are omitted. What Mr. Stangos has attempted to do, however, is to span the poet's entire career in a more subtle way: aesthetically and thematically instead of chronologically. The poems offered here as representative have been chosen to show the diversity of Ritsos's forms—in particular, the interesting combination of short poems and extremely long ones; the variety and range of his modes—elegiac, lyric, ad narrative; the fluctuation, yet deeper constancy, of his attitudes. Hopefully, the multiplicity contained in this selection will suggest its own unity and therefore be an accurate, though miniature, portrait of the artist, one that reveals an integrated poetic personality.

The poems in this volume are generally simple enough on their surface to be "available" to the average reader even on first perusal. Thus, certain individual characteristics of Ritsos's art may be perceived without difficulty, and we may then add these together in an attempt to comprehend the poet's totality. For example, even on a first reading we are immediately aware of how well Ritsos evokes the everyday life of contemporary Greece. We see before us an album of snapshots, not so much of things especially photogenic as of people, places, and events that are completely ordinary and prosaic: a quick plunge into the sea on a deserted beach; a sick man listening to music from a nearby taverna; a driver guarding the load of watermelons in his stalled lorry and combing his hair as some girls admire him on the sly; old fishermen sitting behind the brine-stained windows of a seaside café; rotting fruit; gleaming whitewash under sunlight; a woman cleaning string beans while a corpse lies in the back room; a seamstress closing her shutters at nightfall, her mouth full of pins.[1] No sooner, however, do we establish Ritsos's tireless alertness to the minutiae of life in the Greece of today than we realize his equal interest in the Greek past. Throughout his work, but especially in the collection *Repetitions* (the generic title is significant), there are poems with historical or mythical subjects—the Peloponnesian War, Theseus, Ariadne, Penelope—poems that seem quite different in tone and intent from the simple evocations of contemporary life, and that constitute a second approach to reality. If we look still further, we find that the contemporary and the historical, though separated in certain poems, are used and indeed deliberately confused in certain others, with the result that we have still a third aesthetic approach, one perhaps most characteristic of Ritsos, where apparent simplicity and apparent lucidity

---

1   See the following poems: 'Noon', 'The Day of a Sick Man', 'Working-Class Beauty', 'An Old Fisherman', 'Death at Carlovassi', 'A Three Storey House with Basement' in *Yannis Ritsos: Selected Poems* (Penguin, 1974).

coexist with mystification, complexity, even nightmare. *The Dead House* exemplifies this most strikingly, for in this Pirandellesque mélange of eras, the narrator is both an aged Electra reciting the horrendous events of her father's return to Mycenae, and an aged recluse of modern times recalling the piano and silverware of her once-elegant home, as well as the return of soldiers from some twentieth-century war, their undershirts full of lice. In the shorter poems too, a radio next to the Argives' tent at Troy, or an incongruous statue in an otherwise contemporary landscape,[2] remind us of Ritsos's ability to comprehend Hellenism in its entirety, and to use diverse elements in order to create effects that make us uneasy, despite our continuing conviction that the poetry, though more complex than we first imagined, is still simple enough to be comprehended by the average reader.

All these characteristics should also remind us of the essential role played by metaphor in Ritsos's work. Shelley, in a celebrated passage in his *A Defence of Poetry*, claims that poetic language by its very nature is "vitally metaphorical," and then goes on to define the metaphorical element in a way that bears on Ritsos: "It marks the before unapprehended relations of things and perpetuates their apprehension, until words, which represent them, become, through time, signs for portions or classes of thought instead of pictures of integral thoughts..." This definition helps us to see the various ways in which metaphor operates in Ritsos's verse, ways which correspond to the three approaches described earlier, and which, similarly, move in the direction of complexity and mystification. Insofar as Ritsos merely evokes the minutiae of everyday life, we have a splendid metaphoric capacity that aids this evocation by shocking us into strong sensual awareness. Normally, the tiredness of language and of our own powers of observation prevents us from hearing, seeing, or touching as well as we might. But when a metaphor or simile convincingly relates "before unapprehended" elements of seeming incongruity—when, for example, a shriek remains

> ...nailed in the dark corridor
> like a big fishbone in the throat of an unknown guest

---

2   See 'Necrography' and 'Recollection' in *Yannis Ritsos: Selected Poems* (Penguin, 1974).

—we hear that shriek, see that corridor, and feel the sound's entrapment as never before. This is vitally metaphorical language at its most obvious. If we move to Ritsos's historico-mythical mode and remember the key word "repetitions," we will realize that a poem such as 'After the Defeat,' ostensibly about the Peloponnesian War, is really a metaphorical treatment of other defeats more recent, with a relation established between one element that is mentioned and another that is not. The aesthetic effect of this kind of metaphor begins to be complicated, because here we are being led to an awareness of those portions or classes of events that lie beneath the individual event described. By means of metaphor, the poem offers a universal statement about history, or at least about Greek history. Lastly, insofar as Ritsos fuses and confuses the past and present, the metaphorical element becomes more subtle still. Poems employing this third approach make us uneasy because we feel that we ought to understand them, yet know that our understanding must go beyond (or beneath) either simple sensual acuity or simple historical insight: that the external world, whether present or past, is supplemented by something else. Hopefully, then, our uneasiness will enable us to see that the metaphorical linkages in such poems are between outer and inner, physical and psychic, that the external materials serve as entrées into the poet's internal fears, hopes, wounds, dreams—the configuration of his soul. And it is here, of course, that we realize to what extent the simplicity of Ritsos's work is deceptive.

In adding together these individual characteristics with the hope of comprehending the poet's totality—of feeling an integrated poetic personality—it may be most helpful to think of Ritsos as a painter rather than a writer. If nothing else, the printed words on the page speak much more to our eyes than to our ears. (I say "the printed words on the page" because the poems when *recited* properly, do indeed speak to our ears; but this auditory effect comes primarily from rhythms and euphonies, not from subject matter or imagery.) Even when sounds are evoked, the similes employed tend to be visual, as for example that shriek nailed in its corridor like a fishbone in someone's throat. More importantly, many of the poems are graphic scenes from Hellenic life— I called them "snapshots" earlier, but they are much more like paintings than photographs, because Ritsos's language adds texture, and because he is able to arrange line and color to suit his own aesthetic needs, his aim never being simply to reproduce external reality as such. Even when these scenes are complex and have a narrative plot, so that one might wish to speak of Ritsos as a storyteller or dramatist rather than a painter, the poems are still essentially graphic and relate more to the pictorial than the theatrical arts, because the complexity—the unfolding detail of the narrative—is captured in a single moment and fixed, as on an ancient frieze or urn. In certain at the more subtly pictorial works, the point may not lie in the narration at all. 'Of the Sea,' for example, introduces us to a man cutting up a fish on the wharf. There is much blood involved, and two women remark how well the reddish gore suits the man's handsome black eyes. Then the focus shifts to a street above, where children are weighing out fish and coal on the same pair of scales. If this poem were a snapshot we would justify the children on realistic grounds, and remark Ritsos's accuracy in observing the details of Greek life. If the poem were a storyteller's narrative, we would look for some rational (or even irrational) progression from the wharf to the street, some causal links between the man, women, and children. But perhaps the poem is primarily a painting. As such, it asks us not to proceed in time from the wharf to the scales, but to see both simultaneously, as when we view the two levels of an El Greco, or of a Byzantine icon. Furthermore, it asks us to note, as the primary "meaning" of the poem, nothing more than a visual metaphor marking the before unapprehended relation between the red and black below, emphasized to such a degree by the women, and the red and black above—bloody fish and sooty coal being weighed on the same pair of scales. In short, the poem challenges us to see better. Ritsos, having responded to life with a painter's eye, gives us a small equivalent for life and asks us to respond in the same way.

The more one explores Ritsos's work in terms of this analogy with painting, the more one senses how the poet operates, what drives him, where his uniqueness lies. He is considered rare, for example, because he cultivates both long and short forms, and because he often works simultaneously on both. But the short poems are either distillations from the longer ones or preparatory sketches: an archive of experiments, ideas and observations that will be put to subsequent use in a "grand canvas." (One thinks as well of the epiphanies of that other eye-oriented artist, James Joyce—sudden spiritual manifestations, "whether in the vulgarity of speech or of gesture or in a memorable phase of the mind itself," obsessionally recorded and then systematically inserted in the larger works.) Perhaps the nature of sketches is that they should be suppressed, and indeed critics tend to accuse Ritsos of publishing too much, especially when they compare him to a writer at the other extreme, Cavafy, whose sanctioned works fit within one thin volume. Yet Cavafy, for all his greatness, lacked Ritsos's compulsion to observe and register every nuance of external reality; his imagination was dramatic and historical rather than pictorial, and therefore his sketches, unlike Ritsos's, could not be preserved simply as witnesses, however slight or tentative, to the voraciousness of an eye preying continually on life's colors and forms. The analogy with painting helps us to understand Ritsos's extraordinary prolificness (a poem a day, sometimes several in a day) as well as his decision to publish so extensively, because although not every one of these poems can be a masterpiece, there is no more reason to discard them than there would be to destroy, say, a tiny, hurried sketch of an ugly harridan by Rembrandt, or a sculptor's repeated attempts, with paper and charcoal, to get the shape of a hand just right before attempting it in marble. If we apply the analogy with painting we begin to realize that Ritsos's value lies not so much in those particularly successful poems, large or small, that will become or have already become anthology pieces, as in the totality of his work including the slighter poems, for this totality is what demonstrates most unmistakably his extraordinary aesthetic drive: the artist's urge to observe life, record it, transform everything into beauty.

It would be wrong, however, to apply the pictorial analogy too narrowly lest it darken and distort rather than illuminate. The emphasis on graphic representation, with the eye focused on *external* reality, gives us an incomplete Ritsos, one much more limited than the poet displayed in this volume. I have already stressed that Ritsos's simplicity is deceptive, and that perhaps his most characteristic poems are precisely those in which apparent lucidity coexists with mystification. If he is a realist he is equally a surrealist; indeed, one of his favorite practices is to give us a perfectly observed scene that suddenly, at the end, turns insane: for example a seaside "barbershop" where fishermen walk in one door to be shaved, and then walk out the other with "long reverent beards." Or we have the deliberate confusion of historical eras already mentioned, or poems in which the realistic element is more or less effaced in favor of dream-vision or nightmare ('Way of Salvation' and 'Association' are examples). Yet even in the most mystifying of the poems, the visual quality perseveres; there is always a scene, a graphic concreteness, and this leads us to extend the pictorial analogy rather than to abandon it. What we must realize is that Ritsos's aesthetic drive—the need to observe perpetually and to create on the basis of that observation—has directed his vision inward as well as outward. In this he is of course hardly singular; one might say that the dominant trend in both poetry and prose during Ritsos's formative period between the two World Wars was this inwardness. Far from being eccentric, he exhibits characteristics that place him within the dominant "ism" of that time: expressionism, which has been defined as "a probing search for a deep emotional reality behind appearances—a reality that the artist finds by observing his own subjective reactions, and for which he then fashions an adequate and equivalent formal means to evoke a similar response in the viewer."[3] Ritsos is not just an expressionist—like many writers or painters with long careers he has progressed through various styles, and like any artist of true worth, must be defined ultimately only in terms of himself—yet to consider him part of this school helps to remind us of the degree to which he works from subjective reality, looks inward, establishes metaphors that mark the relations between matter and psyche and that become signs not only for the inner landscape of one particularly sensitive man, but for all men who share Ritsos's love of life and who have been injured, as he has, by forces that deny life. In short, as he wrote in 1946 in a poem called 'The Meaning of Simplicity,'

> I am behind simple things, hiding, so that you may find me;
> if you do not find me, you will find the things,
> will touch what I touched with my hand;
> the tracks of our hands will converge.
>
> . . .
> Each word is an outlet
> for a meeting (often postponed).
> The word is real when it insists upon the meeting.[4]

---

3   Peter Selz, *Emil Nolde* (New York: Museum of Modern Art, 1963), p. 38.

4   See *Ποιήματα Β'*, p. 453.

This simple statement about simplicity helps us to find the complexity lurking behind Ritsos's work. His poems either direct us inward to a psyche obscured by the outward things described, or direct us outward to an external reality validated by the poet's touch. They actualize the ideal and at the same time idealize the actual. Their energy is vitally metaphorical in that they are always arranging meetings between opposites, whether those opposites be self and other, psyche and matter, poet and reader, or subject and object. Yet all this multiplicity and complexity is unified within an integral personality, because the poet Ritsos, whether turning outward or inward, whether impersonal in approach or intensely personal, whether definite in his moral positions or radically indefinite in front of life's intricacy, is always a bridge. His career has been a relentless insistence upon meeting.

Since the method of this volume is to provide a representative selection of Ritsos's poems on aesthetic and thematic rather than chronological grounds, and since the poems here offered cluster in the last third of Ritsos's career, it is appropriate that we attempt, however telegraphically, to survey the poet's background and development. Not surprisingly, this survey will lead both inward to Ritsos's personal life and outward to the political life of his country and era.

Whichever way we look, the story is not a happy one. The great calamity of Greek life, the defeat in Asia Minor, occurred in 1922 when Ritsos was thirteen years old. His father, a well-to-do landowner in Monemvasia, was ruined by this event, and Ritsos spent his adolescence in the decaying family mansion (cf. *The Dead House*) in an atmosphere of sickness and death. His mother and brother had both died of tuberculosis a year before the Asia Minor catastrophe; after it, his father went insane, as did one of his sisters, somewhat later. Ritsos, having finished his secondary schooling, moved in 1925 to an Athens swollen with destitute refugees from Anatolia, all looking for work. After short spells as a typist in a law firm, a clerk for a notary public, and a calligrapher producing law diplomas, he too contracted tuberculosis and was forced to spend three years in the Sotiria Sanatorium in Athens, followed by an additional cure in Crete. Returning to the capital and unable to secure any other employment, he finally placed himself—ashamedly—as a dancer in a theatrical troupe. But these setbacks did not debilitate Ritsos's spirit. At a time (1928) when another Greek poet, Karyotakis, committed suicide out of despair with himself and the world, Ritsos was finding ways to sustain himself. These were two: poetry and socialist revolution. His first slim volume, *Tractor*, in which he collected poems from the period 1930-34, begins with a call to Mother Poetry to receive him, and ends with effusions against a rotten, decadent society that will doubtless abuse and insult him and his verses: the mirror in which the common people will finally discern their true features. Between this prologue and epilogue are excruciating and almost embarrassingly personal poems about his own humiliation by the "hordes of barbarians" who surround him; about his father, incarcerated in an asylum while his son addresses him wearily from the Sotiria Sanatorium; about the acolyte of Art, Beauty, and Ideas who is forced to rattle a tambourine for a few drachmas. There are also hymns to Marx, Engels, and Russia, as well as calls for one world in which all men will be brothers.[5] The same dual orientation—personal and political—continues into Ritsos's next volume, *Pyramids*, published in 1935. An impassioned elegy dedicated to his sister uses the occasion of her deteriorating mental condition to speak of the illness that ravaged the entire family; another elegy directed at his own unhappy boyhood ("Oh, I do not remember ever being young; / Like a paralyzed old man I would hide indoors reading ancient books...") concludes with a vision of himself as a common soldier among the ranks of the workers, fighting on their behalf with "lyre and knowledge."[6]

These early collections are the journeywork of a precocious and gifted youth who still had not found his distinctive voice. The dedications—to Karyotakis, Sikelianos, Palamas—show that Ritsos was reading in contemporary Greek literature and looking for models; the poetic forms—sonnets, impeccable hendecasyllabic or hexametric quatrains rhymed *abab*—show that the prototypes he chose were still the traditional ones of Italian and Greek prosody. On the other hand, these early volumes are a true part of Ritsos's canon, not just juvenilia, because they do establish his abiding attitudes and also give occasional premonitions of later techniques such as impersonal narration.

5   See *Ποιήματα Α'*, pp. 9, 59, 21-2, 13, 31, 58.
6   See ibid., pp. 82-7, 102-5.

Conversely, though he was later to don a mask of impersonality to cover the naked "I" of much of the early verse, his mature poetry has remained intensely personal and autobiographical, as can be seen in the present selection, and though the unquestioning faith in particular political saviors was to be modified later by obeisance to the word "perhaps," the remainder of his career has continued to display energetic devotion to the ultimate goals of freedom, justice, and brotherhood for all men. The unified diversity of personal/political established in the two first volumes endures in the subsequent career, as does Ritsos's vision of the role that the poet must play in society. We may also look upon these early volumes as prophesying his own destiny, for Ritsos has indeed fulfilled the responsibility he announced forty years ago when he offered himself to Mother Poetry; and society in turn, has fulfilled its "responsibility" by abusing him, insulting him—and worse.

These early years, though still scarred by the débâcle of 1922 and its social and economic consequences, were excitingly fruitful ones in Greek intellectual circles. The nationalistic afflatus that had sustained Palamas and his generation was no longer possible; the "Great Idea" of occupying Constantinople and re-establishing Greece as the dominant force in the eastern Mediterranean was so completely dead that everyone realized the need for new directions, new ideologies. Some turned to international communism, others to the chastened humanism of countries that had experienced an equal débâcle in 1914-18. Both turnings had consequences for poetry in Greece, helping it to renew itself. Those with allegiance to the proletariat insisted on extending the domain of "the poetic" to objects and environments meaningful to the working class (note the title, *Tractor*, of Ritsos's first volume); those with bourgeois orientations turned their attention, in a similar way, toward eliminating inflation, rhetoric, and irresponsible lyricism from Greek verse, since all of these were now out of keeping with post-1922 Greek reality. In addition, they looked abroad, to France in particular, and imported into Greece the autonomy, subjectivism, and fragmentation that was western Europe's poetic response to the breakdown of older certainties. The "generation of the thirties" in Greece, stimulated by these foreign trends (and also by the pioneering sarcasm of Karyotakis and the weary irony of Cavafy), effected an important change in Greek poetry. The great year was 1935, which saw the publication of Seferis's *Mythistorema*, the début of Elytis, and the inauguration of Greek surrealism by Embeirikos.

It is against this background that we must view Ritsos as he struggled to find his distinctive poetic voice. He found it in 1936 with *Epitaphios*, a long poem that has remained his most celebrated work and is now in its fiftieth edition. A year later he reinforced this new voice so strongly with *The Song of My Sister* that Palamas himself addressed a quatrain to Ritsos in which he hailed this bitter elegy—in it the poet laments his sister's definitive insanity—and concluded: "We step aside, Poet, that you may pass."[7] By 1937, therefore, Ritsos's career had been launched with the ultimate imprimatur. *Epitaphios* and *The Song of My Sister* taken together—one drawing from political events, the other from private—are representative of much that followed. Both, for example, are elegiac in tone and content, yet at the same time offer hope: the one affirms Revolution, the other Poetry. In both, Ritsos began to discover a way to continue the lyricism of predecessors such as Palamas, but to make this lyricism a responsible confrontation with the problems of post-1922 Greece instead of an escape into self-pity, and also to wed his lyrical impulses to the precision exemplified by anti-lyricists such as Seferis and Cavafy. In *The Song of My Sister*, furthermore, Ritsos liberated himself from rhyme and from metrical strictness, embarking on the free verse that has remained his normal vehicle. However, in neither poem did he liberate himself entirely from rhetorical élan or from what Peter Levi has aptly called "the temptation to draw his passion larger than life-size."[8] These purgations were to come later, especially when Ritsos discovered the dramatic monologue style exemplified in *The Dead House* and when, in the shorter pieces, he began deliberately to squash his flights beneath a mask of impassivity, a neuter expression occasioned by disdain, or tolerance, or perhaps both.

Before looking ahead, however, we must dwell a little longer on *Epitaphios*. I spoke earlier of Ritsos's musicality: the rhythms and euphonies that make his work auditory, when recited, as well as visual. The poem is lyrical in the basic sense of that term: "meant to be sung." Robert Frost once declared that a true poem memorizes itself; by analogy we might say that a true lyric sings itself, hankers after a melody—and *Epitaphios* does precisely this, its

---

7   See *Ποιήματα Α΄*, p. 185.
8   *The Times Literary Supplement*, 10 March 1972, p. 273.

words seemingly vaulting off the printed page in order to dance upon a musical staff. What is crucial to note is that Ritsos achieved this lyricism by grafting his earlier elegiac mode, and also his political fervor, on to the root stock not now of a foreign model but of Greek folksong, the *demotikó traghoúdi*. Employing a fifteen-syllable line and rhymed couplets, he preserved the feel of this superb form: its verve engendered by weariness and hardship, its uncanny back-reaching into the racial and mythical past of a people continually invaded, cheated, and raped. Lyricism became viable because Ritsos's afflatus, controlled by the pattern and spirit of folksong, no longer projected merely his own experiences, nor buttressed the poem with fantasies of success either private, racial, or atavistic, but instead held it rooted in the palpable earth of national tragedy, yet without losing hope.

Epitaphios is overtly political, and as such has had a "political career" of its own. If nothing else, it shows us the inconstant seas—now murderous, now buoying—that Ritsos himself has had to travel. In May 1936, workers in the tobacco industry in Salonika (a city whose proletarian quarter had been one of the focal points of communism in Greece for at least a decade) went out on strike to protest unfair wage controls. Police were called in; they fired on the unarmed strikers, killing twelve and wounding hundreds. The next day the newspapers carried a photograph of a mother clothed in black, weeping over her dead son as he lay on a Salonika street. Moved by this photograph, Ritsos set to work immediately. The dirge that he produced after two days of intensive creativity, wedding his emotion to technical skill, places this particular tragedy in a larger perspective to give it meaning and provide a mirror in which the common people might discern their true features. Though equating the tragedy with Christ's crucifixion (the Epitaphios is the sepulchral lament sung in Greek Orthodox churches on Good Friday) the poem moves at the end from crucifixion to resurrection, thus enclosing sorrow in the sweetness of the poet's abiding hope that injustice may be overcome. At first the bereft mother grieves inconsolably for her son:

Μέρα Μαγιού μου μίσεψες, μέρα Μαγιού σε χάνω

A day in May you left me, a day in May I lost you

She cannot understand why he died, cannot understand his political convictions; but gradually she changes and, at the end, encouraged by her vision of a future in which men shall be united in love, she vows to carry on his struggle:

Γιέ μου, στ' αδέρφια σου τραβώ και σμίγω την οργή μου,
σου πήρα το ντουφέκι σου· κοιμήσου, εσύ, πουλί μου.

My son, I'm off to join your comrades and add my wrath to theirs;
I've taken up your gun; sleep now, sleep, my son.

The event that this poem celebrates was part of the unrest that led to the Metaxas dictatorship several months later, and when that regime made clear its intellectual orientation by publicly burning books in front of the Temple of Zeus, Ritsos's volume was of course included. Though not republished during the two ensuing decades, which saw not only Metaxas's government but also the German occupation of Greece and then two civil wars, this naturally musical poem eventually achieved the widest possible audience when Mikis Theodorakis set the dirge to music in the late fifties, employing the quintessential instrument of the people, the bouzouki, and using rhythms that "carried on the tradition of the elegiac threnody found in the klephtic ballads, the songs of Epiros, the dirges of Mani, the songs and dances of the islands, and the Cretan *rizitika*."[9] This setting, precisely because the bouzouki was at that time condemned in fashionable circles as the instrument of brothels and hashish dens, called forth intense debate, with the result that the music penetrated all segments of Greek society. Ritsos's yearning for poetry that would be known not only to intellectuals, but to dockhands, fishermen, and taxi-drivers, was fulfilled. In addition, the poem became a kind of unofficial "national anthem" of the Greek Left. For example, when in 1963 another tragedy occurred—also in Salonika, also in May—and hundreds of students kept vigil outside the hospital where the parliamentary deputy Lambrakis lay dying after being murderously assaulted by political thugs, it seemed inevitable that the mourners should sing Ritsos's *Epitaphios* in their martyr's honor. The dirge was also chanted through the streets of Athens after the deputy's funeral

9   George Giannaris, *Mikis Theodorakis: Music and Social Change* (New York: Praeger, 1972), p. 132.

at the same time that the slogan "Lambrakis lives" began to appear on every wall. Later, this same poem was presented in dramatic readings in England as a protest against the Colonels. *Epitaphios* lives.

From 1936 until 1952 Ritsos was unable to publish freely, for political reasons. Making the best of his restrictions, he cultivated his lyrical gift at first with intensely personal subjects, as in *The Song of My Sister*, but then increasingly shifted his attention from himself to others, and also to nature itself. As an early, partial, step in this direction, *The March of the Ocean* (1939-40) continues Ritsos's earlier theme of Poetry as a bulwark against misfortune, but recognizes that the strength to resist comes not so much from the poet's individual will in isolation as from that will drawing power from the constancy of sun and sea, the "inexhaustible song of nocturnal waves," a song that refuses to yield to night or to sleep, and that enables the poet, in his turn, to cry: "What if they leave, if everyone leaves. Let them. / I shall remain / across from wide heavens / across from grand seas / without bitterness or complaint— / to sing."[10] This early emphasis on heroic collaboration between man and nature was to bear fruit several years later in *Romiosini*, Ritsos's tribute to the Greek Resistance, where the landscape itself is seen as the principal register, and where the shift from self to other becomes complete.

Meanwhile, Ritsos not only cultivated his lyricism in long poems such as *The March of the Ocean*, but continued to experiment technically, especially in the short or medium-length poems that, characteristically, he was writing at the same time. Two collections of these, covering the years 1935 to 1943, move all the way from Whitmanesque verse-paragraphs ('A Summer's Midday Dream') to a two-line haiku ('April'). Though the lyrical and elegiac modes remain strong, some of these poems lean towards the colloquial diction, staccato rhythms, general simplicity, and elliptical bareness that dominate Ritsos's post-war style.

As the political situation turned from bad to worse, Ritsos increasingly favored overtly political subjects which rendered immediate publication unthinkable. In the winter of 1941-2 Greece was in the clutches of the severe famine that followed Hitler's invasion of the country the previous spring. Mussolini had been repulsed by the Greeks' remarkable campaign in Alba-

10   See *Ποιήματα Α'*, pp. 289, 276.

nia, and the spirit that made that campaign possible, though now temporarily exhausted, was already preparing to resist by means of guerrilla warfare and underground subversion, in order to bring about the country's resurrection. Ritsos did not take to the mountains, his tuberculosis having denied him the necessary robustness, but identifying himself clearly with EAM—a first coalition of various resistance groups, later dominated by the far left—he began to fight with his pen, producing a long series of poems that circulated clandestinely among the resisters and buoyed their spirit. An example is *The Final Century B.H.*; here, Ritsos looks forward to a new era comparable to that begun by Christ, and sees himself—the poet—as a link between old and new, a forerunner who points the way. Written in the summer of 1942, when nature, at least, had revived herself after the bleakness of the previous winter, the poem celebrates the heroes of the Albanian Campaign, weeps over the invasion and famine, rejoices that EAM has been formed, and ends with a sign placed at the crossroads: "This way to the sun," and also the hope that in the future, when people pass freely beneath the sunlight, someone will wonder who painted that sign "with such awkward letters" and someone else will recall that it was "Yannis Ritsos, poet of the final century *Before Humanity*."[11] Another poem that looks at a future resurrection, despite the darkness of 1942, is *The Burial of Orgaz*. Here, Ritsos builds his metaphor upon El Greco's two-tiered painting where surmounting a sombre burial are the effulgent heavens, with an angel already delivering Count Orgaz's inchoate soul to Christ. Packed in on the lower level of Ritsos's own canvas are mutilated veterans of Albania, innocent Athenians dying from the famine, resisters executed by the Germans; on the upper level (the springtime that will come "tomorrow") are workers building a new road. They are naked to the waist, barrel-chested, modern replacements for El Greco's strikingly naked John the Baptist who kneels at Christ's feet. But whereas the miracle of El Greco's painting is the integration of earth and heaven, death and life-everlasting (heaven itself descending resplendently in the persons of Saints Stephen and Augustine to lay Orgaz in the tomb), in Ritsos's poem—in Ritsos's Athens of 1942—the Below and the Above are sundered. Applying metaphor over metaphor like a graphic artist working with layer upon layer of paint, Ritsos speaks of the "ladder" that ought to

---

11   See *Ποιήματα Α´*, p. 521.

unite winter with spring. But the ladder does not exist. Why? Because our mouths, which ought to be sounding the trumpets of salvation, are "stuffed with silence."[12] The implication, if we unite the two metaphors, is once more that the Poet, especially in times when men's hands are tied, may be a ladder or bridge to a better world, and that the material with which he constructs his bridge is Song. We might add, paraphrasing Peter Levi, that perhaps life too, like El Greco's painting, has its dual levels, and that while prisoners and active resisters under an oppressive regime save a people's honor, poets such as Ritsos save a people's soul, because they keep delivering a nation's idealism, however unformed or inchoate its state, to the judgment of Humanity. In any case, this poem, like 'The Final Century B.H.,' uses Christian allusions to assert Ritsos's ultimate faith not in Christ or anything supernatural but in man's best instincts, at the very time when man's worst instincts were temporarily ascendant. The poem is also of interest technically, because it combines complexity of reference—personal experiences, contemporary events, historical or legendary memories, previous expressions in art—with simplicity of language.

Everyone in Greece hoped that resurrection would come as soon as the Germans withdrew. Instead, the sundering of native inhabitants from foreign rulers was replaced by a worse sundering of Greek from Greek. In the first Civil War, which followed almost immediately after Liberation, the leftist-dominated Resistance was routed, in December 1944, with the aid of British tanks. This defeat of EAM's hopes was then exacerbated by repressive measures applied against all radical and liberal elements in the turbulent years that followed, years that only increased the schism between right and left, and devolved into the second Civil War. During the interim period (1945-7), Ritsos joined with other artists in appealing to the United States, Great Britain, and the Soviet Union to recognize what was happening in Greece; more importantly, he set to work on his magnificent tribute to the defeated resistance-fighters and, beyond them, to all previous and future strugglers for Greece's freedom. Appropriately called *Romiosini* ('Greekness'), this tribute sees the men who fought against the Germans and afterwards in the first Civil War as national heroes easily equated with the free besieged of Missolonghi dur-

---

12   See *Ποιήματα Β'*, pp. 203-4.

ing the War of Independence; with that legendary stalwart of medieval times, Digenis Akritas; or with the epic giants celebrated in folksong:

κι όταν χορεύαν στην πλατεία,
μέσα στα σπίτια τρέμαν τα ταβάνια και κουδούνιζαν τα γυαλικά στα ράφια.

and when they danced in village square,
ceilings shook in the houses and glassware jingled on the shelves.
. . .
They treated Death to a raki served in their grandfathers' skulls;
on those same threshing-floors they met Digenis and sat down to dinner
slicing their sorrow in two as they used to slice their barley-loaf on their knees
. . .
On the threshing-floor where one night the stalwarts dined,
the olive stones remain and the crusted blood of the moon
and the fifteen-syllable verse of their guns.[13]

Though eschewing the actual decapentasyllables of *Epitaphios*, that earlier celebrative elegy in folksong metre, Ritsos in this later poem continues the spirit of the *demotikó traghoúdi* with its back-reaching into the racial past of a people—the Romioi—who, despite wave after wave of invasion by foreign troops or usurpation by un-romaic Hellenes, have remained the only true proprietors of the Greek landscape—itself celebrated as the prime resister— and whose ever-renewed energy is the strongest bridge to an improved future. So the poem, though occasioned by disillusion and chastened in tone, is also both defiant and hopeful. It ends by invoking a tomorrow in which others will recognize that the Resistance wished to bring love to Greece, not hate, and its final word is "brothers." Though this tomorrow is not yet visible, the poet articulates the certainty of trees, stars, and men that it shall appear, and asks his brothers, in effect, to keep vigil: to wait for it, watch for it, just as one watches over a corpse in the certainty that the soul will be delivered to "God's heart."

Romiosini could not be published when it was written. It appeared some years after the second Civil War, in 1954, and was reissued in 1966, whereupon Mikis Theodorakis composed settings for several sections, once again bringing Ritsos's verse to an extremely large audience—just before the works of

---

13   See *Ποιήματα Β'*, pp. 65, 62, 68.

both Ritsos and Theodorakis were banned by the regime of 21 April 1967.

By the time of the second Civil War, Ritsos had grown sufficiently danger-ous to the Right to cause his imprisonment. Arrested in 1948, he was sent for detention to Lemnos and then to the infamous "Institute for National Re-ed-ucation" on Makronisos, where the guards administered physical and psycho-logical torture in an attempt to transform communists into "good Hellenes." Lastly, he was transferred to Agios Efstratios. Though released at last because of ill-health, he was picked up again in 1951 and detained for an additional year. The four years in these various concentration camps did not, however, silence him. On Makronisos he placed his poems in a bottle that he buried in the stony ground; on Agios Efstratios ('Ai Stratis') he was able to recite his works to his fellow prisoners—which explains the straightforward style em-ployed during this period. Probably the most celebrated individual piece is the 'Letter to Joliot-Curie,' dated November 1950, a poem that was smuggled out of Greece at the time, unknown to its author. It begins:

> Dear Joliot, I am writing from Ai Stratis.
> About three thousand of us are here,
> simple folk, hard workers, men of letters,
> with a ragged blanket across our backs,
> an onion, five olives, and a dry crust of light in our sacks,
> folk as simple as trees in sunlight,
> with only one crime to our accounts:
> only this—that we, like you, love
> peace and freedom.[14]

As always, Ritsos's prime witness during these years of national and personal suffering was his continued faith in Song as a bridge to decency, a faith reinforced by what he observed in nature, though not always in human nature. "Ah yes," he sighed in another poem composed on Agios Efstratios,

> Ah, yes, the world is beautiful. A man beneath the trees
> wept from the joy of his love. He was
> stronger than death, that man—which is why we sing.
> . . .
> No one will silence our song. We sing on.

---

14   See Ποιήματα Β', p. 99.

The world is beautiful, we insist
—beautiful, beautiful, beautiful—and we sing on.[15]

One might say that these words of affirmation were written with clenched teeth, with the tinge of cynicism and bitterness that begins to darken Ritsos's later poems, although it never wholly dominates the hopefulness at their core. But faith in the poet's role remains, as does faith in a better future, and that is why an entire series of poems from the dark period 1941-53, including *Romiosini* and 'Letter to Joliot-Curie,' was brought together in 1954 under the generic title *Vigil*, beneath an epigraph by the poet of another dark period in Greece's history, Dionysios Solomos: "Forever open, forever vigilant the eyes of my soul." Again the implication is that we keep watch over a corpse, confronting all of life's degradation and injustice not with despair but with hope. Ritsos had been doing this, of course, ever since his very first poems in *Tractor* and *Pyramids*, but he had also grown in the meantime because of the outward circumstances that had fused his own personal misfortunes with those of his people, and because of his inner capacity to extend his elegiac and lyrical gifts to communal subjects.

When Ritsos was released in 1952 he returned to Athens to begin a crucial period of happiness in his personal life and development in his artistry. The return was celebrated exultingly in a long bitter-sweet poem entitled *Unsubjugated City* and in a short lyric called 'Peace,' written in January 1953. Dedicated to Kostas Varnalis, this latter work defines its subject by invoking life's simplest and most genuine pleasures:

Peace is the odor of food in the evening,
when the halting of a car in the street is not fear,
when a knock on the door means a friend
. . .
Peace is a glass of warm milk and a book in front of the child who awakens[16]

The poem is included at the end of the collection *Vigil* as though to vindicate Ritsos's—and Greece's—faithful waiting throughout the preceding years; it also looks forward to Ritsos's own happiness, for in 1954 he married and in

---

15   See *Ποιήματα Β'*, p. 133.
16   See *Ποιήματα Β'*, p. 173.

1955 welcomed an infant daughter into his household and sang her arrival in a "small encyclopaedia of diminutives" called *Morning Star,* the first poem addressed to a member of his immediate family that was not a dirge. These happy events, however, were not enough to erase from Ritsos's life the huge sense of loss that had predominated hitherto; nor had the political situation in Greece, however improved, suddenly become idyllic for a man of Ritsos's persuasions. What we see, therefore, in this next crucial period of artistic development is a continuation, basically, of Ritsos's previous concern with the everyday world of Greece, with his own and his nation's past, with memory and dream, and with social and moral revolution, but also an attempt to make his approach to these subjects more reflective, tentative, responsive to the blatant contradictions and complexities in his experience. We see him moving toward dramatic monologue as a favorite method, because this form lends itself both to reflection and to objectivity; we see him leaning more heavily upon myth alone or myth fused, or deliberately confused, with contemporary events, as a way of universalizing and depersonalizing his themes; we see him preferring the pronouns "he" or "you" to the pronoun "I." All these tendencies are well illustrated in the present selection, and we need not describe them any further here, except to reiterate what was stated earlier: that the style perhaps most characteristic of Ritsos in his later work is one that makes apparent simplicity and lucidity coexist with mystification, complexity, nightmare. We should also add that Ritsos, a poet not normally given to theorizing in prose about his verse, has nevertheless issued some crucial statements of intent. In an unpublished introduction to *Testimonies* broadcast in Prague in October 1962, he spoke about his growing consciousness of all that is "vague, perplexing, incomprehensible and directionless in life...," about his desire to hide the tragic element of the poem behind a "mask of impassivity," about his love for the words "perhaps" and "or," his fear of rhetoric, his continuing gratitude for everything that life has to offer, and his unshaken belief that the role of art is to transform negation into affirmation. In another introduction, this time to a volume of his translations of Mayakovsky (1964), he reaffirmed the positions just cited and placed them against a backdrop of chastened experience. "We have learned how difficult it is not to abuse the power entrusted to us in the name of the supreme ideal, liberty," he stated, "how difficult not to lapse into self-approbation in the name of the struggle against individualism...The first cries of enthusiasm and admiration have given way to a more silent self-communing." These two factors, taken together, have led modern poets to a self-examination that is at the same time self-effacing and hesitant. Thus their reliance on the third person; on dramatic narrative rather than exclamation; on reflection directed toward the past or toward an enlarged field of vision that refuses to speak of the future without considering past and present as well; on language that aspires to the tone of simple, confidential conversation out of fear of being understood, or of not being understood...[17] Perhaps one of Ritsos's poems says all this even more forcefully. Called 'The Disjunctive Conjunction *Or*,' it comments on a passage from the *Iliad*: "...Then brazen Ares / bellowed as loud as nine or ten thousand / warriors in battle...." "O that *or*," cries the poet, that

> equivocal smile of an incommunicable and uncooperative wisdom
> that turns mockingly toward itself and others,
> knowing full well that precision
> is impossible, does not exist (which is why
> the pompous style of certainty is so unforgivable—God preserve us from it).[18]

The period from 1953 to Ritsos's re-arrest in 1967 was an extremely productive one in which he published no less than twenty-eight separate collections of new work, not to mention three large volumes of his *Poems, 1930-1960*, and nine volumes of translations. In 1956 he received official recognition—a tardy complement to the unofficial recognition awarded him earlier by the public and by critics such as Palamas and Kleon Paraschos—when his *Moonlight Sonata* won the National Prize for poetry. The Prize also gained him recognition outside Greece; after the poem was translated into French, Louis Aragon eulogized Ritsos in the following terms:

> *...C'est un des plus grands et des plus singuliers parmi les poètes d'aujourd'hui.*
> *Pour ma part, il y avait longtemps que quelque chose ne m'avait donné comme*

17   These excerpts from the Mayakovsky introduction are available in French translation in the Poètes d' Aujourd'hui series, no. 178: *Yannis Ritsos, Étude, choix de texes et bibliographie par Chrysa Papandréou* (Paris: Éditions Seghers, 1968).

18   In the collection *Repetitions*, poem dated 18 June 1969. *Petres, Epanalipseis, Kinglidoma* (Athens: Kedros, 1972), p.91.

ce chant ce choc violent du génie... D'où vient cette poésie? d'où ce sens du frisson? où les choses telles qu'elles sont jouent le rôle des spectres...Il y a, dans cette poésie, le bruit...d'une Grèce qui n'est plus celle de Byron ou de Delacroix, d'une Grèce qui est soeur de la Sicile de Pirandello et de Chirico, où la beauté n'est point des marbres mutilés, mais d'une humanité déchirée...la décadence d'une époque.[19]

[...He is one of the greatest and most singular of today's poets. I for one had gone a long time without encountering the violent shock of genius given me by this poem. Where does this poetry come from? This thrill in which things as they are play the role of ghosts? There is, in this poetry, the sound...of a Greece no longer that of Byron or Delacroix, a Greece now the sister of the Sicily of Pirandello and De Chirico, with a beauty not at all of mutilated statues but a humanity torn apart...an era's decadence.]

As a result, Ritsos suddenly found himself an international celebrity, at least in the socialist world. In 1956 he journeyed to the Soviet Union, after that to Hungary, Bulgaria, Czechoslovakia, Romania, and Germany; in 1966 to Cuba. Meanwhile, inside Greece, he continued his "testimonies" in active as well as poetic ways. One example will suffice. When the Bertrand Russell peace movement spread to Greece, Ritsos became one of its advocates along with Theodorakis and the parliamentary deputy Lambrakis. In April 1963, the Greek Committee for Peace organized an Easter march from Marathon in imitation of Lord Russell's Aldermaston marches. Ritsos participated in this and was among the two thousand who were consequently detained by the authorities. We have already spoken of Lambrakis's fate a month later in Salonika, but it should be noted as well that Ritsos, together with Theodorakis, personally joined the vigil held for the dying deputy outside the university hospital when *Epitaphios* was sung.

Given this continuing activism on top of the earlier allegiance to EAM, not to mention the fact that some of Ritsos's works had been adopted by progressives as central articulations of their ideals, it is hardly surprising that the poet was among those arrested on the very first night of the 1967 coup or that his writings were promptly banned. Once more he found himself in various detention camps, this time for a period of a year and a half, followed by exile

19   *Les Lettres Françaises*, 28 February–6 March 1957, p. 1. [English version by Mary Feeney]

in Samos, where contact with the outside world was denied him and he was prevented from accepting invitations extended by the Festival of Two Worlds at Spoleto, for example, or the Arts Council of Great Britain. Eventually, owing certainly to protests from abroad, the government did release him, and even granted him a passport, but with restrictions that Ritsos felt he could not accept. Besides, he knew that in the years left to him—his health had remained precarious—he needed to stay in Greece, close to the language and the people that had formed him. So he continued to live in a depressing neighbourhood of Athens in a street called Koraka ('Crow'), observing the life around him:

> Dental surgeries have multiplied in our poor suburb,
> so have chemists, coffin makers…

> …A tap
> has been forgotten running all night at Crow's sidestreet
> in front of the flowershop, the barbershop.[20]

He concentrates on 'The Essentials':

> Did you eat your bread? Did you sleep well?
> Were you able to talk, to stretch your arm?
> Did you remember to look out of the window?[21]

'Athens 1970' is not the same as the unsubjugated city that Ritsos greeted so exultingly upon his return in 1952. Then, to be sure, there was hunger—old ladies scrambling in the marketplace for soup-bones, blinded veterans playing accordions on street corners—but there was also the hope and impetus born of hunger: "Mothers, the bread-troughs are waiting for you to knead loaves of peace." People had a voice then, an audible voice, whereas now, when they are no longer hungry, their hunger has been replaced by aimlessness, by the futile bustle of humans without ideals:

> …they are in a hurry
> to go away, to get away (where from?),
> to get (where?)—I don't know—not faces—

---

20   From 'Desertion.'
21   See *Ποιήματα Β'*, p. 266.

vacuum cleaners, boots, boxes—
they hurry.

As for the poet himself:

You must tighten your tie. Like this.
Keep quiet. Wait. Like this. Like this.
Slowly, slowly, in the narrow opening, there
behind the stairs, pushed against the wall.[22]

This is where a long life of personal and communal vicissitude left "Yannis Ritsos—poet of the final century B.H." He became free in body as he had always been in spirit, having survived imprisonment, exile, misunderstanding, isolation and disillusion—as well as adulation, perhaps the greatest trial of all. Measured against such hardships, the bitterness of his later poems is scarcely excessive, especially when we feel, as we continually do, an optimistic and affirmative energy still at work. And, of course, we have much to be thankful for. True, there is still no ladder uniting winter with spring (will there ever be? does such a ladder exist?); true, the mouths are still stuffed with silence. But precisely because of repeated disillusion, precisely because the wheel of crucifixion-resurrection-crucifixion has kept turning so inexorably in Ritsos's life, and in Greece's, Ritsos was forced to grow. He started, as did so many writers in the twentieth century, by confronting a disintegrating culture and by responding to that disintegration with the fervour and narrowness of certainty, with a recipe for moulding existence to his own liking. Poetically, this encouraged compassionate involvement, but also a tendency toward grandiloquence and rhetorical flourish, the temptation to draw his passion larger than life-size. As his career developed, however, he learned that present vicissitudes and future hopes are but visible functions of timeless rhythms in nature, history, and human psychology. He realized more and more that the words in a poem must become "signs for portions or classes of thought," that they must receive their meaning from what they would conceal, at the same time that they employ metaphorical power to make us see the objects and events of everyday reality. Poetically, this encouraged in him the need to register and validate existence—as opposed to the need to mould it—so that

22   From 'The Meaning Is One.'

32

Ritsos passed from the self-absorption and self-assertion of his earliest verse to the increasing objectivity, hesitancy, and reticence that we have seen as his career unfolded.

What remained unaltered throughout all this development is Song. Ritsos's poetic personality, seen in its totality, is an organic whole, despite fluctuations of attitude or technique, because—whether his stance is moral outrage or forgiving acceptance, whether his stylistic mode is magniloquence or elliptical understatement—the original allegiance to Mother Poetry has never vacillated. This means three things: (1) unshaken faith in words: in each word as an outlet for a meeting between the reader and the poet's inner or outer world, no matter how often that meeting is postponed; (2) realization that although poetry ultimately treats universal and general classes of thought, it must do so through the senses, not the intellect, and must therefore cling to individual, palpable objects of experience, operating by means of language that is vitally metaphorical in that it establishes relationships between the single and the generic; (3) gratitude toward life in its totality—its ugliness and evil included—for providing the materials of poetry and the human consciousness that transubstantiates those materials into art. In short, what we see unchanged in Ritsos, throughout his growth, is the primal aesthetic drive: the obsession with seeing life and articulating what has been seen. This drive is so vital in him that it turns even his bitterness into affirmation. "I mark Henry James' sentence," Virginia Woolf wrote in her diary at the height of her own chagrin. "Observe perpetually. Observe the oncome of age. Observe greed. Observe my own despondency…I insist upon spending this time to the best advantage…"

That is what Ritsos continued to do.

PETER BIEN

2. Myth in Modern Greek Letters, with Special Attention to Yannis Ritsos's *Philoctetes*

I
N EUROPE, GREAT CLAIMS HAVE BEEN MADE for the role of myth, and these have produced equally great attacks. Eliot, Joyce, Mann and Lawrence reacted to the emptiness of their transitional age by filling its hollows with myth, in the hope of providing a core not simply of meaning but of a special kind of indefinable, irrational (or meta-rational) meaning appropriate to the general bewilderment of their times. Myth became doubly useful: It eliminated a vacuum, and did so in a complex way. This of course produced a double target for the attackers. The famous meaninglessness of the West, they asserted, was not an objective emptiness at all but just a failure of nerve, since abundant meaning existed in contemporary economic, social, and class struggles. Furthermore, the particular fill chosen—namely myth—manifested an unfounded distrust of rationality and an equally unfounded doctrine that human affairs are basically universal and non-historical.

This happened in Europe. Greece is obviously a part of Europe; Greek intellectuals (though not the common people) have always maintained contact with France, for example, and have imported the literary movements of the West. In Greece, we encounter the same claims for and against myth that have been observed in European letters. Seferis, heavily influenced by both France and England, placed his hopes in myth as a way of "softening" the living horror of his own age;[23] the arch-irrationalist Kazantzakis, an intellectual product of Paris and Berlin, scorned realism and considered myth the "simple, composite expression of the most positive reality." Conversely, Greek Marxists such as Markos Avyeris and Galatea Kazantzaki accused the mythifiers of evasion. To some degree at least, the trends seen in Western Europe were

23   "Si je te parle par légende et parabole, c'est qu'elles sont plus douces à entendre. L'horreur, on ne peut pas en parler parce qu'elle est vivante, parce qu'elle est silencieuse et qu'elle avance." (1944). Cited in Chrysa Papandréou's Introduction to *Yannis Ritsos*, Paris, Seghers, 1968, "Poètes d'aujourd'hui," No. 178, p. 37.

34

transplanted to Greece unchanged.

Greece, however, stands outside of Europe in very important ways. Language is an indication. When a Greek announces a trip abroad to France, Austria, or Germany, he says "I am going to Europe," as if he were not already there. Despite what I said earlier, crucial differences exist between Greece and Europe (which I shall henceforth distinguish from Greece) in connection with the role of myth in contemporary letters.

In England, France, and Germany, when a writer wishes to employ myth he turns most often to Greek tradition or some other foreign source. In at least one country where native myths have been favored—Ireland—these derive from a past sufficiently dead to be almost foreign, and certainly to require miraculous resurrection. The situation in Greece is entirely different. Greek myth is obviously not foreign to Greece. One could object that it is foreign because ancient, but the ancient Greek past, far from having to be dragged forcefully back into relevance by literary miracle-workers, is if anything too pervasively alive in contemporary Greece, too unavoidable. "No region of the [modern Greek's] homeland calls forth a disinterested quiver of aesthetic appreciation. The region has a name; it is called Marathon, Salamis, Olympia, Thermopylae, Mistra, and it is bound up with a memory: here we were disgraced, there we won glory." What Kazantzakis says here about famous locales may be applied equally to famous personalities, both historical and mythical. Modern Greece's topography, place names, educational curriculum, racial memories, folksong traditions, the unbroken continuity of the Greek language from mythical times to the present, and a long, "fabulous" history that has encouraged continual myth-making, all combine to cause Greek myth to affect a modern Greek in a stronger and necessarily different way than it can ever affect a non-Greek. The Greek does not reach Achilles, Helen, Prometheus, Daedalus and the rest by leaping over a myth-less divide, but rather steps easily across to them upon the numerous stones of subsequent incarnations. Achilles, Alexander the Great, the border-fighters of Byzantium, Constantine Palaiologos immured in Hagia Sophia, the klephts, pallikaria and noble women of Zalongon in the War of independence—all have become equally mythic for the Greeks, and each suggests the others, particularly because the three millennia of Greek history have been so extraordinarily cyclical.

What we must remember in distinguishing a Greek's reaction to myth from a European's is this: Whereas Europeans acquired Greek myth largely during the Renaissance, modern Greeks inherit a tradition that their ancestors never really lost.[24] In Europe, furthermore, Greek myths have been meaningful chiefly to the educated class and, indeed, were often a mark of highbrowism. It is true that when Greece underwent a so-called enlightenment in the early nineteenth century, artificially acquired knowledge of ancient lore became a guarantee of status; but this situation did not alter the fact that the same mythic heroes, though perhaps under different names, continued to live in the hearts of the uneducated, "suckled through the bloodstream by racial memory in an indigenous environment of landscape and inscape."[25] Moreover, once the nation was cured of its self-destructive fantasy of producing another Golden Age on the exact model of Periclean Athens, the archaizing education predominant in Greek schools actually helped to crumble the wall between intellectuals and common folk, because the particular form of highbrowism involved—immersion in the literary monuments of the Greek past—inclined poets and scholars to look with admiration upon a peasantry that itself was immersed in the same past, albeit unknowingly. It is hardly accidental that by the end of the nineteenth century folklore had joined classics as a major ingredient of intellectual life in Greece, or that an immensely sophisticated poet of our own time such as Seferis should cite as his initial esthetic nourishment the snatches of seventeenth-century epic and drama (all mythical) that he heard declaimed by the uneducated servants of his household when he was a child.[26]

~

Hopefully, these observations will begin to explain the ease with which modern Greek literature has produced in Yannis Ritsos a Marxist poet at once

24   On the direct transmission of modern folksong from ancient tragedy via pantomine and paralogés, see S. P. Kyriakidis, *Ai istorikai archai tis dimodous neoellinikis poiiseos*, Thessaloniki, 1954, summarized in Linos Politis, *A History of Modern Greek Literature*, Oxford, 1973, pp. 88-9.

25   Kimon Friar, *Modern Greek Poetry*, New York 1973, p. 120.

26   See Seferis's interview in the newspaper *To Vima* (Athens), 29 August 1971.

immensely popular with the masses and immensely sophisticated, a poet who can employ mythical subjects nonchalantly with no fear whatsoever of restricting his audience to highbrows or of deserting contemporary reality for either some fantastical vision of the past or some disinterested quiver of esthetic appreciation. This means that he stands in a relationship to Greek myth that would be difficult for any European poet to duplicate. But Greece, as I indicated earlier, is still associated with Europe and reflects its intellectual movements. A part of Ritsos's fascination for comparatists is that he, too, like Eliot, Lawrence and the others, employs myth to add meaning to hollowness and to do so in a largely indefinable, meta-rational way consistent with his vision of life's complexity. Yet to accuse him of a failure of nerve because of this, or of a retreat to non-historicity and universalism, would be unthinkable. On the contrary, Ritsos's mythic poems are so firmly moored to his nation's and his own contemporary, specific experience that they do not cut loose from that experience when the winds of ancient legend puff out their sails. Myth leads his work neither to evasion nor diversion, but to revelation.

Ritsos's own experience has been a tragedy of sickness, hardship, exile, imprisonment, and censorship. His nation's has been even worse: one decade of war from 1912 to 1922 ending in disastrous defeat by the Turks, and a second decade from 1940 to 1950 ending in brutal hatred of Greek for Greek. No wonder, then, that Ritsos became obsessed by that other decade-long conflict involving internal dissension, the Trojan War. Starting in 1962 he published a series of long poems that meditate either openly or covertly upon various mythic personalities affected by the dreadful events of Mycenaean times, personalities such as Clytemnestra, Electra, Orestes, Helen, and Philoctetes. His treatment of the last my be taken as representative.

The myth is simple enough in outline. Briefly, Philoctetes, on his way to Troy with the others, suffers a snake-bite when he accidentally invades a sacred precinct. The resulting wound is so disgusting that the Achaean generals abandon him on the deserted island of Lemnos. Ten years later, however, with Troy still unconquered, they send an emissary to fetch him, because an oracle has informed them that only with Philoctetes's bow and Neoptolemus's prowess will Troy ever fall. Philoctetes goes to Troy and the prophecy is fulfilled.

The extant sources are few, yet we know that this myth fascinated the ancients. Recently, critical discussion of the surviving play by Sophocles has ranged from Edmund Wilson's pioneering essay in 1941 to Jan Kott's treatment in 1973. This is not the place to summarize the various interpretations at any length. It is sufficient to note that they contradict one another decisively. Wilson stresses the conflict between private justice and public duty, relating the play to Sophocles's family life. Bowra insists that defiance of the gods is central, while Kitto deems the gods irrelevant and considers the play a study of human character, specifically of Neoptolemus's nobility. For Kott, Neoptolemus is a base villain, while the drama is political, mirroring Athens' degeneration during the Peloponnesian War.[27] One can only conclude that the myth as elaborated by Sophocles can mean anything, or perhaps everything. We should also remember the abundance of uncanny motifs that reach far down into universal mythic consciousness: an incurable wound, a compulsive or ritualistic withdrawal, magically effective weapons, strength united to disability. These too are subject to multiple interpretations. In sum, Ritsos chose a theme that could be assimilated easily to his own needs but that at the same time anchored him to some deep (if elusive) truths about Greek national life and life in general.

His version reduces the characters to two, mature Philoctetes and young Neoptolemus. The latter has come with his ship (the crew are off-stage but audible) to transport the recluse to Troy. Philoctetes greets the youth with a long account of his chagrin, but this we do not hear. The entire poem—a dramatic monologue—consists of Neoptolemus's reply. Though the characters and their accouterments are ancient, we cannot be too sure. The setting is Lemnos "...perhaps." Occasionally Ritsos adds temporal incongruities with the arbitrariness of a surrealist. Neoptolemus's home (i.e., Achilles's palace) has colonnades and statues, but also French doors with frosted glass. These devices create an atmosphere of imprecision and synchronism.

The poem exhibits so many themes fused into such a complicated unity that to isolate them all, much less analyze the unifying relationships among them, would require an extended monograph. I shall simply try to describe some of the most important.

---

27   Edmund Wilson, *The Wound and the Bow*, Cambridge, Massachusetts, 1941, pp. 272-95. C. M. Bowra, *Sophoclean Tragedy*, Oxford, 1944, pp. 261-306. H. D. F. Kitto, *Greek Tragedy*, London, 1961, pp. 296-308. Jan Kott, *The Eating of the Gods*, New York, 1973, pp. 162-85.

The basic situation dramatically involves one generation confronting another. On a personal level, Ritsos himself, having survived the terrible decade
1940-50, confronts his father's generation, victims of the incessant warfare of
1912-22. But the synchronism goes further. The internal squabbling of the Trojan chieftains, for example, suggests the breakdown of unity in the resistance
coalition EAM during World War II. Most importantly, however, Ritsos as-
serts that the modern Greek defines himself by encountering his nation's past.
As Neoptolemus recites his story to the elder Philoctetes, we begin to discern
three stages in his life: (1) a psychic preparation in childhood—in this case a
psychic wound; (2) a call to experience—in this case the summons to Troy;
(3) conscious understanding of both the childhood preparation and the adult
experience, this understanding catalyzed by interchange with the older man
who arrived at the same understanding previously by another road. Ritsos is
telling us that Greeks discover themselves by twisting round like snakes and
biting their own historical tails.

If the basic situation in the poem is the confrontation between generations,
the basic action is Philoctetes's departure for Troy. In Sophocles's play this
had to be engineered by the *deus ex machina*, a device that Ritsos retains but
utterly transforms. Both Philoctetes and Neoptolemus are obsessed with life's
pillage, with senseless, gratuitous violence that never achieves its supposed
goals and only confirms the futility of human endeavor. Confronted with this
vision of omnivorous death, Neoptolemus as an unreflecting youth suffers a
hidden psychic wound, while Philoctetes deliberately inflicts upon himself a
visible fleshly wound. Both withdraw (as long as they can) from life's sinister
call. One might classify them as brooding intellectuals—like Ritsos himself.
But the world is not populated solely by intellectuals. There are also the common people, and they, when confronted with the threat of extinction, react
not with paralysis and withdrawal but rather with sexual vitality or vulgarity—with increased bodily energy in defiance of the worst that life can do to
them. It is this group—the common people, here represented by the crew of
Neoptolemus's ship—that Ritsos employs as his *deus ex machina*. Destiny for
him (and we must remember his Marxist orientation) is the people; hence the
force that makes Philoctetes decide, just as mysteriously as the god Heracles'
exhortation made him decide in Sophocles's version, is the affirmative Greek

folksong sung off-stage by Neoptolemus's sailors. It is right for intellectuals to understand life's futility, Ritsos is saying, provided they also participate in the world whose contingency they know so well. This participation is their ultimate responsibility (their ultimate mask, as we shall see in a moment). Philoctetes must go to Troy.

Anyone who appreciates the dilemmas faced by Ritsos and other Greek intellectuals during our own era of pillage will realize how revelational, rather than evasive or diverting, Philoctetes's problem and its solution have become in this poem. When a Greek contemplates the three millennia that define his personality, when he looks back at the Trojan War, the Peloponnesian War, Byzantine strife, the War of Independence, EAM fighting the Germans, he sees so much senseless pillage and petty divisiveness, so many betrayals, false goals embraced, true goals neglected, that he is revulsed. Yet all this is also his culture's vitality, its destiny, the whirlpool that tossed certain great figures (such as Sophocles; such as Ritsos) onto the serene ground of wisdom. In addition, this history, however discouraging, shows the best men always hoping that decency will come in the end.

Any thinking Greek is caught between these two equally valid perceptions, the one encouraging contemplative withdrawal, the other self-conscious participation. He may withdraw for a time, and this will be good. But emissaries will come to fetch him sooner or later from his barren Lemnos, offering as a cover for his diaphanous face an opaque "mask of action"—what Ritsos in the subtitle calls the "ultimate mask." He will receive this mask, but then— overhearing the people's song as it "takes…stars, bitterness, valor, endurance, the whole murkily sparkling sea in its boundlessness, and encloses all these in human dimensions"—he will set the mask down. His face will slowly grow younger, more positive; it will become the mask. And he will follow his magical weapons as Neoptolemus carries them to the ship, for these are his, and his culture's, only defense against death.

Ritsos solves his dilemma with an affirmation resting on multiple paradoxes. The fiction of positive action to support the goals of one's country, to help Greece achieve its destiny, is our ultimate path to self-realization. But when an undeluded person accepts that fiction knowingly, it ceases to be a mask. Fictive hope becomes a man's, and a nation's, authenticity.

~

It has been said that literature is a culture talking to itself. Greek culture is such a skein of contradictions and paradoxes extending over so long a time that when it wishes to talk to itself most meaningfully it is almost forced to employ literature impregnated with myth, because myth guarantees to an artist themes, symbols and personalities that somehow became, and have remained, meaningful to an entire people. Greek writers are particularly fortunate. Their culture not only developed abundant mythic materials at an early stage but kept those materials alive ever since for both the learned and the illiterate segments of the population. Add to this a language that can draw freely from any and all periods of its long evolution, and we see why poets such as Ritsos find in myth an irresistible means to range broadly and deeply over Greece's collective experience as a way of discovering themselves.

3. Yannis Ritsos's *Philoctetes*: Approaching a Modern Poem through Its Ancient Prototype. A Methodology and a Demonstration

METHODOLOGY

CLASSICAL SCHOLARS ARE APT TO BE PERPLEXED by Yannis Ritsos's *Philoctetes*.[28] Comparing this poem to Sophocles's play, they will be struck, for example, by various omissions: Odysseus does not appear; Philoctetes himself neither speaks nor exhibits physical pain; there seems to be no *deus ex machina*. On the other hand, classical scholars will be the first to recognize how clearly Ritsos's poem invokes the larger traditions, mythological and literary, associated with Philoctetes; they will also presumably recognize that the major question posed in Sophocles's version—Why should Philoctetes go to Troy?—is also the major question posed in Ritsos's poem. They might even conclude that the two poets, across a span of 2,374 years, provide the identical answer.

Neohellenists, in their turn, would be foolish to examine Ritsos's poem apart from the Sophoclean prototype, despite all the differences. The modern work so clearly echoes the ancient one that the neohellenists' problem is not *whether* they should bring Sophocles into their discussions but rather *how* they should do this so that the exercise is not just pedantically mechanical. The most obvious method strikes me as the worst. I mean the process of cataloging similarities and differences. This is the worst for the simple reason that whether Ritsos differs from Sophocles or fails to differ is unimportant in itself. We may know fifty differences and as many similarities without un-

---

28   Much of the impetus for this essay, and also subsequent counsel that helped eliminate many gaffes, came from Professor Harry C. Avery of the Department of Classics, University of Pittsburgh, to whom this thrice-amateur classicist gives sincere thanks. In addition, I thank Professor Karelisa Hartigan for bibliographical and other suggestions. An earlier version of the essay was printed in: Peter Bien, *Αντίθεση και σύνθεση στην ποίηση του Γιάννη Ρίτσου* (Athens: Kedros, 1980), 77-109.

derstanding Ritsos's poem a jot better than before. The important thing is whether the comparison with Sophocles can alert us to aspects of Ritsos's poem that we might not have noticed otherwise, and can therefore enable us to understand Ritsos's poem better. Wary, therefore, of cataloging similarities and differences for their own sake, I shall try something else. The methodology I propose is merely to discover what questions are normally asked about Sophocles's play and then to apply those same questions to Ritsos's poem. If, in this manner, we isolate some of the issues relevant to Sophocles, we may discover how the same issues are treated by Ritsos, or at least may recognize their existence in the modern poem. For example, classicists like to debate whether the chorus in Sophocles voices the author's own views or speaks in character. Ritsos has no chorus as such, but he does include stage directions. Alerted by this issue as it relates to Sophocles, we shall probably now wonder whether these stage directions come from the author himself or from a fictive narrator—a problem that might not have concerned us otherwise.

The objection will doubtlessly be raised that since the problem of a reliable narrator/chorus/set of stage directions is a staple of literary criticism, the trained neohellenist should not have to read essays on Sophocles written by classicists in order to become aware of such a problem in Ritsos. But in the case of a poem like *Philoctetes*, clearly derived from a classical prototype, it is fitting for our methodology to come at least in part from classical scholarship, fitting not only for sentimental reasons but also for more substantive ones that I shall now attempt to formulate.

Literary criticism is an amphibian coexisting in water and on dry land. Unthinkable without the literary text being criticized, it nevertheless claims autonomy as an intellectual discipline in its own right. How can we reconcile its subordination with its asserted independence? If literary criticism existed only as a servant of the text, as a lamp illuminating an icon, then of course we would not think of it as autonomous. If it existed only as a theory of meaning, discussing cunundrums in the abstract and not illuminating specific works, then we might not think of it as literary criticism any longer but instead might call it philosophy, psychology, or linguistics. At its best, however, literary criticsm avoids these extremes. It reconciles the incompatibles because, although subordinating itself to a specific work or author, it nevertheless acquires a

PETER BIEN

form of independence since what it does is to attempt to re-create and re-articulate in another mode of discourse, this time an analytical one, the thought process, world view, and/or aesthetic principle of the icon it is illuminating. The relationship between poet and critic is surely not that of master and slave. I like to think of it, instead, as a relationship between angel and human, where the angel (the poet, of course) employs intuitive reason and the human critic discursive to arrive at the same goal.[29] Whether consciously or not, the critic treats more than the specific work; in re-creating the artist's vision, he necessarily parallels in his method and concerns the artist's way of viewing the world.

All this may be used to argue further the proposition that in a criticism of Ritsos's *Philoctetes* it is fitting for us to derive our methodology from studies of Sophocles.

To see this, we must first ask why Ritsos chooses to base poems upon ancient prototypes that rest, in turn, upon the great themes of Greek mythology. Does he resort to myth primarily to avoid censorship? Does he employ ancient themes because he hates the present and loves the past? The answer in each case, I believe, is "Certainly not." Does he feel compelled by the chaos of modern life to turn to myth for coherence, as Joyce did in *Ulysses*? Does he, like D. H. Lawrence, need myth in order to reach some level of human experience too deep for mental understanding? This time the answer in each case is "Possibly" or even "Probably." Does he utilize myth to make private experience public and, at the same time, his vision of public experience private? In this case the answer must be strongly "Yes." I would contend, however, that none of these explanations gives us the primary reason for Ritsos's use of myth. Primarily, Ritsos employs myth as an economical way of speaking about the entire Greek experience. It is often claimed that myth is a-historical or, worse, that it evades history. But Ritsos employs myth because he wishes to explore history. He knows that each myth has displayed great adaptability in relation to historical factors, taking on many different forms yet always retaining enough of its basic characteristics to be recognizable as that myth and not a different one. As Lévi-Strauss reminds us, a myth consists of all of its

---

29   Compare Milton, *PL* 5.488-490, where Raphael instructs Adam regarding the two types of reason: "Discursive, or Intuitive; discourse / Is oftest yours, the latter most is ours, / Differing but in degree, of kind the same."

versions. Ritsos, fascinated by the combined versatility and stability of myth, wishes to discover what form the eternal myth will take in twentieth-century Greece. We could say that myth enables him to remain within the Greek tradition while at the same time renewing it.

It is fitting for a criticism of Ritsos's *Philoctetes* to draw its impetus from classical scholarship because this methodology enables the critic to duplicate (in his own mode of discourse) the most basic presuppositions of the poet and the poem. Now the critic as well as the poet will remain within the Greek tradition, renewing it for himself (and, one hopes, for his readers) as he ranges back and forth between the ancient prototype and the modern variation in an attempt to discover issues relevant to both. A criticism that takes its lead from classical scholarship will have the potential not only to illumine Ritsos's mythic poems, thus exercising its subordinate role in relation to those poetic texts, but also to re-create in its own language the mentality that gave rise to the texts in question. By fulfilling this latter potential, such a criticism will acquire a kind of independence, or at least the integrity of a (subordinate) parallel.

DEMONSTRATION

Let us proceed, then, to some of the questions normally asked about Sophocles's play. We have already encountered the problem of the chorus's reliability as an authorial voice, and the central question of why Philoctetes should go to Troy, why he ultimately *does* go to Troy. Classical scholars continually debate, as well, the role of the *deus ex machina*, a problem that obviously relates to the two cited above. The meaning of Philoctetes's wound is examined repeatedly in the critical studies, as is the question of whether the hero himself must be brought to Troy or whether his weapons alone are sufficient. Furthermore, the relation between Philoctetes and Neoptolemus is scrutinized, leading to controversies over which of these two is the true hero of the play.[30] To an-

---

30   For general bibliography on Sophocles, see the annotated list by H. Friis Johansen in *Lustrum* 7 (1962): 94-288. For a survey of criticism of *Philoctetes* in particular, see P. E. Easterling, 'Philoctetes and Modem Criticism,' *ICS* 3 (1978): 27-39. Discussion of the specific problems that I have singled out may be found in the following sources, among others:

swer many of these questions, scholars ask another, namely whether certain linguistic patterns—recurring or obsessive words, double meanings, verbal antitheses, ubiquitous figures of speech—may be discerned in the play.[31] Lastly, the scholarly literature on Sophocles's *Philoctetes* includes a considerable number of articles debating the political significance of the play: what it suggested politically to an audience viewing it in 409 B.C. in the midst of the Peloponnesian War.

Although this list obviously does not include all the questions asked or askable, it does I trust represent the kinds of inquiry found in classical scholarship. In the demonstration that follows, I shall arbitrarily confine myself to the issue mentioned last, the political significance. We shall find, however,

Reliability of the chorus: B. M. W. Knox, *The Heroic Temper* (Berkeley: U of Cal Pr, 1964), 135. Why Philoctetes goes to Troy: R. G. A. Buxton, *Persuasion in Greek Tragedy* (Cambridge: Cambridge U Pr, 1982), 128-129; Easterling (above) 33, 34, 35-36; Philip Whaley Harsh, 'The Role of the Bow in the *Philoctetes* of Sophocles,' *AJP* 81 (1960): 410-414; Knox (above) 141; Jan Kott, *The Eating of the Gods* (Evanston, Ill.: Northwestern U Pr, 1987), 184-185; George Meautis, *Sophocle, essai sur le héros tragique* (Paris: A. Michel, 1957),56; Pierre Vidal-Naquet, 'Sophocles's *Philoctetes* and the Ephebeia,' in Jean-Pierre Vernant and Pierre Vidal-Naquet, *Myth and Tragedy in Ancient Greece* (New York: Zone Bks, 1988), 173-174.

The *deus ex machina*: Easterling (above) 31, 35; David Grene and Richmond Lattimore, eds., *The Complete Greek Tragedies* (Chicago: U of Chicago Pr, 1959-1960), vol. 2, *Sophocles*, 398-399; Harsh (above) 412-414; John S. Kieffer, 'Philoctetes and *Arete*," *CP* 37 (1942): 38-50; Knox (above) 141; Norman T. Pratt, Jr., 'Sophoclean "Orthodoxy" in the *Philoctetes*,' *AJP* 70 (1949): 285-286; Sophocles, *Philoctetes*, ed. T. B. L. Webster (Cambridge: Cambridge U Pr, 1970), 156; Oliver Taplin, 'Significant Actions in Sophocles's *Philoctetes*,' *GRBS* 12 (1971): 39; Edmund Wilson, *The Wound and the Bow* (Cambridge, Mass.: HM, 1941),283.

Meaning of the wound: Grene and Lattimore (above) 392; Harsh (above) 414; R. C. Jebb, *Sophocles, the Plays and Fragments*, part 4, *Philoctetes* (Cambridge: Cambridge U Pr, 1908), xiii; Kott (above) 167, 169; Knox (above) 131; Ivan M. Linforth, 'Philoctetes: The Play and the Man,' *University of California Publications in Classical Philology* 15.3 (1956): 106.

The hero or the weapons, or both: Penelope Biggs, 'The Disease Theme in Sophocles's *Ajax, Philoctetes* and *Trachiniae*,' *CP* 61 (1966): 223, 231-235; Easterling (above) 30, 31-32; Harsh (above) 412-414; Kieffer (above) 48; Knox (above) 126-127,131; Linforth (above) 102; David Robinson, 'Topics in Sophocles's *Philoctetes*,' *CQ*, n.s. 19 (1969): 46; Wilson (above) 287f.

Relations between Philoctetes and Neoptolemus: Harry C. Avery, 'Heraclcs, Philoctetes, Neoptolemus,' *Hermes* 93 (1965): 286-290; Easterling (above) 29, 35, 37-38; Knox (above) 120; Taplin (above) 27f.

31   I have followed this approach, applying linguistic analyses by classicists such as Knox and Avery (above, note 30) in my 'Αντίθεση και σύνθεση στην ποίηση του Γιάννη Ρίτσου' in Bien (above, note 28) 111-145.

that this inquiry, like the rest, cannot be sealed off hermetically from the others. Thus, in pursuing a political analysis we shall find ourselves considering the role of the *deus ex machina* and also the problem of why Philoctetes goes to Troy.

Classicists seem unable to agree on a single political interpretation of Sophocles's *Philoctetes*; nor can they agree on whether a political interpretation is even possible. But this does not stop them from trying.

They begin (1) by cataloging the important political events during Sophocles's lifetime, especially those close to 409, when the play was produced. Then (2) they try to determine the extent, if any, of Sophocles's direct participation in these events. Finally (3), they sometimes claim to see in the play reflections of the events themselves and of Sophocles's personal attitude. Needless to say, the first of these steps is relatively easy while the second is extremely difficult and the third well-nigh impossible.

Across the span of Sophocles's lifetime the primary change, politically, was the dissolution of Greek unity as we move from the victories against the Persians in his youth (480, 479), to the final defeat of Athens by Sparta in 404, soon after his death. Close to 409, the noteworthy events were Alcibiades' maneuvers during his exile (415f.), the disaster at Sicily in 413, the revolution of the Four Hundred in 411, the counter-coup of the Five Thousand in the same year, Alcibiades' victory at Cyzicus in 410, restoration of democracy in the same year, and preparations for another Athenian campaign in 409.[32]

When we turn to Sophocles's direct participation in these events, things become extremely speculative. It is best simply to admit our ignorance despite numerous attempts to make the meager evidence yield some results.[33] We are

32   The events are conveniently summarized by Michael H. Jameson, 'Politics and the Philoctetes,' *CP* 51 (1956): 217-227, and also by Jebb (above, note 30) xi-xii, where references to the primary sources may be found.

33   Speculation on Sophocles's participation in the turbulent events close to 409 depends on a passage in Aristotle's *Rhetoric* (3.18.6) about a certain Sophocles who may or may not be the poet. If he is the poet, then one can construct the following sequence of events: Elected in 413 as one of the ten commissioners in charge of Athens after the Sicilian disaster, Sophocles voted in 411 for the Four Hundred as the least of various evils (οὐ γὰρ ἦν ἄλλα βελτίω) but soon regretted his action and supported the counter-coup of the Five Thousand (see P. Foucart, 'Le poète Sophocle et l'oligarchie des Quatre Cents,' *RP* 17 (1893): 1-10, and Michael H. Jameson, 'Sophocles and the Four Hundred,' *Historia* 20 (1971): 5~1-568). But since these "facts" are so speculative, it is not surprising that the various political interpretations of

on firmer ground when we try to relate the play to the political events preceding its production. We know that *Philoctetes* was mounted at a moment when a long and discouraging war looked as though it might be concluded. Hence we may surmise that, for an Athenian audience in 409, the play, because it focused on a time when another long and discouraging war looked as though it might be concluded, would have seemed to be using that earlier war to say *something* about the current one, even if we cannot know exactly what. It is tempting to strengthen this analogy between the Trojan and Peloponnesian wars by recalling that Sophocles's mythical plot takes place in the tenth year of the former conflict, and by suggesting that perhaps Sophocles's audience thought of themselves as living through the tenth year of the Peloponnesian War, since hostilities had resumed in 419 following the peace, negotiated by Nicias in 421, that had ended the Archidamian War (see Thucydides 5.17-20; 5.52). But the argument based on decades is probably too neat, since other dates besides 419 can be advanced for the actual resumption of hostilities. We are left with the vague but nonetheless suggestive analogy stated above: Sophocles's mythical situation, the Trojan War, relates *somehow* to the real political situation of 409. Let us be content to know neither exactly how it relates nor exactly what personal attitudes or experiences of the playwright's lie hidden behind the action.[34]

Philoctetes are contradictory. On the one hand, we are told that the bitter, intransigent hero on his island "equals" a self-justifying portrait by Sophocles of himself, the decent man of principle tricked by deceitful politicians. The play's political "message" would then be that honorable men should mistrust and oppose the politicians' new schemes in 410/409 to defeat the Spartans (see William M. Calder III, 'Sophoclean Apologia: *Philoctetes*,' *GRBS* 12 [1971]: 153-174). On the other hand, the hero is said to portray not Sophocles himself but the exiled Alcibiades, in which case the "message" would be precisely the opposite: everyone should rally to the common cause despite justifiable personal grudges. (This "Alcibiades hypothesis" was first stated by M. Lebeau le cadet in 1770. It is vigorously refuted by Jameson [above, note 33] 219.) Against this view, other critics assert that Philoctetes cannot "equal" crafty Alcibiades, who has more in common with crafty Odysseus in the play. Still others argue that Alcibiades is seen in Neoptolemus (see Calder [above] 168-169)—unless that son of the noble Achilles "equals" the son of the noble Pericles! (Jameson [above, note 5] 222-223).

34   This is the position taken by Jebb (above, note 30) xii. Cf. Kott (above, note 30) 183: "Sophocles's tragedies are not historical parables, but their contemporaneity, although hidden, does not cease to be significant. Like Shakespeare's *Tempest*, *Philoctetes* seems to be a personal confession but the autobiographical touch, which one can hear at times in the bitter confessions and outbursts, is the whole of human experience."

For a political interpretation of Ritsos, this conclusion, however vague, is nevertheless significant because it alerts us to the hidden presence of the Peloponnesian War in a poem that seems to deal exclusively with the Trojan War. When we remember that the most important political change in Ritsos's own experience, as (presumably) in Sophocles', was the dissolution of Greek unity, we can begin to see why the Philoctetes myth, as elaborated by Sophocles in 409 B.C. at a particularly optimistic moment in the Peloponnesian War, was so politically suggestive to this modern poet writing in A.D. 1963-1965.

In Ritsos's lifetime, Greek unity dissolved not once but twice. It is perhaps not irrelevant that a decade was involved in both instances. The first decade, from 1912 to 1922, began with a united Greece victorious against foreign enemies in two Balkan Wars. By 1917, however, the country was so divided that it had two separate governments, the king's in Athens and Eleftherios Venizelos's in Thessaloniki; after that, each successive government attempted (unsuccessfully) to restore unity by invading Asia Minor. Ideologically, the wars of 1912-1922 were motivated by a single purpose: the irredentist desire to incorporate into the Greek state the ethnic Greek populations of Macedonia, Thrace, and Asia Minor. Known as the Μεγάλη Ιδέα (Great Idea), this purpose, along with the glory that would have accompanied its realization, went up in smoke with the burning of Smyrna in 1922. The second decade, 1940 to 1949/1950, likewise began with a united Greece, in this case a Greece unified in its effort to repel Mussolini and then to resist the German occupiers. But by 1943 the Resistance forces were fighting each other; after the Germans withdrew (1944), the country endured two periods of civil war.

Ritsos lived through this, just as Sophocles had lived from the victorious unity of Salamis to the catastrophic disunity of the penultimate years of the Peloponnesian War, culminating in Aegospotami shortly after his death. And, although we shall probably never know how directly Sophocles was involved, or what his precise attitude was in 409, we do have clear evidence regarding Ritsos's involvement and also, luckily, regarding his personal attitude precisely at the time that he was beginning his *Philoctetes*. In relation to the first decade we know, for example, that the Asia Minor disaster of 1922, and the economic problems it created for Greece, gave the *coup de grâce* to the already dire economic situation of his father, forcing the adolescent son to seek work in an

Athens seething with refugees. It was this situation that led directly to Ritsos's communist allegiance. In relation to the second, we know that Ritsos identified with the anti-German Resistance in 1941, celebrated the defeated leftists in his poem Ρωμιοσύνη ("Greekness") directly after the 1944-1945 phase of the civil war, was arrested in 1948 after the civil war's resumption, and was detained in concentration camps for four years. His attitude toward all this at the precise time he began to draft *Philoctetes* (May 1963) is revealed in an essay called 'Περί Μαγιακόβσκη' ('Concerning Mayakovsky'), to which I shall refer later.

What I have attempted to show so far is that in our attempt to see in the modern poem reflections (1) of the political events themselves, (2) of Ritsos's direct participation in those events, and (3) of his attitude at the time, we possess much more material than we do for Sophocles. In addition, we have Sophocles's play to tell us what to look for. Here I have space to cite just a sampling of the many political and personal reflections that appear.

The wars of 1912-1922 were motivated, as noted above, by the Great Idea.

Ritsos's most unmistakable hint that he is using the Trojan War to speak about twentieth-century irredentism comes when Neoptolemus bitterly describes the Achaean leaders as setting forth

> ...καθένας χώρια...: καθένας
> για ένα δικό του λόγο, μια ξεχωριστή φιλοδοξία, στεγασμένη
> κάτω από μια μεγάλη ιδέα, έναν κοινό σκοπό....

> ...each one individually...: each
> for a private reason, a distinct ambition sheltered
> underneath a single great idea, a common purpose...
> (377-379)[35]

Less obviously, the parallel is established in the opening lines as Neoptolemus, called to end the Trojan War after ten years of fighting, sounds like a young Greek being sent out to Smyrna shortly before the débâcle of 1922, as

---

35   Γιάννης Ρίτσος, *Φιλοκτήτης* (Athens: Kedros, 1965). A second printing appeared in 1970. The poem was then included in the collection of Ritsos's longer poems entitled *Τέταρτη Διάσταση* (Athens: Kedros, 1972), 247-265. A translation by Peter Bien appeared in *Shenandoah* 27.1 (Fall 1975): 68-87. The following rendering is taken from that version, as are all subsequent ones.

he complains to Philoctetes:

> ...Εμείς οι νεότεροι
> που κληθήκαμε, όπως λένε, την ύστατη στιγμή για να δρέψουμε τάχα
> τη δόξα την ετοιμασμένη με τα δικά σας όπλα,
> με τις δικές σας πληγές, με το δικό σας θάνατο,
> ...
> Μια τέτοια δόξα μας έλειπε·—ποιός τους την ζήτησε;

> ...We of the younger generation,
> called up at the very last minute, as they say, supposedly to reap
> the glory that all of you prepared for us
> with your arms, your wounds, your deaths:
> ...
> We could have done without such glory! Did we ever ask for it?
> (1-4, 9)

If we consider the Peloponnesian War as well as the Trojan, the parallel is strengthened. When Bernard Knox describes Sophocles's Athens as attempting "to impose its political will ... on all Hellas," we think as well of irredentist Greece in the twentieth century, and when the same critic continues by describing the Sicilian Expedition as "a megalomaniac venture," we have an apt description of modern Greece's disastrous attempt to control Smyrna and its hinterland. Sophocles's Athens rose "to a height when the mastery of the whole Greek world seemed within its grasp," only to fall catastrophically;[36] in 1918, Ritsos's Greece seemed to have the mastery of Constantinople itself in its grasp, only to lose everything four years later. Once the two parallels—the Trojan War and the Peloponnesian—enter our consciousness, passage after passage unveils the relationship between Ritsos's poem and the horrendous decade of 1912-1922. For example: the common soldiers being transported across the sea to Troy (i.e. to Anatolia) "like lambs / being led to the slaughter for others' profit" (389-390); the squabbles of the lenders, each filled with "the savage passion for preeminence" (398); Neoptolemus's sarcastic invitation to Philoctetes: "The ten years are over now.... / Come to see... / ...for what internal hatreds / we exchanged our former enemies" (524-527); or the youth's articulation, at the end, of the "inescapable fear of asking / why we went, why

36 Knox (above, note 30) 59-60.

51

we fought, why we are going home—and where" (540-541).

Anyone familiar with modern Greek history will recognize how strongly, for someone of Ritsos's leftist orientation, many of these same passages also evoke the decade 1940-1950, when once again unity gave way to factionalism, hope to disillusion, and the communists' near-mastery of Greece to their utter defeat. Now, if we take these same lines that were just cited in relation to 1912-1922 and re-read them in relation to 1940-1950, we shall see that the Great Idea and common purpose of irredentism are metamorphosed into the socialist vision of a people's democracy as Ritsos describes the disillusioned heroes who went full of idealism to their "Troy" in the guerrilla strongholds of the Greek mountains:

> ...κι αυτοί ξεκίνησαν κάποτε...
> ...ν' αναμορφώσουν τον κόσμο. Ξεκίνησαν
> όλοι μαζί, καθένας χώρια, ...καθένας
> για ένα δικό του λόγο, μια ξεχωριστή φιλοδοξία, στεγασμένη
> κάτω από μια μεγάλη ιδέα, έναν κοινό σκοπό,—διάφανη στέγη
> που κάτω της διακρίνονταν καλύτερα του καθενός το κομμάτιασμα

> ...these too set forth one day...
> ...to reform the world. They set forth
> together, each one individually, ...each
> for a private reason, a distinct ambition sheltered
> underneath a single great idea, a common purpose whose transparency
> made that much clearer every man's fragmented self.

> (375-380)

During the periods of enemy occupation and civil war, the common people were once again led to slaughter for others' profit; the squabbling leaders were once again filled with the savage passion for preeminence, and the Greeks exchanged their common enemies—the Germans now instead of the Turks—for their own internal hatreds. The "myriad-eyed machination" (313) of the rank and file against their leaders, the desire "to take back whatever they stole from us, to commandeer it, even" (314), perhaps suggests the bitter resentment felt by the guerrilla forces in the mountains against the official government in Athens following the German withdrawal. More terrible still is Ritsos's evocation (always in terms of the Trojan expedition, of course) of the disparity between (a) the original exultation of the resistance fighters, when one and all "set forth.../ ...to reform the world" (375-376), and (b) the later dejection of those who realized that everything had gone wrong:

...αυτοί οι ίδιοι
που χόρευαν τα βράδια πάνω απ' τις φωτιές κι αστράφτανε
τα γυμνά πέλματά τους ολοπόρφυρα,—τώρα ζαρώνουνε
ανάμεσα στα βράχια, χολώνουν, γκρινιάζουν, βάζουν την παλάμη
μπροστά στα σκέλια τους, ντρέπονται, κρύβονται,
σα νάχουν φταίξει, σα να τους έχουν όλοι φταίξει.

             ... those same who
danced at night vaulting campfire flames
their bare soles flashing vermilion—they cower now
amid the crags, they sulk and whine, they place their palms
over their thighs, they hide in shame as though they'd done
some wrong to others and all the others had done some wrong to them.
                 (366-371)

Anyone familiar with Ritsos's poetry cannot fail to connect this passage with the exultant dancing of the guerrilla forces evoked in Part 4 of *Romiosíni* and thus to feel the contemporaneousness of Neoptolemus's account.[37] This feeling of contemporaneousness is strengthened by another passage in which Ritsos introduces topography and other conditions that clearly suggest, not the encampment outside of Troy, next to the ships in which the Achaeans arrived, but instead the long, grim, thirsty marches of the guerrilla army during

---

37   κι όταν χόρευαν στην πλατεία.
           μέσα στα σπίτια τρέμαν τα ταβάνια και κουδούνιζαν
             τα γυαλικά στα ράφια.
           and when they danced in the square
           ceilings shook in the houses and glassware
             jingled on the shelves.
Ρωμιοσύνη is collected in *Ποιήματα Β'* (Athens: Kedros, 1961), pp. 59-72. The lines quoted above appear on p. 65. A translation by N. C. Germanacos first came out in *Chelsea* 30-31 (1972) and was reprinted in *The APR* 2/5 (September–October 1973): 13-17.

the periods of occupation and civil war (and/or the marches of the retreating troops in Anatolia):

Κείνος ο δρόμος ερημώθη ώς το βάθος. Απ' τις δυο πλευρές του
πηγάδια σκεπασμένα, μολυσμένα απ' τους νεκρούς...
...
                                    ...Μέσα στην ανελέητη λιακάδα
σπίθιζαν στά σαμάρια των τειχών, όρθια, σπασμένα τζάμια,
χωρίζοντας συντρόφους, φίλους, συμπολεμιστές...
                              ...Είδα άντρες γενναίους
να ρίχνουν στάχτη στα μαλλιά τους· κ' είδα τη στάχτη
ν' ανακατεύεται με τα δάκρυά τους.

That road was ravaged along its entire length. Its wells on either side
were covered over, polluted by cadavers ...
...
              ... Atop the coping of the walls
stood bits of broken glass that sparked in unrelenting sunlight
as they divided comrades, friends, and fellow-fighters...
                              ...I saw courageous men
throw ashes in their hair and saw the ashes
mingle with their tears...

                                        (354-355, 357-362)

This disillusion experienced by Neoptolemus, and brought up into his consciousness during his long monologue, is the necessary prelude to his sympathetic understanding of Philoctetes's withdrawal from the war. "How, my friend, could you have brought some order / to that chaos?" he asks the older man (381-382), and then: "How could you stand by them?" (382).

Yet we know that Philoctetes did stand by them at the end. We know that Neoptolemus's mission to bring Philoctetes to Troy was accomplished. The poem's basic question becomes: Why does Philoctetes condescend to participate despite his awareness of the distressing truth of war? The answer, I believe, is that Philoctetes has learned that contradiction is positive. Why is it positive? *Because when we erect a bridge between thesis and antithesis we achieve the possibility of a new, albeit fragile, synthesis that will redeem the fragmentation and futility of human history, if only momentarily.*

I have purposefully stated this in the abstract terminology of dialectical philosophy because the poem, although utilizing concrete visual and auditory images, is predominantly a philosophical meditation. Its principal subjects are (1) the opposition of freedom and necessity, absence and presence, the ideal and the real, the metaphysical and the physical, (2) the fusion of these opposites in life and (especially) in art. But the poem is also political; hence the abstractly philosophical answer "Because he has learned that contradiction is positive" should speak as well in a political way to the poem's basic questions. And so it does.

To appreciate *politically* why Philoctetes must go to Troy, why he must stand by them, we shall have to proceed to the final stage of our analysis, namely the examination of Ritsos's personal attitude at the time of the poem's composition.

I have already referred to the essay 'Concerning Mayakovsky,'[38] written in May 1963 just as Ritsos was beginning *Philoctetes*. Although ostensibly discussing the work of another poet, this essay obviously expresses Ritsos's personal position. Less obviously, it glosses *Philoctetes*; at a minimum we should note that the essay and the poem share the key verbal images "bridge," "silence," and "shouting," among others, indicating that Ritsos's deep thought-patterns were similar in these two works written at the same time.[39] But the

---

38   In: Yánnis Rítsos, *Μελετήματα* (Athens: Kedros, 1974), 9-33. The essay originally appeared as the introduction to Ritsos's translation of Mayakovsky's poems (Athens: Kedros, 1964).

39   Compare:
Essay: Είναι οι γέφυρες απ' το αόριστο στο ορισμένο, απ' το άπειρο στο πεπερασμένο και αντίστροφα. Παντού και πάντα τούτη η "γέφυρα," που κάποτε τη βλέπουμε...ακριβώς τη στιγμή που έχει πατήσει...τις δου αντίθετες όχθες (p. 22).
Poem: σα νάμαι μια μπουκιά σταματημένη στο λαρύγγι του απείρου καί ταυτόχρονα μια γέφυρα
πάνω από δυό, τό ίδιο απόκρημνες κι άγνωστες, όχθες—
(lines 341-342)
Essay: Οι πρώτες κραυγές...παραχωρούν τη θέση τους σε μια πιό σιωπηλή περίσκεψη...Οι σημερινοί ποιητές..."φτιάχνουν τις φράσεις τους πάνω στο πρότυπο της σιωπής" (p. 29).
Poem: ανάμεσα στους γόους...
                         ...θα μας είναι...
                η δική σου...σιωπή, μια πυξίδα.
                              (lines 530-532)
Essay: Κ' εδώ η ίδια λαμπρότητα...είναι, άν όχι μια σύνθεση και ένωση των φυσικών,

similarities appear as well if, quite aside from verbal echoes, we consider the actual position taken in the essay. Looking back over the political events of the past few decades, Ritsos concludes that they belie the mechanistic Marxist perception "της άμεσης, αστραπιαίας και ολοκληρωτικής αντανάκλασης του οικονομικοκοινωνικού φαινομένου στο πνευματικό υπερεποικοδόμημα." (of the direct, instantaneous and thoroughgoing effect of socioeconomic phenomena on the intellectual superstructure.)[40] In simple language, this means that neither socialism nor any other political system automatically changes human culture for the better. "Πολλοί μύθοι παλαιότεροι και νεότεροι," Ritsos insists, "γκρεμίστηκαν...Μάθαμε πόσο δύσκολο είναι να μην κάνεις κατάχρηση της εξουσίας που σου δόθηκε στ' όνομα τού μεγαλύτερου ιδανικού της ελευθερίας, να μην κάνεις κατάχρηση περιαυτολογίας στ' όνομα του αντιατομισμού, να μην κάνεις αγώνα προσωπικής επικράτησης στ' όνομα της σεμνής, ανώνυμης μάζας." (Many of the older myths, and also the newer ones, have been demolished...We have learned how difficult it is not to abuse the power given us in the name of that great ideal, freedom, how difficult to avoid boasting in the name of the campaign against individualism, to avoid fighting for personal domination in the name of the modest, anonymous masses.)[41] Although ostensibly explaining why Mayakovsky's simplistically overconfident poetry is no longer possible, these sentiments obviously derive from Ritsos's own experience of the savage passion for preeminence motivating those who set forth one day to reform the world. The remainder of the essay, however, shows that this direct experience of the human weakness infecting all idealism has not tempted Ritsos to become cynical or defeatist; it has simply impelled him to call for an abandonment of facile optimism. In responsible poetry, he says,

ηθικών και κοινωνικών αντιθέσεων, είναι τουλάχιστον ένα *γεφύρωμα* ανάμεσα στο παρόν και στο μέλλον, ανάμεσα στο πραγματικό και το φανταστικό, ανάμεσα στο άτομο και στην ομάδα, ανάμεσα στον άνθρωπο και στον κόσμο, ανάμεσα στη ζωή και στ' όνειρο...(p. 20).

Poem: ...το φώς του λυκόφωτος είναι...

...

        ...μια ολότελα ανεξάρτητη σύνθεση
της νύχτας και της μέρας...
        (lines 485, 488-489)

These and other verbal motifs, such as hands, masks, and transparency, are explored in my linguistic analysis of *Philoctetes* noted earlier (above, note 31).

40   Ritsos, *Μελετήματα* (above, note 38) p. 30.

41   Ritsos, *Μελετήματα* (above, note 38) p. 29.

the "πρῶτες κραυγές του ενθουσιασμού... παραχωροὑν τη θέση τους σε μια πιό σιωπηλή περίσκεψη" (the first shouts of enthusiasm...have given way to a more silent circumspection).[42]

Once we know this attitude, we can register the way in which Ritsos's poem reflects the author's political vicissitudes in the period 1940-1950 and afterwards. The question asked Philoctetes, "How could you stand by them?" now calls up Ritsos's own dilemma: his recognition of the problematical nature of human activity, on the one hand, and his determination to avoid cynicism, defeatism, and permanent withdrawal, on the other. We know that Ritsos himself did continue his active involvement. In the very month that he wrote the essay and began the poem (May 1963, as noted earlier), he kept vigil outside the hospital where the peace activist Gregory Lambrakis lay dying after the attack on him by rightist thugs. Philoctetes's withdrawal and Neoptolemus's agonized meditation would seem to reflect Ritsos's need for circumspection, while the conclusion of the poem, where Philoctetes hands over his weapons to Neoptolemus and goes off to Troy so that his "επιείκεια και σιωπή" (clemency and silence) may become "μια πυξίδα" (a compass) for vanquisher and vanquished alike (532, 530),[43] would seem to reflect Ritsos's refusal to lapse permanently into withdrawal or individualism.

Synthesizing these antitheses, we may attempt to articulate the author's to-

---

42   Ritsos, Μελετήματα (above, note 38) p. 29.

43   We have an *ex post facto* gloss on the important word επιείκεια in another essay, written a decade later, in which Ritsos describes his collection Θυρωρείο as follows: "Εκεί, η αβάσταχτη 'σπανιότητα' του ατομικού, διαλύεται πραϋντικά μέσα στην αθωωτική καθολικότητα που στεγάζει συντροφικά τους πάντες και τα πάντα. Η ασυννενοησία και ακατανοησία κατακαθίζει σε μιαν επιείκεια και συχώρεση, αν όχι σε μια παραδοχή και συνεννόηση,...κάτι σαν μια εκτεταμένη, πέρα απ᾽ τις διαφορές και τις αμοιβαίες μομφές, ευγενική αδελφοσύνη." ("There, the unbearable 'rarity' of individualism is soothingly alleviated within the exonerative catholicity that jointly shelters everyone and everything. Disagreement and incomprehension subside into clemency and forgiveness, if not into acceptance and agreement...something like a gentle brotherliness extending beyond various and mutual reproaches." Ritsos, Μελετήματα [above, note 38] 106.) All this would seem to gloss not only this particular word but also the general wisdom acquired by Philoctetes as a result of his solitude and meditations. As for his former method of dealing with distressing reality, a method symbolized by his famous weapons (Ritsos changes Sophocles's single bow into three lances in accordance with the poem's basis in Hegelian dialectic), we should note that this method is not abandoned completely but rather is transferred to the younger generation—Neoptolemus opens his monologue with a phrase that generalizes his status: "Εμείς οι νεότεροι" (We of the younger generation).

tal political vision as projected in the poem: Human nature and human activity will always be problematical. This is our fate; to be alive means to participate in a problematical world.[44] We must go to Troy, but we must go there no longer deluded by a mechanistic or simplistic Marxism that history itself has refuted, or by any other slogan or discredited myth that creates a facile optimism. If, however, we do go in this knowing way and allow our "silence"—so sterile and suicidal when sequestered on an island of withdrawal—to reside at the core of the shouting, a kind of miracle will take place, a fusion reaction releasing new energies that will serve mankind as a "bridge" to the future. Ritsos seems to move from a mechanistic justification for action toward a transcendental justification expressible only in the language of the saints. Indeed, the poem bursts into a fully orchestrated mysticism in the epilogue, as Philoctetes's transparent face "[γ]ίνεται...πιο παρόν" and the mask of action glows with "ακατανόητη κατάφαση" in the "μυστηριώδη μακαριότητα της νύχτας."[45]

Now we can begin to understand why a *deus ex machina* is needed in Ritsos's *Philoctetes*. To move from a realization of the problematic nature of human existence—i.e. to move from a revulsion from history because of its contradictions—to a sense that contradictions are bridgeable, synthesizable, and positive, requires "insanity,"[46] what Kierkegaard would call an illogical leap of faith. This leap, in turn, demands an extra source of propulsion, a nudge from the outside similar to the transcendental energy that determined Philoctetes to go to Troy so suddenly and illogically in Sophocles's play, or that converted Saint Paul. In the modern equivalent, however, the transcendental becomes chthonian; the energizing god does not descend from above but ascends from below. Herakles is replaced by the common people of Greece; the Olympian

---

44   Cf. Ritsos, Μελετήματα (above, note 38) 30: "αυτό που έλεγαν άλλοτε Μοίρα, και που και σήμερα ο όρος είναι θεμιτός με την έννοια του προβληματισμού της καταγωγής του ανθρώπου, της θέσης του μέσα στο σύμπαν και του αναπότρεπτου του θανάτου" (that which used to be called Fate, a term that today may legitimately mean the problematical origin of man, his position in the universe, and his inevitable mortality).

45   As Philoctetes's face "becomes more present" and the mask of action glows with "incomprehensible affirmation" in "the mysterious beatitude of the night."

46   Compare the essay, where Ritsos glosses a poem in which Mayakovsky hails his "τρέλλα" (insanity) as the characteristic that paradoxically enables him to return to earth, to men, to love. (Ritsos, Μελετήματα [above, note 38] p. 21).

pronouncement becomes a folk song; the redeeming principle is no longer outside of life; it is life itself, finally accepted by the intellectual in its problematical wholeness and unity as a given, as his Fate. In Ritsos's words applied to Mayakovsky, this insane leap into acceptance makes one feel resurrected, but the modern resurrection experienced by the modern Philoctetes is "an inversion of the Christian resurrection,"[47] since the movement is not from the physical to the metaphysical, but the other way round. It is a return to earth, to men, to love, to community.

Viewed politically, then, Ritsos's *Philoctetes* traces a journey away from an old myth, the mechanistic conception of social amelioration redeeming human nature, and toward a mystical socialism whose transcendental principle governing history is still the Hegelian dialectic of thesis-antithesis-synthesis but whose supreme teacher is now the common people of Greece, the modest, anonymous masses who so effortlessly synthesize contradictions and whose good-natured endurance—that affable smile illuminating the dark tragedy of human endeavor—is the real lesson of Greek political history.

Politically, the poem attempts to come to terms with Ritsos's own annealment in the furnace of Greek history: the cruelties and disillusionments of 1940-1950 in particular, and also of 1912-1922, periods that taught him the realities behind political crusades and that, instead of destroying his ideals, tempered them into a different kind of strength: a clemency and silence meant to serve others as a compass.

Ritsos chose to explore these problems in terms not simply of twentieth-century Greek history but of history in general, as typified by the full span of Greek experience across the ages. And what better way to do this—to make private experience public, Greek experience universally human—than through myth, employed not as an evasion of history but as a means of ranging back and forth between ancient and modern times to see what form the eternal story (that of Philoctetes in this case) would take in our own day? The form is different: no Odysseus, no physical pain, some very surprising *homines ex machina*. Yet the substance is strikingly similar. Why should Sophocles's Philoctetes go to Troy? Why should Ritsos's Philoctetes do the same? Why should, and did, the two heroes stand by their inadequate, even hated, fellow

---

47   Ritsos, Μελετήματα (above, note 38) p. 20.

beings? The answer that Jan Kott applies to Sophocles is equally applicable to Ritsos: "The island was a refuge from cruel history....One cannot run away from history."[48] That is the political significance of Yannis Ritsos's *Philoctetes*.

---

48   Kott (above, note 30) pp. 184-185.

4. Antithesis and Synthesis in Yannis Ritsos's *Philoctetes*

I

Ritsos's *Philoctetes* is a very difficult poem. My effort to teach it to university students has shown me that although it exercises an emotional influence upon them especially when recited aloud, its intellectual content remains uncertain and confusing. "What does the poem mean?" they ask me. "What is it trying to say?" I am tempted to reply that a poem does not mean anything; it simply exists. However, this would be a faulty presentation of Ritsos's art. In *Philoctetes* we are dealing with an intellectual text and not with one that is simply aesthetic or emotional. Indeed, Ritsos's achievement is precisely that he succeeds in assimilating thought to emotion in a way that causes the poem's feeling to deepen its intellectual content and the intellectual content to restrain and direct the feeling.

I conclude that we need to confront the intellectual content of *Philoctetes*. The problem is a methodological one. We could read the text carefully, separate out specific passages, and present these as the poet's "message." This methodology is extremely dangerous for many reasons. First, the speaker throughout the poem is Neoptolemos, not Ritsos. It is a mistake to assume that a character's opinions are necessarily those of the author himself. (This holds true as well for the prologue and epilogue, both of which are "dramatic" even though they are not spoken by a specific character.) Second, although certain passages of a didactic nature exist in the poem, Ritsos's general tendency for many decades was to be wary of didactic pronouncements, We no longer find ourselves in the nineteenth century, when a poet such as John Keats, thanks to a totally clear aphorism, could summarize the thoughts he enclosed in his 'Ode on a Grecian Urn' as "Beauty is truth, truth beauty." Third, in a poem like *Philoctetes* in which thought, emotion, and imagination are so expertly integrated, every attempt to isolate the threads of thought and to examine them apart for everything else will surely lead to distortion.

These reasons lead me to suggest a more suitable methodology for discovering the poem's intellectual content—namely, examining its tropes and imagery. This will enable us to confront the poem's intellectual content no longer as a separate category but as something inextricably connected with the very elements that transmit the poem's emotion and give the poem its aesthetic shape. We will acquire a still greater power to penetrate more deeply into Neoptolemos's thought and thus to reach Ritsos's as well, since it is logical to accept that, even if the ideas of a certain character in a poem are not necessarily the ideas of the author, the imagery and tropes by which these ideas are expressed may open a pathway toward the author's own thought. This methodology, which has been successful in the examination of ancient Greek drama and Shakespeare's plays, as well as difficult texts by contemporary poets, should also illuminate what is dark in Ritsos.

II

In the special case of Sophocles's *Philoctetes*, the usefulness of lexical analysis is demonstrated by Bernard Knox's *The Heroic Temper*. Isolating key words that recur frequently, Knox uses them to ferret out the work's basic ideas. The most obvious examples are φύσις (nature; ll. 874, 1310) and γενναῖος (noble-minded; ll. 798, 1068). In Ritsos's case it is easy to pinpoint repeated words and tropes that seem to be significant; consequently, we may attempt the sort of lexical analysis that I am suggesting. Modern Greek writers are the only ones in the contemporary world who can quote excerpts from ancient Greek texts with the expectation that they will be comprehensible to a Greek audience and that the hints they furnish will be recognized. In this case, our first hope is that Ritsos employed some of the very same words that are so important in Sophocles's play. But he apparently did not wish to link his contemporary poem to the ancient model by means of a common vocabulary. The only words that frequently recur in both texts are μόνος (alone) and ὅπλα (weapons). These probably do not testify to any deliberate effort by Ritsos to employ lexical echoes from Sophocles; they appear in both texts simply because of similarity in theme. It is noteworthy that the ancient Greek terms φύσις and γενναῖος, both of which survive unchanged in modern Greek and could easily have been used, do not occur at all in Ritsos's text. Consequently, if our analysis is to proceed, it must be satisfied with non-Sophoclean words.

A useful procedure established by Knox draws our attention to words that equate one person with another—a process that I will call "transference." "Neoptolemos," Knox says, "is a prey to emotions that he can no longer conceal, and they force from him a sudden cry—παπαῖ (l. 895). It is no ordinary exclamation; it is the same cry of agony we have heard Philoctetes utter [thrice] in his torment" (ll. 745–746).[49] According to Knox, this "transference" is a key to interpretation. The unpremeditated cry by Neoptolemos convinces us of his equation with Philoctetes.

In Ritsos's poem, lexical "transference" plays a significant role because it is often our only indication that a specific person or idea is equated with another. It acts as a skeleton providing both structure and meaning to a poem that otherwise might seem chaotic and/or incomprehensible.

We see this in the case of hands that are transparent, initially applied to Neoptolemos's mother (ll. 193–197). The relationship between mother and Philoctetes is strengthened when we read that his face is transparent (l. 516).[50] In order to acquire a clearer understanding of the meaning hidden behind this image, we may benefit from the "transference" of another key word: απουσία (absence). This broadens transparency until it becomes complete non-appearance. It is used in connection with the mother (l. 143), with Neoptolemos, who is tormented by the absence of his voice (l. 434), and with Philoctetes, who also has this awareness of absence (l. 428). The relation to the transparent face becomes clear in the poem's Epilogue when Philoctetes accepts, yet afterwards rejects, the "mask of action" (l. 514) offered him by Neoptolemos as an opaque covering for his face before he leaves for Troy. Indeed, his face becomes more "present," overcoming his absence.

In addition, the reason why Philoctetes must go to Troy becomes clear if we consider the relationship with Neoptolemos's mother that is created by means of the lexical "transference." She is obviously dead— nonexistent—owing to her insulation from life's threats. Philoctetes has chosen the same road: his

---

49   Bernard Knox, *The Heroic Temper* (Berkeley: University of California Press, 1964), p. 132.

50   The Greek text of *Philoctetes* is printed in Ritsos's *Τέταρτη Διάσταση* (Athens: Kedros, 1976), pp. 247–265. The line numbers that I cite begin with the actual verse, not with the prose prologue.

wound, as interpreted by Ritsos, was occasioned by himself as a pretext for him to be rescued from the war and accordingly to withdraw into "freedom" and philosophical reflection in order to comprehend life's essence. Neoptolemos could not save his mother, yet now he manages to save Philoctetes, restoring him to life by taking him to Troy. To be alive, for Ritsos, means to renounce freedom, expose oneself to the "pillage" of life, participate in the necessary errors, the waste—the unavoidable ten years of the Trojan War (l. 546). When Philoctetes decides to leave his island, he is released from his transparency and absence. He no longer requires the mask. Unlike Neoptolemos's mother, he is indissolubly "present."

Other instances of "transference" might be mentioned, but I trust that the details presented above are sufficient to indicate the usefulness of this lexical approach derived from Bernard Knox's analysis of ancient texts. It might have been simpler, perhaps, to attribute this approach to the leitmotif technique employed by modern poetry, without mentioning Sophocles. This however would distort Ritsos, whose strongest connections are with ancient texts rather than with West European models despite those models' generally strong influence on contemporary Greek literature.

In Sophocles, key words seem to operate in still another fashion, creating strange combinations. An example is the double meaning of πόνος first as pain and secondly as an achievement, the fruits of labor. When Neoptolemos expresses his sympathy to Philoctetes, he employs the word in its first, more common meaning:

ἰὼ ἰώ, δύστηνε σύ,
δύστηνε δῆτα διὰ πόνων πάντων φανείς. (ll. 759–760)

oh, wretched you,
wretched you indeed, as pain of every kind reveals you.

When, however, the same word is repeated toward the end in Herakles' speech, it takes on the nuances of the second meaning and, thanks to the aorist participle πονήσας, is juxtaposed in the same verse with the first meaning in a way that projects the following paradox:

καὶ πρῶτα μέν σοι τὰς ἐμὰς λέξω τύχας,
ὅσους πονήσας καὶ διεξελθών πόνους
ἀθάνατον ἀρετήν ἔσχον... (ll. 1418–1420)

To start with, I will tell you my own fortunes—
how by hard work and endured toil
I won immortal fame . . .

A somewhat different lexical game shows us still another paradox. It consists of the words νόσος (disease) and νῆσος (island). The paradox consists
in the fact that the island, symbolizing Philoctetes's isolation—which in turn
conveys his superior ethical stature compared to the ethically diseased generals in Troy—is truly Philoctetes's disease.[51]

We do not encounter such key words or such paradoxes everywhere in
Sophocles's work; nevertheless, they serve to make us aware of something
that in Ritsos's poem is everywhere present, and that I intend now to investigate in depth.

III

Examining the language and imagery of *Philoctetes*, we immediately observe antithesis as a much-repeated characteristic. If we look still further, we
discover a second prominent characteristic: synthesis. Let us examine each
of these in turn.

A rhetorical trope that seems to be especially favored by Ritsos in this poem
(as in others) is the oxymoron, which may be defined as a form of antithesis
in which opposing elements are juxtaposed in order to emphasize their contradictory nature. A perfect oxymoron in *Philoctetes* is ανάλαφρο βάρος (l.
421; imponderous weight, light heaviness). More often, Ritsos is satisfied with
creating an oxymoron by assigning a noun two adjectives of contradictory
meaning. Here are some examples: a gesture is superfluous and necessary (l.
14; μιάς περιττής κι αναγκαίας χειρονομίας); knowledge is sweet and terrible

51   Cf. William H. Calder III, "Sophoclean Apologia: Philoctetes," *Greek, Roman and
Byzantine Studies* 12 (1971): 153–174: "Odysseus knows too that Philoctetes's 'tragic flaw' is his
loneliness—the νόσος-νῆσος motive" (p. 161). Calder also refers to the opinion of Andreas
Spira: "Νόσος-νῆσος bleibt das beherrschende Motiv: Qual der Krankheit—Qual der Einsam-
keit und Heimatferne" (*Untersuchungen zum Deus ex Machina bei Sophokles und Euripides*
[Kallmünz/Opf., 1960], p. 17).

PETER BIEN

(l. 451; μελιχρή και τρομερή); soldiers are sexually aroused and innocent (l. 90; ερωτικοί κι αθώοι); the glimmer of twilight is "so brief and yet immortal" (l. 490; τόσο σύντομο, κι αθάνατο ωστόσο); Helen's veils are somber, sparkling (l. 553; σκοτεινά, σπιθίζοντα); a layer of air is invulnerable, most thin (l. 492; άτρωτο, λεπτότατο). In other cases, the impression of an oxymoron is preserved even though the lexical structure is more diffuse. Neoptolemos's mother is present in her constant absence (l. 142–143; παρούσα / μέσα στη διαρκή απουσία της); freedom squeezes tight (l. 500; περισφίγγει); Neoptolemos claims to hear his own silence (l. 434; ν' ακούσω τη σιωπή μου); the soldiers are immobile upon the ever-mobile sea (l. 418; ακίνητοι...πάνω στο αεικίνητο πέλαγος); a bee is as though beleaguered by bliss (l. 210; σαν πολιορκημένη); a shadow is a circle of light (208; κύκλος φωτεινός).

These details of antithetical expression are so frequent that it is impossible to avoid noticing them. As soon as we do notice them, we begin to wonder whether they exist solely for their own sake or, more broadly, in order to furnish hints that lead to the poem's deeper meaning. Our curiosity increases as we perceive that many of the poem's descriptive passages reflect not only the form but also the essence of these lexical tropes. Neoptolemos continually describes situations involving striking antitheses: his father as opposed to his mother, life at home and life in the bivouac, Apollo's chariot above and oxcarts below (ll. 273–275), food for corpses and food for the living (ll. 25-26), knowledge of nothingness and the impression of a well-shaped knee (ll. 405, 408), the leaders and the common soldiers, silence and shouting, the soldiers' laughter and their weapons (l. 101), sweaty hunters and a serene gardener (ll. 172, 178–180), light and darkness. It becomes increasingly clear that these antitheses are not present simply for the sake of form. They reflect the poem's chief thematic motifs, let alone its basic symbols and its two basic protagonists. In other words, the similarity of form between lexical and descriptive elements, a similarity that is observed without great difficulty, is a major hint that directs us to investigate deeper meanings and themes that otherwise would perhaps be difficult to perceive. We begin now to appreciate Neoptolemos and Philoctetes not simply as two characters in the Sophoclean drama upon which Ritsos's poem is based, but as youth and maturity, another pair of antitheses. We begin to suspect that antitheses such as light and dark or silence and shouting do not serve simply a descriptive purpose in the poem but also a symbolic one. The antithetical relationship of mother and father becomes clearer as does the relationship between the soldiers' laughter (life, joy, sex) and their weapons (death). The opaque mask of action becomes less incomprehensible when we realize that it is meant to cover Philoctetes's diaphanous face. If we proceed to a general view of all the specific antitheses in the poem, we discover that this work is thematically concerned with pairs of antithetical meanings such as action and contemplation, necessity and freedom, the physical and the metaphysical.

Thus we advance step by step from a minimal oxymoron such as "imponderous weight" toward a knowledge of the poem's basic subject. On the other hand, if we stop here and conclude that *Philoctetes* has as its principal content the existence of antitheses, we will make a bad mistake. Oxymorons serve as an initial indication that will lead in a faulty direction if we fail to look beyond them—that is, beyond antithesis. Let us not forget that an oxymoron is a form of antithesis that emphasizes a paradoxical contradiction. It may be stark and uncompromising like John Milton's famous "darkness visible" (*Paradise Lost* I.63). However, since an unresolved contradiction creates discomfort, we often find in the oxymoron a playful tone that dissolves away this discomfort, as for example in Romeo's outcry to Benvolio (*Romeo and Juliet* I.i.175-179):

> O anything of nothing first create!
> O heavy lightness, serious vanity,
> misshapen chaos of well-seeming forms!
> Feather of lead, bright smoke, cold fire, sick health,
> still-waking sleep that is not what it is!

In both of these types—the serious and the playful—we sense the mutual clash of the antitheses, and that is all, since the opposites remain firm in their contradictoriness. Ritsos's oxymorons are different in that they do not remain firm in their contradictoriness but transcend opposition via synthesis. The oxymoron is a clue leading to the refutation of the oxymoron.

I will be able to show this better with a careful analysis of the way in which the poem's most important symbols are developed. Before commencing such an analysis, however, I would like to remark that Ritsos's interest in synthesis may be highlighted if we compare his poem with its model, Sophocles's work, which, like Ritsos's, presents contradictory themes, for example withdrawal and action, good and evil, a person who is simultaneously accursed and blessed. However, in Sophocles the contradiction is solved by eliminating one of its elements. Philoctetes's wound (evil, a curse) will be cured when the hero goes to Troy. Edmund Wilson is mistaken when he says that the Greek forces "cannot have the irresistible weapon without its loathsome owner"—mistaken because when they finally acquire the weapon, its possessor will cease to be loathsome.[52] In Ritsos's poem, on the contrary, the contradiction is resolved via assimilation and not elimination. It is characteristic that Ritsos eliminates the prophecy concerning Philoctetes's cure. Indeed, Neoptolemos states that the wound is incurable (l. 72),[53] which is fine seeing that the wound, for Ritsos, is the existential curse/blessing of consciousness. Another noteworthy change in Ritsos's text confirms his interest in synthesis. In Sophocles, Homer, and elsewhere in the mythical tradition, Philoctetes is a great archer whose weapon is the splendid bow given him by Heracles. In Ritsos, strangely, the bow is replaced by three spears. Yet this is not so strange when we remember that three is the dialectical number of the progression thesis-antithesis-synthesis. As such, it was cherished by Ritsos,[54] just as it was by Nikos Kazantzakis, who needed 33,333 verses in order to make his retelling of Homer's Odyssey incorporate a Hegelian dialectic of history.

IV

What I wish to maintain is that the oxymorons in *Philoctetes* reveal that the poem's intellectual content includes, above and beyond paradoxical contradiction, a dialectical vision of existence in which the principal movement is the reconciliation of thesis and antithesis into synthesis. In order to provide a foundation for this assertion, I will need to proceed to a careful analysis of

52   Edmund Wilson, *The Wound and the Bow* (Cambridge, Massachusetts: Houghton Mifflin, 1941), p. 294.

53   Although Ritsos departs from Sophocles here, he does not depart from the broader mythical tradition. In Pindar's brief narration of the story (Pythian I.53–55), as in Ritsos's more extensive version, there is no indication whatsoever that Philoctetes will be cured. On the contrary, after sacking Priam's city, Philoctetes «ἀσθενεῖ μὲν χρωτὶ βαίνων» (went on his way with a frame that was diseased).

54   Personal communication by Ritsos to the author.

the means by which certain pairs of antithetical symbols are developed from the beginning of the poem to its end.

One of the most significant pairs is silence-shouting. Throughout the poem, silence is equated with withdrawal and shouting with action. Neoptolemos tells Philoctetes that, cut off from social problems as he has been on his island, he has become "the great silence of your own existence" (l. 458). Neoptolemos himself, suddenly discovering a fourth dimension to existence—a metaphysical one—becomes speechless, hearing his own silence (l. 434), and for this reason (among others) develops a feeling of kinship with Philoctetes. (We should recall here the technique of "transference" mentioned earlier.) Contrariwise, the simple soldiers, when stimulated in the same way, react with shouts. Throbbing with life, they continually make noise. Compared to this, Philoctetes's withdrawal is a form of death despite the opportunities for wisdom that it offers (l. 59, "the snake of wisdom, maybe?"). The identification of silence with passivity and death is strengthened by the appearance of the same antithetical motifs elsewhere in the poem. In the strange tenth stanza, for example, a hero who has returned from battle "did not shout" at the moment when he was being killed by the "frenzied mob" that was supposedly acclaiming him (ll. 80–84). Throughout the poem, the clash of silence with noise is emphasized, as is the clash of withdrawal with action, passivity with liveliness. Yet at the poem's end the contradiction is resolved—not by obliteration of one of the opposites but by the synthesis of silence and noise, hence of contemplation and action as well. Once again, Ritsos departs from the Sophoclean prototype. Sophocles brings Philoctetes's isolation to an end, just as he has Heracles promise to cure the loathsome wound. Ritsos, contrariwise, makes Philoctetes bring his isolation with him to Troy. The poet shows this in many ways, but the clearest is by means of the specific thesis and antithesis that we have been examining. When Philoctetes departs for Troy, his silence will accompany him—a silence now joined to the noise—the wailing and groans—of action:

ανάμεσα στους γόους των νικημένων και των νικητών, το δικό σου
νοητικό, μειλίχιο χαμόγελο θα μάς είναι ένα φέγγος,
η δική σου επιείκεια και σιωπή, μια πυξίδα. (ll. 530-532)

amid the groans of vanquisher and vanquished,
your affable, intelligent smile will be a light for us,
your clemency and silence a compass.

Philoctetes must go to Troy so that his silence may be assimilated into the noise of victory, creating a deeper understanding. Action is hollow when not accompanied by metaphysical wisdom gained through the silence of individual meditation. Yet meditation is suicidal if divorced from action. The two opposites must join.

Light and darkness constitute an additional pair of symbols whose development provides us with yet another indication of the poem's dialectical apprehension of existence.

Light, sunshine, daylight, resplendence, etc. are generally linked with situations that strengthen life such as peace, commerce, food, laughter, sex, the daily chores of typical housewives. Darkness, shadows, nighttime, etc., contrariwise, are linked with elements that deny life such as war, shields, and death itself. The dichotomy is introduced very early in the poem when Neoptolemos recalls his childhood years in Achilles' palace during a period of constant warfare and speaks about dead heroes but also about the festive banquets of the living and about their shouting, which reminds him of the veil of a dancing-girl "whirling / between life and death" (ll. 20–21) and "dispersing the shields' shadows" (l. 23). Although the images of light and dark are introduced here only indirectly, we begin—perhaps unconsciously—to form groups of associated terms. Shadows relate now to shields and death; light, which disperses shadows, relates to dancing, shouting, vitality.

The same images are strengthened afterwards. Once again a division is created between the soldiers' weapons, martial plans, struggles, and ambitions on the one hand (ll. 101, 89) and, on the other, their laughter, manly shouting, sexual innocence (ll. 101, 87, 90). This division is paralleled with the other pair immediately afterwards as young Neoptolemos imagines the soldiers' shouting to be crossing "successive galleries /…of alternating light / and dark" (ll. 107–108).

In the first stage of his monologue, Neoptolemos remembers the childhood years when he naturally was still very far from achieving the profound understanding attributed to the mature Philoctetes. Ignorant at that point of the possibility of synthesis, he believed that he needed to choose between the soldiers' laughter and their weapons, just as Philoctetes had chosen previously. At least he believed this with one part of his conscious thought. At the same time, however, he was aware of the impossibility of choice (l. 85; η εκλογή, θαρρώ, ακατόρθωτη). He felt "so lonely then, so perplexed" (l. 99), and was especially frightened by Achilles' huge shadow, which prevented him from seeing sunlight (ll. 115–116). Although he did not possess any real solution in this initial phase, he instinctively followed the correct path—at least with regard to the symbolism of light and dark—because he withdrew into semi-darkness (l. 118), the union of light and dark. Naturally he did not possess any conscious awareness of dialectical movement; nevertheless, this action may be considered a subconscious preparation for the deeply conscious apprehension of synthesis that he acquires later in "a glorious dusk at sea" (466; ένα ένδοξο λυκόφως στον ωκεανό), upon which he comments as follows:

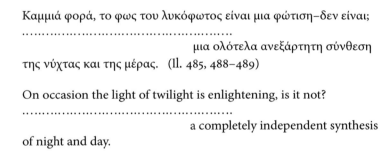

Καμμιά φορά, το φως του λυκόφωτος είναι μια φώτιση–δεν είναι;
....
                              μια ολότελα ανεξάρτητη σύνθεση
της νύχτας και της μέρας. (ll. 485, 488–489)

On occasion the light of twilight is enlightening, is it not?
....
                              a completely independent synthesis
of night and day.

In this first stage, at all events, the young man does not possess any solution. Despite the fact that his instinct sends him into the half-light of dusk, he continues to view life dualistically. Thus his narration of his childhood experiences continues by emphasizing the dissociation between light and dark. Accordingly, wherever he speaks about his mother, he repeatedly identifies shadows with death. The shadow of a rope (the hangman's noose) is discerned on her face (l. 152) as she sits inside the "somber frame" (l. 147) of the west window. In the yard behind the house, "where mountain-shade already / fell" (l. 168–169), the servant girls are plucking slaughtered birds for dinner. A plume with a red blot at its root settled on the mother's hair and "shaded her completely" (l. 189). When Neoptolemos removed it, it was as though "a dagger had been taken from her breast" (l. 192). Equally significant here is the young man's explanation: he removed the plume because he could not bear to see her "shaded by the sins of others" (l. 191). His youthful instinct naturally guides him to sunlight or at least to twilight. He wishes to avoid shadows or to do away with them. In other words, he wishes—like his mother and also like Philoctetes—to escape the sins of others and consequently to escape death. The poem as a whole, however, tells us that all those who attempt to escape life's negatives—sin, atrocity, warfare—become, just like the mother and Philoctetes, transparent and absent, lose their substance, their presence— in sum, die. In a strange way, therefore, a person's effort to keep himself far from sin and death is another form of death, whereas a person's acceptance of negatives is synonymous with life. As the poem progresses, we discover that to be alive requires not just light but also shadow. That is why Philoctetes must go to Troy.

As Neoptolemus's narration continues, we see that he is mobilized in turn (l. 211) and sent to a training camp in Oeta's shadow (l. 271). His first comment regarding this transfer from home to camp is "the lighting changed" (l. 217). He describes the bivouac at night with its bright red fires and vibrant sexuality. In addition, at night he is awakened by a fear, no longer of "the customary thieves / that might vault into our rooms," but now of "some thief unseen and undefined" (l. 250), a fear that is immediately generalized into an abstract "sense of perpetual thievery—pillage rather" (l. 257), something, as he now realizes, that was also present in his home (ll. 258–263). He is increasingly in a position to dull the sharp lines of division between the antitheses of peace and war, home and bivouac, day and night—increasingly able to apprehend the simultaneous existence of contraries without being tormented by contradiction. We are beginning to advance toward the final stage of the dialectical journey in which the clashing elements of thesis and antithesis advance to synthesis.

It is now difficult for Neoptolemos to avoid this journey since, despite his wishes, he is no longer able to invoke one side without the other. An example is his recollection of the opposite to life in the bivouac—namely, the serene daily routines of a neighboring village. Here, in the abundant daylight, fruit-sellers arrange their wares in piles, a philosopher goes for a stroll, women shake out bed sheets, athletes do short trial-laps "almost like birds in the air," temple metopes glow brightly (ll. 273–287). Many of the positive life-giving images of his childhood years are repeated here: nourishment (for living people, not for corpses), athletes (instead of slaughtered heroes), birds flying in the air (instead of being plucked for dinner), art, and above everything else the splendor of Greek light. But, he continues:

> Τούτη η λαμπρότητα,
> τυφλή, εκτυφλωτική, σ' αυτήν της ακριβώς την επίδειξη,
> σαν κάτι να μας έκρυβε—κι αλήθεια μάς έκρυβε·—
> μήπως εκείνη την κλοπή;   (ll. 288–291)

> This blind and blinding
> brightness seemed—precisely in its ostentation—
> to be holding something back from us (which truly was the case).
> That thievery perhaps?

The thievery previously separated from brightness now begins to be incorporated into brightness. At least to a minimal degree, Neoptolemos is apprehending the simultaneous existence of contrary antitheses.

As the poem advances and this apprehension is converted into profound comprehension, Neoptolemos becomes increasingly less frightened by paradox. Consequently, he no longer agonizes so much over the need to choose either one path or the other. (We should remember his previous awareness of the impossibility of choice.) Of course, he continues to be cognizant of the differing antitheses; yet the fact that he grasps their mutual relationship and not, as before, just their existence, moderates the clash within each pair to such a degree that he is soon in a position to understand—and indeed to experience with intense fullness, owing to a series of ecstatic discoveries—the full dialectical progression in which contraries unite to form a synthesis.

We should not be surprised to discover that this finally happens only when light and dark come together to form twilight. Then and only then is Neoptolemos empowered to utter his supreme appeal to Philoctetes: "Return with us" (l. 511).

The synthesis of light and dark enters the poem for the first time five stanzas above, as the youth declares to Philoctetes, "I've just recalled a glorious dusk at sea" (l. 466). The ensuing five stanzas, filled as they are with paradoxes, are difficult, perhaps even incomprehensible; hence we must venture a careful analysis.

All together, the five stanzas may be divided into three parts. In the first, Neoptolemos testifies to the same actualities of infinitude, freedom, and unshadowed joy that Philoctetes felt in his isolation. In the second, he brings to the surface these actualities' danger and inadequacy. In the third and last, the two clashing views come together in what constitutes, I believe, a theory of art. Thus, from the point of view of form, the five stanzas present the dialectical progression of thesis-antithesis-synthesis and consequently abbreviate the entire poem's content. If we examine them using psychological criteria, we will recognize that they first express Neoptolemos's ability to sympathize with Philoctetes's mystic knowledge. This is important for Neoptolemos because, in order validly to criticize the mature man's stance he must first experience the "unshadowed" actualities himself. Ritsos seems to be telling us that a movement outward toward infinitude is a necessary precondition for a contrary movement leading to concrete reality. All of this was already foreseen to some degree in Neoptolemos's monologue when he spoke of the exhilarating feeling arising "from the touch of everlastingness and nothingness" (l. 405) and then immediately turned to an opposite pleasure: the privilege of discerning "a well-shaped knee" (l. 408). On the other hand, in these stanzas the same dualistic movement—outward and inward—is expanded to include Philoctetes as well as Neoptolemos and finally to be metamorphosed into synthesis.

The first of the five stanzas we are examining moves outward toward the mystical sense of infinitude thanks to images that have already been presented in the poem. Dusk—combining light and dark, hence possessing a double symbolic capacity—is employed here in order to mythologize and "refine" reality, transforming the sea into a "fabulous rose-garden" in which triremes are propelled by "noiseless oars…like moistened sunbeams" (ll. 470–471), handled by sailors who, when they open their mouths to sing, emit no sound— only silence.

Given such surroundings, it is not strange that Neoptolemos, in the next stanza, should convey "the authenticity of metaphysics" (l. 477) via an action. This is because his action, in this setting, seems unavoidable. Undoing his belt, he allows one end to etch a line "within the infinite" (l. 480) of the water. Then, feeling greatly relieved, he secures the belt once again around his waist. How shall we interpret this strange action? Soon afterwards, the belt is clearly equated with "freedom" (l. 500). This encourages us to conclude that Neoptolemos, having sensed the feeling of freedom transmitted by half-light, mythical triremes, noiseless oars, and the like—that is, having sensed the transformation of complicated reality into something entirely mellow and forgiving—feels the need to plunge his belt, the symbol of his (limited) freedom, into the unlimited or perhaps also "metaphysical" freedom symbolized by the transformed sea—as though, we might say, he were seeking support. This action naturally gives him great satisfaction. Yet my interpretation is called into question owing to his observation, in the same stanza, that when he undid his belt it was as though he were "removing / a primeval noose" from round his neck (ll. 477–478). We presumably remember the rope that shadowed the face of the "hanged" mother (ll. 151–152), a remembrance that allows us to apprehend, together with Neoptolemos, that freedom, although it constitutes a release—a movement outward toward the authenticity of the metaphysical—at the same time constricts, threatens, and finally kills, since most basically the release it brings is from the rituals of history and from participation in human concerns. This clearly applies to the mother, whose keys are abandoned on the stone steps (l. 198) and whose hands, delivered from all forms of release, even from the solid consistency of human flesh, are "locked forever / inside their very own transparentness" (ll. 201–202). In this way, we are prepared for the paradox that freedom is able to curtail and threaten, just as we have also been prepared for the analogous paradox that inexplicable bliss is able to encircle us like an enemy army beleaguering a city (l. 210). On the other hand, when freedom has its other, more familiar, meaning of release, absence of coercion, flight toward the unknowable kingdom of imagination, then it, too, is a part—indeed an essential part—of Neoptolemos's experience (and naturally of Philoctetes's as well). At this point in the dialectical progression, Neoptolemos's movement seems to be chiefly centrifugal. Yet a centripetal force is simultaneously present.

As we proceed now to the third stanza, we learn more about the synthesis of light and dark into twilight or dusk. We learn that this special twilight unites not only night with day (ll. 488–489) but also a previous physical phenomenon with its own image mirrored in the infinite sea. This brings to mind the yoking of reality and "representation" that occurs quintessentially in art. Ritsos is preparing us for the fifth and final stanza. Right now, however, he develops the idea of synthesis via an entirely unexpected metamorphosis of the preceding images of the noose and the belt. Both participate in the twilight while "this glimmer / so brief and yet immortal" (ll. 489–490) becomes first "a cuirass of pure gold / secured around our breasts" (ll. 490–491) and afterwards a "layer of air / between the cuirass and our flesh" (ll. 492–493). Synthesis is piled upon synthesis, the achieved synthesis of twilight governing all the others. In reality, the glimmer is brief and fragile, yet in imagination it assumes magical powers that make it seem immortal, capable of dematerializing the triremes, oars, and sailors' shouts. As for the cuirass, it literally squeezes. Furthermore, since it is a part of the weaponry, it shares with the poem's other weapons something of darkness, shadows, menace. On the other hand, it is scintillating: it consists of pure gold. In this respect, it strengthens the sense of release and splendor contained in twilight. The layer of air is equally contradictory. Although "thinmost," it is also unexpectedly "invulnerable" (l. 492).

Ritsos exploits both the cuirass and the layer of air as he develops still another paradoxical symbol: inward and outward breathing. This seems to match the overall symbolism of the five stanzas because the movement of breathing is outward at first, when the chest swells during a deep inhalation, and then inward once again. Indeed, we read that the layer of air "turns inward again / the outward motion of our breath" (ll. 493–494). Our spirit is curtailed since the layer is not only invulnerable but is also strengthened even more by the tight cuirass that encircles it. Sometimes, however, "during the deepest inhalations, we feel the tips of our chest / covertly graze the cuirass' metal"—feel them, in other words, approach nonexistence "with the extreme delight of tactile sensuality" (ll. 494–497). The layer of air is now no longer invulnerable; it is still most thin, since the tips of our chest (the same word, αιχμή, is used later for the well-sharpened tips of Philoctetes's weapons) are capable of penetrating it and touching the cuirass, which, in turn, is no longer a threatening, squeezing suit of armor but now a scintillating, golden raiment symbolizing infinity, myth, imagination, nonexistence. Indeed, the contact of chest with cuirass—which, let us not forget, is most deeply the contact of Neoptolemos with the "deep, fabulous rose-garden" that the glorious twilight has fashioned out of sea, ships, oars, and sailors—is so absolutely delightful, so tactile, that it resembles the touch of two bodies at the moment of sexual union.

This complex cluster of images develops the twilight's initial paradox—the combination of night and day, immortal and ephemeral, material and imagined—in order to enable this first paradox to include our spirit's motion outward toward a certain freedom that paradoxically brings us into tighter contact with a certain necessity (the inflexible cuirass) that, again paradoxically, brings us more freedom. What is perhaps most important is that the cluster of images develops the initial paradox in a manner that enables it to include as well the artistic process. An artist, after all, takes specific aspects of materiality—that which exists—and, using them to transcend material existence, touches non-existence. He or she achieves this not via abstract thought, the mode of philosophy, but via representation, employing tactile, concrete means in order to unite the real with the imaginary, the finite with the infinite. Or, if we refer to the Trojan horse, another image employed earlier in the poem, the artist is "a bridge / above two embankments equally precipitous and unknown" (ll. 341–342).[55] All of this will be applied to Philoctetes, as we see in the fifth and last stanza.

A short fourth stanza intervenes. This emphasizes the ambiguous nature of freedom and prepares for Neoptolemos's final advice to Philoctetes. The young man returns to the belt that the glorious twilight had encouraged him to undo and insert in the boundless sea as though to seek some strengthening. At the same time, however, he refers to it as a noose that he removed from his neck. This threatening aspect of the belt—of freedom—is now developed

55   Compare the following from Ritsos's essay 'On Mayakovski,' which is included his Μελετήματα (Athens: Kedros, 1974), pp. 9–33: "Mayakovski's small, everyday details…are lexical…bridges…from the indefinite to the definite. . . These 'bridges' are ubiquitous; they occur everywhere,…precisely at the moment when [Mayakovski] sets foot…on two antithetical shorelines" (pp. 21–22). Written in May 1963, exactly when Ritsos began *Philoctetes*, this essay is extraordinarily useful for interpreting the poem since it is concerned with many ideas that resemble those in the poem, and indeed utilizes many similar turns of speech.

further. The belt is so narrow and tight that it incises the flesh. It is "always buckled and taut / round the entire body, including without fail the heel" (ll. 500–501); hence it makes whoever wears it invulnerable and deathless yet at the same time, negatively, it isolates him from dependency upon life and "obliges the chest to expand" (l. 502), to stretch outward toward infinitude. We remember the tips of the chest pleasurably touching the all-golden cuirass during one's deepest inhalations; nevertheless, the word "obliges" here makes the action seem less pleasing. Indeed, we read in the next verse that the belt is a "painful estrangement" that nonetheless "grows tractable in time" (l. 503). Freedom, consequently, is protective and becalming, yet dangerous in the final analysis and all the more so because it protects even the Achilles heel and because the situation it provides may finally become very seductive. It seems that Ritsos is directing himself at this point to intellectuals who withdraw entirely from the struggle, erroneously believing that only thus can they succeed in discovering what they deem indispensable if they are going to grasp life's profoundest meaning.

One such intellectual is of course Philoctetes. Neoptolemos, whose mission is to bring the mature man once again into contact with life, now begs the gods to keep the two of them "from falling prisoner / to even the most beautiful of revelations" (ll. 504–505). This begins the fifth stanza of the section we are examining, a stanza that takes all the previous approaches and applies them to Philoctetes—applies them to a figure who is an artist threatened and imprisoned by his own intellectuality. The remainder of the stanza contains some of the poem's most difficult verses, their meaning being so compacted that periphrastic explanations are required if this portion is to be comprehended analytically. Why must we protect ourselves from the revelation of profound meaning? The reason is that if we remain in ecstatic condition within a rose-garden that stays permanently transformed for us, we face the danger of forever losing our ability to transform reality ourselves (ll. 505–506). In addition, we face the danger of forever losing "the ultimate action: speech" (l. 507). The meaning of this last verse derives from two principal thematic elements in the poem: "silence," which we have already analyzed at length, and the "mask of action" (l. 514). Silence is imposed on us by revelation. Whenever silence is assimilated into a life of energetic participation, it may become, as we have

seen, a compass for others; whenever, on the other hand, the intellectual perseveres in his isolation, he is then hemmed in by silence. Previously, silence
had been juxtaposed to the shouts of the simple soldiers, shouts used by them
to express their vivacious contempt for the revelation given them by a mo-
mentary sense of eternity and nonexistence. Now, Philoctetes is called upon
to take refuge in the Word, clearly implying that he, too, like the common
people, will express in this way his vivacity vis-à-vis the revelation of eternity
and nonexistence. The difference, naturally, is that Philoctetes's "Word" will
be not the uncoordinated shouts of the masses but an elevated, controlled
expression. Poetry, perhaps? The remainder of the stanza encourages this
view. But Word is also assimilated into action, indeed into the "ultimate action," and our thought proceeds to the next stanza, where Neoptolemos offers
Philoctetes a "mask of action" (l. 514) to conceal his transparent face—a mask
that in the poem's subtitle is termed "the ultimate mask." On the one hand,
Philoctetes is being called upon to abandon his political isolation, to go to
Troy, and to participate in the life of his people, even though he knows full
well that the war is entirely unjust. Parallel to this, Philoctetes is being called
upon, as it seems, to abandon his artistic isolation, to return to society, and
to participate in its concerns, guiding it correctly with the aid of poetry even
though he knows full well that all similar guidance is futile and that creativity itself is easily defeated in its struggle with nonexistence. The rest of the
stanza, as I noted, strengthens this artistic parallel. Neoptolemos suggests to
Philoctetes that perhaps the most terrible aspect of his absolute isolation is
his "lack of objects" (l. 508). An artist needs objects more than anything else.
They are not required for use in the usual sense, "but for coming into contact,
for figures of speech, depictions" (l. 509). What this means, I believe, is that
objects are the artist's means—his or her only possible means—for coming
into contact with the indefinite immaterial kingdom of infinitude. Our embrace of nonexistence must involve, we will remember, the tactile immediacy
of sexual contact. How do artists realize this contact, this union? They do so
by representation— the key to art—since art fulfills its purpose by represent-
ing abstraction through concretion. This explains the stanza's final verse. It
gives us two definitions: art is that which unites in brotherhood the actual
with the infinite by means of figures of speech, and art is that which makes

possible the "measurement of the immeasurable" (l. 510).

In order to fulfill his duty as intellectual, artist, and human being, Philoctetes must abandon his "uncompanioned saintliness" (l. 512) and his freedom's "unmarred joy" (l. 514). He must go to Troy. But no, he must not abandon them; on the contrary, he must take them with him to Troy, just as he will take his silence. He must join these to action in a finite world governed not by freedom but by necessity—the necessary ten years of the Trojan War (l. 546). Philoctetes had attempted to escape the war, to escape death, only to find that his isolation, revelations, and freedom were simply another form of death. If, however, antitheses unite, then creativity is capable of resulting. This is why Neoptolemos hands the mask of action over to Philoctetes as he calls him to depart. But union has not yet been achieved: the opaque mask will simply conceal Philoctetes's transparent face (ll. 515–516). For the dialectical movement to be completed, the oxymoron must be dissolved by the power of synthesis. This is precisely what happens in the epilogue. Against a background of the sailors' splendid folksong, which places everything in "human dimensions," Philoctetes takes the mask and rests it on the ground. Afterwards, his face is transformed little by little, as though duplicating the mask. The apparent rejection of action leads once again to participation. Yet Philoctetes is not just a pendulum swinging from one extreme to the other. Having discovered the truth regarding participation and also the truth regarding its opposite, isolation, he is now in a position to rise to a level higher than these two stances, a level that nevertheless includes them both.

V

"Sometimes," asks Neoptolemos, "the light of twilight is enlightening, is it not?" (l. 485). We answer: Yes it is, because the synthesis of antithetical symbols that is projected so clearly not only here but in other portions of the poem illumines the poet's more general dialectical vision of life.

In Sophocles's play, the contradiction is removed by means of the disappearance of one of its elements. In order for the earthly clash to be terminated, a god is required to descend from a machine. This seems to indicate that

Sophocles viewed human affairs as incurably contradictory and as rectified only by divine intervention. In Ritsos's poem, contradiction is removed by the synthesis of contrary elements, not by the disappearance of one of them. Silence is incorporated into noise; light and darkness are merged into twilight; the transparent face assumes the presence and solidity of the opaque mask. For this to happen, no divine appearance is necessary; nor is it possible, since for Ritsos God does not exist (although the dialectical process seems to possess for him an eternal power on a par with something divine). Synthesis for Ritsos is not an extraordinary situation foreign to the nature of life. On the contrary, it is the realization of life's profoundest dynamism. For this reason, art is so properly a major subject in this poem that seems to be concerned first of all with life—with the realistic and not the imaginary. Why? Because the realistic, for Ritsos, includes the imaginary. What we call "real" is the merger of inanimate, meaningless materiality with insubstantial, subjective values that we impose upon that materiality. Our life on earth is thus a play, not a theatrical play but a "life-play"[56] and our participation in this life-play affixes upon our faces the characteristics of the ultimate mask that determines our personality. Art properly constitutes a major subject in a poem that seems to speak about life; yet art not only does not differ from life, it is life's intensification. In Ritsos's view, both art and life constitute a synthesis of antitheses, both are marvelous "mythic" fusions, and neither can blossom if the natural powers leading to synthesis encounter resistance.

That, finally, is why Philoctetes must go to Troy.

---

56   Ritsos, Μελετήματα, p. 106.

5. Ritsos's Painterly Technique in Long and Short Poems

BEFORE DISCUSSING RITSOS'S "PAINTERLY" TECHNIQUE, I shall have to speak about the technique that preceded it. For the purposes of this discussion, I shall call the previous technique "non-painterly." My thesis is that Ritsos, in evolving from non-painterly to painterly technique, improved his art.

Starting out from personal and family anguish, Ritsos managed by the end of the first decade of his career to create in *Επιτάφιος* (1936) a style appropriate for a poet who had sided with the communists and who consequently wished to express not only his own anguish but the overall suffering and hope of the oppressed working class. It is well known that the inspiration for *Επιτάφιος* was a photograph published after a demonstration in Thessaloniki in which several tobacco workers were killed by the police. Ritsos describes this photograph in the poem's epigraph: "Μια μάνα, καταμεσίς του δρόμου, μοιρολογάει το σκοτωμένο παιδί της. Γύρω της και πάνω της, βουΐζουν και σπάζουν τα κύματα των διαδηλωτών—των απεργών καπνεργατών."[57] The mother's progress in the poem coincides with the poet's own progress up to that point: she begins with personal and family anguish but modulates to a feeling of solidarity with the overall suffering of the oppressed working class. Like Ritsos, she moves from personal grief to public purpose. Ritsos was obliged to create a technique appropriate for this poem, a technique sufficiently flexible to (1) correlate with the the subject matter's progress toward the working class's common interests, (2) be at once private and public, and (3) speak to the common man as well as to the intellectual. His solution was brilliant. Drawing from the cultural treasures of ordinary people—nature, the demotic language, the passion of Christ, the rituals of the Orthodox Church—he placed all this in the format of the demotic folk song and lament. The poem employs the metrics,

---

57   See *Ποιήματα Α'*, p. 163.

diction, and imagery of popular art; it is a splendid example of λαϊκισμός. Yet we must ask ourselves if *Επιτάφιος* is entirely successful aesthetically. My own view is that it is not—because the young poet still had not learned "painterly technique." Despite the admirable way in which the new method does correlate with subject matter, the poem's non-painterly technique is incapable by its very nature of corresponding to the chief goal of the mother's successive emotions, for the mother's modulation from her consideration of death and loss leads not merely to solidarity with the oppressed working class but also, primarily, to a vision of a paradisaical future in which all people—the policeman as well as the worker—will be permanently united in mutual love. To say this in Greek, her modulation proceeds from the reality of φθορά (corruption, wastage, decay) to a vision of αφθαρσία (incorruptibility). But the technique, for its part, does not incarnate a corresponding progress in a way that allows the poem to become what it proclaims. Ritsos was still unable to match his style perfectly to his persistent theme of αφθαρσία overcoming φθορά. To do this, he had to discover painterly technique.

∼

Although I have invoked this term repeatedly, I have neglected to define it. Nevertheless I am going to let it tantalize the reader a little longer while I continue with a new period in the poet's career. This commenced on 4 August 1936, three months after the writing of *Επιτάφιος*. The change was caused by the dictatorial régime of Ioánnis Metaxás, which burned *Επιτάφιος* along with other "dangerous" books in a public ceremony beneath the columns of the Temple of Olympian Zeus. Under conditions such as these, a militant poet like Ritsos was forced to choose between keeping silent or changing direction. He changed direction. Unable to continue the political form of his persistent theme, he replaced revolution with poetry itself as the wonder-working power that would bring redemptive incorruptibility.

We see this change in *Το τραγούδι της αδελφής μου*, published one year after *Επιτάφιος*. This new elegy begins with the poet's personal melancholy. Lamenting the fate of his sister, who had become insane, he bewails his own fate as well:

Αδελφή μου,
δεν είμαι πια ποιητής,
δεν καταδέχομαι να 'μαι ποιητής.
Είμαι ένα πληγωμένο μυρμήγκι
που έχασε το δρόμο του
μες στην απέραντη νύχτα.[58]

Little by little, however, the poet realizes that his insane sister does not drag him down into the darkness with her but, contrariwise, gives him the opportunity to save himself in the process of saving her. Why? Because by addressing her in poetry he converts his own decay, as well as hers, into incorruptibility. As in Επιτάφιος, the subject matter moves from a distressing past to an eternally happy future. But this time, as noted above, the magical power that transmutes reality is poetry instead of revolution:

Δεν μπορώ πια να κλάψω.
Το Τραγούδι με υπέταξε.
Το Τραγούδι μού χάρισε τη νίκη.
…
Κι εγώ που δε δυνήθηκα
να σε σώσω από τη ζωή,
θα σε σώσω από το θάνατο.
…
κι αλλάζω την οδύνη σ' έκσταση
και την κραυγή σε προχευχή.[59]

The great poems of Ritsos's first and second periods, respectively, Επιτάφιος and Το τραγούδι της αδελφής μου, are a pair because they treat the same basic theme, the first in a public mode, the second in a private one. But they are also a pair in their non-painterly technique, which means that neither is able to incorporate into its own being the αφθαρσία that each tells us about so insistently and, at times, stridently. If we wish to comprehend the difference between painterly and non-painterly technique we may compare Το τραγούδι της αδελφής μου with yet another lament, Η σονάτα του σεληνόφωτος, written almost two decades later, in 1956. In this mature elegy, the poet removes

---

58   See Ποιήματα Α', p. 190.
59   See Ποιήματα Α', p. 210, 212.

his own emotions thanks to a complicated system of ironic narration that allows him to address his readers in a painterly fashion. We shall return to *Η σονάτα του σεληνόφωτος* later, when we reach the technical methods that Ritsos applied to his long poems in order to make them painterly.

~

For the moment, let us examine his short poems. Turning the restrictions imposed by the Metaxás regime to good advantage, Ritsos began a systematic review of his poetic practice, aspiring to develop a technique in which there would be no trace of stridency, importunity, or rhetoric. Understandably, he (like a painter) commenced with small sketches. For subject matter he favored nature and the daily life of the common people as opposed to the tribulations of his own family. It is in these exercises composed during the Metaxás years that we find for the first time the technique that I have been calling painterly. Now, at last, I shall attempt to define this term—but gradually, step by step.

To start, let us recall that in *Το τραγούδι της αδελφής μου* Ritsos invokes poetry as the wonder-working power capable of transforming wastage into incorruptibility. I have already argued that although he does this triumphantly, he fails to incarnate in the poem's very technique that which is advanced in its subject matter, so that the work of art might actually become redemptive instead of merely speaking about redemption. To become redemptive it would have to embrace in its technique the characteristics of incorruptibility and avoid the characteristics of decay. The most basic characteristic of decay is time; the most basic characteristic of incorruptibility is timelessness. Hence poetry, if it is to *be* incorruptible, must manage to halt time's inexorable flow. Said in another way: it must transmute reality into beauty.

This is the lesson of John Keats's celebrated 'Ode on a Grecian Urn.' In this poem, all the figures depicted on the ancient Greek jar—boys and girls kissing, a shepherd playing his pipe, trees covered with leaves—all, in real life, are condemned by time to decay. But painted as they are on the urn the lovers will never grow old, the leaves will not fall, the shepherd's music will continue forever. Reality (hence time) is conquered by art, by beauty. This is why the poet addresses the urn as follows:

Thou, silent form, dost tease us out of thought
As doth eternity: Cold Pastoral!
    When old age shall this generation waste,
        Thou shalt remain, in midst of other woe
    Than ours, a friend to man, to whom thou say'st,

(here he appends the well-known lines in which the urn speaks to men, telling them:)

"Beauty is truth, truth beauty,"—that is all
    Ye know on earth, and all ye need to know.

Keats's lesson, then, is that art liberates us from decay because *beauty freezes the flow of time*. We are progressing toward a definition of painterly technique. Yet this formulation, useful so far as it goes, is still not complete because it neglects to specify the precise process involved. We must ask *how* beauty accomplishes the miraculous transformation. To move another step forward in our investigation, we must realize that beauty delivers us from decay by *converting time into space*.

To understand how it does this, we should think again of the wailing mother who inspired *Επιτάφιος*. In real life, "the waves of demonstrators roar and break around and above her." But in the photograph there is no motion, no sound; we are reminded of the "silent form" invoked by Keats. In the photograph, sound is transformed into sight. This means that time is transformed into space. Why? Because the presupposition of sound is motion and the presupposition of motion is time. The meaning of any given sound depends upon the sounds that precede and follow. A note in a piece by Beethoven, for example, becomes meaningless the moment it is extracted from the previous and subsequent notes of the entire composition. Conversely, the presupposition of sight is immobility and consequently space. A photograph or painting is meaningful on its own, independent of the flow of time.

We have reached the point where we can formulate a pair of equations to summarize the above:

1) wastage = time = motion = sound (nonpainterly)

2) incorruptibility = space = immobility = sight (painterly)

How, then, does beauty deliver us from decay? It does this by converting time into space, as we have already said. And how does it convert time into space? *By converting sound into sight.* This is the essence of the technique developed by Ritsos in short exercises written during the Metaxás dictatorship. These exercises resemble snapshots; however, I prefer to liken them to paintings because they do not restrict themselves to the objective representation of external reality. Thanks to this technique that transforms sound into sight, time into space, motion into immobility—in sum, reality into beauty—Ritsos began to write poems that not only *talk* about incorruptibility but *become* incorruptible because they embrace as much as possible the characteristics of incorruptibility and avoid as much as possible the characteristics of wastage. These poems overcome decay because, like the urn in Keats's ode, they freeze the warm flow of events, enabling us to see life aestheticized upon the "canvas" of the poem. They do this by challenging our spatial apprehension more than our temporal apprehension owing to a painterly technique that addresses itself to our visual faculty (which apprehends space) as opposed to our auditory faculty (which apprehends time).

～

To illustrate this change in technique, I wish to offer a short poem written around 1938 and published in the collection Σημειώσεις στα περιθώρια του χρόνου, a title that is not irrelevant to our discussion since it too converts time into space via a spatial metaphor. As for the poem's title, I shall withhold that for the moment so that it may come as a surprise later. Here is the poem:

Καμπάνες μονάχες μιλούν τη σιωπή,
παρέες-παρέες οι θύμησες κάτου από τα δέντρα,
οι αγελάδες λυπημένες στο σούρουπο.

Πίσω από τους μικρούς βοσκούς
ένα σύγνεφο βέλαζε στη δύση.[60]

---

60   See Ποιήματα Α', p. 480.

At first this poem seems to escape neither time nor sound. The bell-towers are speaking, even if they speak silence; the cloud is bleating. Gradually, however, we begin to understand that the poem offers a composition (in the painterly sense) that resembles Keats's cold pastoral. In real life, all the forms described in the poem are subject to decay: bell-towers fall, memories fade, cows are led to slaughter, young shepherds grow old. Yet in their poetic representation the figures are arranged as in a painting; we perceive them as though they were in the foreground and background of a canvas—soundless, immobilized in space, delivered from time.

What is the poem's theme? Does it have a theme? We might conclude that this brief exercise is meant to offer nothing more than simple description. On the other hand, as soon as we take into consideration the poem's painterly technique, we realize that a theme does exist, indeed the same theme that we observed both in *Επιτάφιος* and *Το τραγούδι της αδελφής μου*—the conversion of decay into incorruptibility. Now, however, Ritsos does not *say* anything regarding this persistent theme; he does not force the theme upon us via stridency or rhetoric. Instead, he presents the theme indirectly and silently via a technique that removes itself as much as possible from time in order to embrace space, so that the poem *becomes* incorruptible. Without uttering a word about poetry's redemptive power, the poet expresses this power by incorporating αφθαρσία into his poem's very being.

We have reached the appropriate point for the surprise that I promised earlier. The poem's title is 'Χαλκογραφία' ('Engraving'), proof that Ritsos himself was thinking of his new technique as painterly.

～

Let us proceed now to the long poems. In the case of a painting or engraving, the work of art is apprehensible as a single, unified object in space as opposed to a series of objects encountered successively in time. The same is true for a short poem such as 'Χαλκογραφία.' Although we may begin by registering the bell-tower, memories, cows, shepherd, and cloud successively in time, we then easily compose all of these images into a single, indivisible arrangement in space. But how can painterly technique be utilized in a poem that stretches over many pages and therefore cannot be comprehended all at once? The answer is that such technique cannot be utilized to the same degree. Nonetheless, long poems can acquire certain painterly qualities—which means that they can be given characteristics equatable with space rather than time.

Having developed his painterly technique through experimentation with brief sketches, Ritsos proceeded to experiment with ways to apply the technique to longer compositions. He found at least four, as follows:

1. the use of figures of speech that convert the auditory element into an optical one;
2. the use of an actual painting as the skeleton of a poem;
3. the use of a prologue and epilogue to frame the body of a poem;
4. the use of a well-known myth as the skeleton of a poem.

Sometimes these techniques are combined, as when a mythic poem framed by a prologue and epilogue includes figures of speech that convert time into space. For analytical purposes, however, it is easiest to illustrate each of the four ways separately.

To demonstrate the first, I will present an excerpt from the lengthy elegy *Το Νεκρό Σπίτι*, written in 1959. The passage in question describes a piercing scream uttered by the slaves in the "dead house." Yet this auditory element is made visual thanks to two figures of speech, a metaphor followed by a simile. The scream remains

...καρφωμένη στο σκιερό διάδρομο
σαν ένα μεγάλο ψαροκόκκαλο στο λαρύγγι ενός αγνώστου μουσαφίρη[61]

The metaphor takes the auditory (hence temporal) scream and immobilizes it as an object wedged in the passageway; the simile converts the now-frozen scream into the even more visual and less auditory image of the fishbone. The terrible cry, the sign of decay, is transformed into beauty because it participates in the spatial characteristics of incorruptibility.

It may be objected that a large fishbone in your throat is anything but beau-

---

61   See *Τέταρτη διάσταση*, p. 97.

tiful. We must remember, however, that artistic beauty is not necessarily pretty, It does not satisfy because it removes us from ugliness *per se* but rather because it removes us from the wastage of time. In this case, both ugliness and pain are aestheticized by being spatialized so that the temporal factor is overcome or at least reduced.

A long poem filled with images of this type will assume a painterly quality to some degree even though such a poem cannot be apprehended instantaneously as an integral composition in the way that a painting or a short poem can.

Proceeding now to the second technique, the use of an actual painting as the skeleton for a long poem, let us consider the famous canvas by El Greco known in Greek as *Η ταφή του Οργκάθ* and in English as *The Burial of Count Orgaz*. This painting is so complicated, with so many figures, that we necessarily begin to comprehend it temporally, part by part. Yet if we are ever to appreciate the canvas fully, we must proceed at some point to a spatial apprehension, registering the work as a single, indivisible composition. It follows that if a painting—even a complicated one—is used as the skeleton for a long poem, we will be encouraged to try to comprehend that poem, too, in this same way, instantaneously and integrally. Ritsos employed this technique in a complicated poem written in September 1942, shortly after the severe famine that followed the German invasion. The poem and the painting bear the identical title, *Η ταφή του Οργκάθ*.

We have already noted that Ritsos was unable to write political poems after the establishment of the Metaxás dictatorship in 1936. Conditions changed radically, however, owing to Greece's occupation by the Axis powers in the spring of 1941. Ritsos joined the Greek resistance movement, EAM—not as a combatant (his long history of tuberculosis precluded that) but in the educational branch, with the goal of encouraging his fellow resisters. Under these new conditions he returned to political subjects in poems that were circulated clandestinely. He did not return, however, to the style of *Επιτάφιος*, since in the meantime he had developed the technique we have been calling painterly.

If we wish to comprehend *Η ταφή του Οργκάθ* we must first comprehend the painting that serves as its skeleton. What does this painting show us? It has two levels. On the bottom level is the melancholy funeral of Count Orgaz, the faithful Christian. On the upper level we see heaven, where an angel is already presenting the dead man's embryonic soul to a Christ enthroned in radiant glory. A semi-nude John the Baptist kneels at Christ's feet. I remarked earlier that in order to appreciate the painting we must surpass the temporal mode in which our eye travels from one figure to the next. If we do this, registering the entire canvas as an integral whole in space rather than as a series of fragments in time, we will realize that the painting presents the co-existence of earth and heaven, in other words the co-existence of death and immortality, decay and incorruptibility, φθορά and αφθαρσία. Wastage exists but does not exist independently, El Greco is telling us, since real life is merely one part of a fuller and more essential Truth that guarantees to man that at the end of his journey he will find hope and (to use the appropriately religious term) salvation.

This entire process by which we apprehend the painting—namely, an initial temporal survey followed by a deeper spatial understanding—must be repeated when we attempt to apprehend the poem that is built upon this skeleton. The poem as well, like the painting, is divided into two levels. On the bottom level, which of course is that of decay, injustice, death, and time, we see the horror of the defeated Athens of 1942: a waste land in which veterans of the Albanian campaign, hungry men with amputated legs, move about in wheelchairs:

ολάκερος στρατός καρότσια
…
μόνο καρότσια
μες στα καρότσια τίποτα
μονάχα μια φωνή «πεινάμε».
Ήταν άνθρωποι.[62]

These victims of war who "used to be men" are the faithful who have died—at least spiritually. They correspond to Count Orgaz in the painting. There, <u>death is conquered by the merciful Christ who re</u>igns in glory on the upper

62   See *Ποιήματα Β'*, p. 188.

level. But what miraculous power of salvation operates on the upper level of
Ritsos's poem? Ritsos does not share El Greco's Christian faith; in his poem
Christ cannot be found (*Ποιήματα Β'*, p. 95). When at the poem's conclusion
we see the heavens, all radiant with light, we accordingly find neither Christ
nor John the Baptist, but instead workers whose beautiful bodies, "γυμνούς
ως τη μέση" (*Ποιήματα Β'*, p. 204), identify them with El Greco's Forerunner:
they are the proclaimers of Ritsos's own faith not in Christian redemption but
in radical social reformation. Characteristically, they are not sitting in glory
but are working—constructing the Marxist heaven that will exist sooner or
later for the oppressed. Ritsos's faith is that injustice is part of a fuller, more
essential Truth that assures the tormented resistance fighters in their wheelchairs that justice will come. As for us, the readers, we will share this vision
of redemptive Truth to the degree that we register, with the help of Ritsos's
painterly technique, the poem's integral totality in which evil and good are
interconnected—to the degree that we surpass a fragmented perception. This
needs to be emphasized all the more because on the surface the poem is so extremely episodic, as though in conformity with the purposeless anarchy of the
veterans and of defeated Athens. Yet this incoherence is merely a conscious
deception perpetrated by the painterly technique, which challenges us in this
modernistic way to advance beyond apparent incoherence to the instantaneous, indivisible perception of a meaningful whole.

I cannot devote adequate space to the third and fourth ways developed by
Ritsos to apply elements of painterly technique to his long poems. In brief,
I'll say that the crucial evolution took place in the decade 1956-1966. I have
already mentioned *Η σονάτα του σεληνόφωτος*, written in June 1956, and have
noted that in this work, thanks to a complicated system of ironic narration,
the poet tames the self-indulgent lyricism of previous laments. The poem's
ostensible theme is deception—more precisely, self-deception. Accordingly,
its technique becomes deceptive in its own right, confusing us. We do not
know which narrator to trust. If we seek the author's genuine voice, we seek it
in vain—as a voice.[63] But we do find it—voiceless, so to speak—in the poem's

---

63   If the author does insert his voice anywhere, it is perhaps in the three bars of
Beethoven's *Moonlight Sonata* that he prints at the poem's conclusion. Has anyone wondered
why Ritsos chose those particular bars? My own conjecture is that he chose them because the

overall form, the painterly form in which a prologue and an epilogue are employed to frame a dramatic monologue. As soon as we become aware of this form, the poem's deepest meaning is released. We now understand that the major theme is not deception; it is, once again, mankind's yearning to be delivered from decay and to participate in incorruptibility. In this case, decay is represented not by the murder of a striking worker, the insanity of a beloved sister, or veterans with amputated legs, but by the self-deception of a romantic woman who tries to sustain herself by means of the illusion that ο χρόνος και η φθορά του do not exist beneath the redemptive moonlight:

Τι φεγγάρι απόψε!
Είναι καλό το φεγγάρι,—δεν θα φαίνεται
που ασπρίσαν τα μαλλιά μου...[64]

She seeks her salvation in places where it does not exist: in the idealized past, the day-dreamy present. But although *she* cannot escape time, the *poet* can. He knows full well that deception is subordinate to an incorruptible Truth that converts deception into beauty. He does not utter a word about this, however. He cannot utter a word, because his own voice is nowhere to be found. Instead, he takes this monologue that is so beleaguered by time and frames it in such a way that the poem acquires, to some degree at least, the characteristics of a painting. As soon as we become actively aware of this, we begin to suspect that the poem's chief meaning resides not in what is *said* but in what the poem *is*: in the form, the painterly construction. When we encounter the narrator in the epilogue, we are encouraged to recall the narrator in the prologue and thereby to register the poem not just as a succession of fragments unfolding in time but as a single composition immobilized in space. The very artificiality of the form reminds us that we are not hearing about life in the raw, despite the woman's anguished lament, but are instead seeing life painted as though upon an urn, by an invisible master. We are registering life re-presented in a manner mysteriously empowered to "tease us out of thought / As doth eternity."

 Regarding the fourth way in which Ritsos applies painterly technique to third and last bar includes the direction *misterioso*. Could this be the one and only time that Ritsos steps out of the dramatic mode and speaks "directly" (via indirection!) to the reader?

64   See *Τέταρτη διάσταση*, p. 45.

long poems, I shall confine myself to the assertion that in a work such as *Φιλοκτήτης*, which Ritsos began in May 1963, we reach the zenith of his painterly technique. Here he employs all of his strategies: figures of speech that transform acoustical elements into visual ones, a frame around a dramatic monologue, and, instead of a complicated painting, a complicated myth known to all educated people by virtue of Sophocles's play of the same name. Since the myth is more generally accessible than is El Greco's painting, it provides a more effective skeleton. In any case, it functions in the same way as does the painting since a myth, like a canvas, and despite the complication of its details, is comprehensible as a single integral thing, indeed derives its power from our instantaneous intuition of its wholeness.

~

We have traced Ritsos's career over a period of almost thirty years, from 1936, when he composed *Επιτάφιος*, to 1965, when he completed *Φιλοκτήτης*. We have noted that his persistent concern has been redemption from decay by means of revolution or poetry. At the same time, we have observed an evolution from the non-painterly technique of his beginnings toward the painterly technique of his maturity, initially in short exercises and then in long poems that acquire painterly characteristics owing to various technical impositions, all of which give these poems the power to *become*, to a greater or lesser degree, that which they assert.

6. A Ritualistic View of Ritsos's *The Moonlight Sonata*

T HIS IS THE FIRST TIME I EVER THOUGHT about a literary text in relation to ritual. I wondered whether I had any relation to ritual in my personal experience. We all partake of the rituals of breakfast, supper, our daily needs, etc. But my own life offers at least three additional instances.

First: I am a practicing Quaker, which means that on every Sunday morning I sit for an hour in silence. This strange silent liturgy is ritualistic because it is repeated each week, because it is crazy (deeper than merely rational), and because it is an imperative activity, which means that if I am absent I feel unfulfilled.

Second: For fifty years I have participated in a very different ritualistic act on our farm: the mowing with a large tractor of about twelve acres of meadow. In this case, as in the Quaker liturgy, the characteristics are repetition, craziness (since the fields really do not need to be mowed every year), and— perhaps most important—a sense of unfulfillment (which cannot be logically explained) if the mowing does not take place. Thus this annual mowing, like the weekly Quaker liturgy, is imperative for me.

Third: on two occasions I was privileged to view the fire-walking ritual of the *Anastenárides* on May 21st in Langadas, Macedonia. However, I was not seated in the grandstand along with thousands of other spectators. Because my brother-in-law then served as the agriculturalist for that region, the *Anastenárides* allowed me to enter their sanctuary where they danced themselves into trance. This ritual displays the characteristics to which I referred above: repetition, craziness, and the imperative need for it to take place. For example, young *Anastenárides* who were doing their military service would return on May 21st in order not to miss the magical dance. And, at the end, the expression on everyone's lips was "May it happen again next year," indicating that even though the necessary ritual had happened this year it needed to be repeated on each and every subsequent May 21st. As for me, each time I complete the mowing on our farm, I always say—feeling beyond rationality— "May it happen again next year!"

These are the three kinds of personal experiences that helped me think about ritual in relation to the poetry of Yannis Ritsos. But I also resorted to some scholarly aids. I once happened to hear a lecture by Margaret Alexiou on ritual approaches to Greek literature.[65] Alexiou says that ritual "involves the *repetition*...of actions, gestures, utterances, which *do not mean by words alone*" (italics added)—i.e., which are beyond rationality. I was pleased to find here a confirmation of two of the findings from my own experience: repetition and craziness. Beyond this, Alexiou stresses that "ritual is an attempt, by a group or by an individual, to control the...outside world." That factor I did not meet in my personal experience, but now I realize how it relates to Quaker worship, the mowing of my fields, and—perhaps most obviously—to the *Anastenárides*. In each case, the ritual is bankrupt if it does not somehow impose itself upon the world outside.

Alexiou then proceeds to additional factors. She says that literary texts may become ritualistic if they incorporate liturgical language, follow a ritual schema such as passion/crucifixion/resurrection, link our everyday activities to a cosmic dimension, blend fantasy with realism, perceive time and space in a non-linear manner so that a plot no longer has a beginning, middle, and end.

Examples of all these factors are not difficult to find in Greek and non-Greek literature. Liturgical language is incorporated in Elytis's *Axion esti*. Ritual schemata govern Ritsos's *Epitáfios* and Kazantzakis's *Christ Recrucified*. Everyday activities are linked to a cosmic dimension in Sikelianos's poem 'Pan.' Fantasy and realism are co-existent in the short stories of E. M. Forster. Time and space are not linear factors in James Joyce's *Finnegans Wake*, which has neither start, middle, nor end.

Each of these works shares at least one of the three characteristics of ritual that I identified from my own experience: repetition, craziness, and urgency. Some of them also incorporate an attempt to control the outside world.

But my subject today is not a general survey of either Greek or Western

65   Margaret Alexiou, "'Not by Words Alone': Ritual Approaches to Greek Literature." Lecture delivered at the Center for European Studies, Harvard University, 9 November 2000.

literature. It is an examination of ritual in the poetry of Yannis Ritsos. I cannot attempt to generalize on his immense *oeuvre*. It will be better for me to concentrate on a specific work and perhaps on one that does not seem to incorporate a ritualistic dimension.

I have chosen *The Moonlight Sonata*.[66] I translated this masterpiece more than thirty-five years ago[67] and attempted to describe its "painterly technique"[68]— that is, the method by which the poet transforms time into space and sound into sight as a painter does, in order to bring into the actual technique of the poem something incorruptible. Now I am going to try to extend this analysis by means of a ritualistic approach, hoping thereby to "broaden our aesthetic criteria and enrich our understanding of literature."

The previous approach is not irrelevant. Let's remember one of the characteristics I mentioned earlier: the ability of ritual to link our everyday activities to a cosmic dimension. This is precisely what Ritsos accomplished in *The Moonlight Sonata* through his painterly technique. The poem is difficult. Its ostensible theme is the Woman in Black's self-deception. But the real theme is the existence of incorruptibility, the opposite of deception and corruption. The poem is ritualistic because it links the daily action of the Woman's self-deception to the cosmic dimension of Beethoven's Sonata, which is continually heard in the background. The technique becomes deceptive in its own right, thus imitating the ostensible theme. We do not know which of the various narrators to trust. We cannot verify which is the author's voice; nevertheless, we do find his "voice"—*voiceless*—in the poem's painterly form, namely in the prologue and epilogue that form a frame around the Woman in Black's dramatic monologue. As soon as we register this form, we begin to understand that the poem's deepest meaning is not deception; it is humanity's yearning to be delivered from decay and to participate in a cosmic dimension characterized by incorruptibility. In this instance, decay is represented by the self-deception of a romantic woman who does her utmost to sustain herself by means of lies. She says for example that "time and its decay do not exist

66   Yannis Ritsos, «Η Σονάτα του Σεληνόφωτος», in *Τέταρτη Διάσταση* (Athens: Kedros, 1972).

67   "Yannis Ritsos, *The Moonlight Sonata*, translated from the Modern Greek by Peter Bien," *New England Review* (Spring 1979), pp. 301-309.

68   Peter Bien, 'Ritsos's Painterly Technique in Short and Long Poems,' *Το Γιοφύρι* (Sydney, Australia) no. 11 (1990-91), pp. 5-11.

beneath the redemptive moonlight":

Τι φεγγάρι απόψε!
Είναι καλό το φεγγάρι,—δεν θα φαίνεται
που ασπρίσαν τα μαλλιά μου...

What a moon tonight!
The moon is good,—that my hair's turned gray
will not show.[69]

She seeks her salvation where it does not exist: in the idealized past and day-dreamy present.

Although the Woman in Black cannot recognize the timeless cosmic dimension, the poet can. He has the unswerving belief that deception is subordinate to an incorruptible Truth that converts deception into beauty. However, he does not utter a word about this. He cannot utter a word, since his own voice is nowhere to be found. Instead of words, he presents us with a frame around the Woman in Black's monologue, giving the poem in this way the traits of a painting, which occupies space rather than time. When we encounter the narrator in the epilogue, we recall the narrator in the prologue and thereby register the poem not just as a succession of fragments unfolding in time but as a unified composition immobilized in space. The painterly technique reminds us that we are not hearing just about everyday activities or about life in the raw despite the Woman in Black's anguished lament. No. In addition, we are seeing life as it is described in John Keats's poem 'Ode on a Grecian Urn,' immobilized so that it may "tease us out of thought as doth eternity." In other words, thanks to the painterly technique we sense that the contents are also ritualistic.

Let us ask now if this text also contains some other ritualistic elements. Very obvious is the element I called "craziness": that which, surpassing rationality, requires a work to speak not by words alone. The lament of the Woman in Black is certainly crazy—frenzied, neurotic—but it belongs to a *pseudo* ritual. What, then, is the real ritual that contains an element of craziness? It is the process by which the *poet* (certainly not the narrator) deals with wastage not with words but in a manner that may be termed *misterioso* (I use the direc-

69   See *Τέταρτη διάσταση*, p. 45.

tion that the poet adds to the music printed at the end and that is not found in Beethoven's Urtext). The true ritual employs the painterly frame-technique, as I explained above; more importantly, however, it also counterpoints the entire lament against *The Moonlight Sonata*, placing the Woman's false ritual within a second frame, that of a true ritual. This true ritual reaches out beyond the Woman in Black, beyond the narrator, and beyond us, the readers, confirming that wastage may be conquered or at least mollified by the incorruptible Truth of art. By means of this unshakable faith, the poet aspires to control the outside world. In other words, if he declares his faith repeatedly, either straightforwardly or *misterioso*, perhaps this ritualistic declaration will influence reality. All of this obviously surpasses rationality. It is craziness: that which obliges a work to communicate in a bizarre manner—not just with words.

Let's now continue to discuss repetition, which was the first characteristic of ritual that I identified owing to my personal experience as a Quaker, a mower of twelve acres, and a privileged observer of the *Anastenárides*. Repetition is obvious in the Woman's lament. She sighs "Let me come with you" so many times and has an insistent monomania regarding her disemboweled armchair. But all this, as I claimed above, is embedded in a false ritual. The repetition that belongs to the true ritual is announced by the narrator in the epilogue: "this entire scene has been accompanied pianissimo by *The Moonlight Sonata*, the first movement only." This is indeed *misterioso*! Beethoven's Sonata has three movements. Yet in the poem, instead of hearing the standard sequence—beginning, middle, and end—we hear nothing but the first movement, which is repeated interminably, consequently giving the poem a flavor that we must call ritualistic.

Regarding the third characteristic that I identified from my own experience as a Quaker—its imperative nature—I can report only a subjective impression. I believe that Beethoven's music, subordinating as it does the wastage of the woman's life, is just as necessary for us as for the Woman in Black. Why? Because its absence will discourage us. Insofar as we identify with the Woman (which we should, given that we all are subject to wastage), the ritualistic therapy of Beethoven's Sonata reminds us, urgently, how imperative it is for us not to forgo the redemptive rituals of our own lives.

Returning now to additional characteristics of ritual listed by Margaret Alexiou, I need to ask whether Ritsos's poem incorporates liturgical language or a liturgical schema. I do not find liturgical language in it, even though the Woman submits that she conversed with God on many a spring night. But I do find in the poem a basic liturgical schema: darkness giving way to light—the light of *The Moonlight Sonata*. I need to ask again, furthermore, whether the poem controls the outside world. The Woman in Black aspires to do this, but futilely. Hers, I insist, is a false ritual. But the *poet* offers us a true ritual that has the power to make the vicissitudes of the outside world—none of which the Woman can conquer—sink down under the quiet, gentle assault of Beethoven's first movement. Does this assault approach a cosmic dimension? Yes, insofar as we consider as given an incorruptible realm unbounded by either space or time. Perhaps some of us will wonder whether such a realm exists, but that is not the proper question. The proper question is: Do we have the *faith* that an incorruptible realm exists? We may say *No*. Yet Ritsos shouts out *Yes*. In poem after poem he affirms to his readers that the negatives of human life lie in an eternal cradle that can rock them into peace.

Margaret Alexiou claims that we may broaden our aesthetic criteria and enrich our understanding of literature by exploring the characteristics of ritual. I hope that my brief approach via ritual to Ritsos's *Moonlight Sonata* has strengthened this claim by revealing to us some interesting new dimensions.

7. ORESTES' COW

T HE MAJOR THEME OF YANNIS RITSOS'S DRAMATIC monologue *Orestes* is the conflict between action and contemplation.[70] The poem leads its mythological protagonist along a contemplative path at the end of which he is willing to act even though he has understood the deepest complexities of life. In a sense, then, Ritsos revises *Hamlet*. There,

> ...conscience does make cowards of us all,
> and thus the native hue of resolution
> is sicklied o'er with the pale cast of thought (III.i.83-85).

For Orestes, on the contrary, resolution is not inhibited by thought but strengthened. He is momentarily paralyzed by his meditations, it is true; in the end, however, he slays Clytemnestra and does so not in spite of his deeper understanding but because of it.

The "plot" of the poem is simple enough. Orestes and Pylades arrive at Mycenae at night and halt at the Lion Gate, where they hear Electra lamenting incessantly inside the palace. In the monologue that follows, Orestes struggles against the external fate that has made him the unwilling instrument of Electra's revenge, concluding in the exact middle of the poem that he will go away again and lead his own life. But then Electra's cries cease. The physical silence of the night reinforces Orestes' previous meditations about silence so that he is slowly able to comprehend the abhorred act of revenge within a larger context that makes his fate acceptable to him. As dawn arrives he enters the palace and slays both Clytemnestra and Aegisthus, whose screams are immediately swallowed by the various sounds and silences of ordinary life. Lastly, a large

---

70   This is an expanded version of an essay that first appeared in the Greek periodical *Αυτί*, July 19, 1975, pp. 36-37. Ritsos's poem was written between 1962 and 1966 and was published in 1966 by Kedros, Athens.

cow places herself at the center of the Lion Gate and gazes at the sky.

Although the poem's plot may be simple, its ideas and images are complicated. I link ideas to images because the ideas are conveyed chiefly through imagery. There are some didactic statements, to be sure—for example Orestes' affirmation to Pylades that he will do the deed not for revenge, hate, or punishment (ll. 497-498)[71] but

ίσως για κάποιο «ναί», που φέγγει αόριστο κι αδιάβλητο πέρα από
σένα κι από μένα.

perhaps for some sort of "yes" that shines vague and incorruptible
beyond you and me. (l. 501)[72]

Yet statements such as these are still very cryptic. Instead, our own deeper understanding, like Orestes', is achieved through a profusion of striking images that, although they may seem disparate embellishments at first, are neither disparate nor embellishments, for all of them cooperate eventually to weave the pattern of thought that, much more than the surface plot, is the poem's central subject.

If the images are the key to the ideas in *Orestes,* the cow that seals the poem's end so strangely is the key to the images. But we cannot analyze the cow in isolation because the meaning that is ultimately conveyed through this major image is constructed slowly by virtue of the minor images that precede it. What Ritsos attempts to articulate through all of them is a paradoxical union of opposites. Hence it is not surprising that the omnipresent rhetorical figure in the poem is the oxymoron:

μια κίνηση ακίνητη (a *motion without* motion; l. 291), αόριστο, κι ωστόσο ορισμένο (vague, yet fixed; l. 377), μια βουβή κραυγή (a speechless cry; l. 378), το απαρηγόρητο... / ...τόσο παρηγορητικό (inconsolable... / ...so consoling; ll. 435, 436). This is not clever word-play for its own sake but rather a linguistic reenforcement of thematic material seen as well in paradoxical lo-

---

71   In counting lines I have begun at the first line of verse, after the prose prologue.
72   Wherever possible, I have employed the English translation by Martin McKinsey and Edmund Keeley in *The American Poetry Review,* July/August 1981, Special Supplement, pp. 21-28. But I have also been helped by the version published by Philip Pastras and George Pilitsis in the *Journal of the Hellenic Diaspora* 12/1 (Spring 1985), pp. 52-81. In both cases, I have made adjustments when necessary in order to produce a more literal rendering.

cutions such as την αδιαλλαξία...μέσα στη συμπωνία (the intransigence... [found] in agreement; l. 414). These figures and locutions should alert us to the nature of the images; indeed we find them to be obsessively dualistic and paradoxical. When we examine them further, however, we discover that they subdivide into two categories. In the first, the dualism is limiting and/or destructive. This is evoked most brilliantly by the simile of the clapper and bell that describes Electra's alienation from her own lamenting voice:

κ' είναι η ίδια κρεμασμένη μέσα στη φωνή της
σα γλωσσίδι καμπάνας, και χτυπιέται και χτυπάει την καμπάνα.

and she herself hangs there inside her voice
like the tongue of a bell, and she is struck and she strikes the bell. (ll. 19-20)

Her voice is that of just revenge, or so she thinks. But Orestes, initiated gradually into the deeper meaning of things, realizes that she is "walled up in her narrow justice" (l. 404). These figures convey the paradox that the normal motives for vengeful action—namely unreflective "duty," "punishment," and "justice"—imprison or limit the self. Thus young Electra is already old (l. 189). Her belt is "like a vein without blood around her belly" (l. 194).

Orestes refuses to be trapped in the same way. Seeking some άνοιγμα προς τα έξω / και προς τα μέσα(opening outward / and also inward; ll. 358-359), he achieves this by means of a second category of dualistic vision in which the individual self that wishes to act (the clapper) no longer collides with some obdurate, finite circumscription (the bell) but is absorbed instead in some vague and regenerative infinitude. Once he understands that all human struggle—even the murder of Clytemnestra and Aegisthus—"elevates life" (l. 494), he can willingly perform the deed.

The images in this second category, culminating in the cow, yoke together opposites such as tumult and serenity, motion and motionlessness, the determined and the indeterminate, death and rebirth. Here are some examples: The serene night, broken by Electra's cries, is like a dark river that πορεύεται κατά τη θάλασσα / ...με τυχαία σκιρτήματα (ίσως κάποιος / να ρίχνει πέτρες στο ποτάμι (flows toward the sea / ...with unforeseen leaps (maybe someone's / throwing stones into the river; ll. 32, 35-36); a farmer walking at the edge of a field holds beneath his arm the shadow cast by a cloud—a shadow that traces a distant landscape of infinitude (ll. 86-92); mice fall into wells and drown, yet the same wells reflect the constellations as they move slowly across the sky (ll. 370-371). In all these cases, something small, definite, and often destructive is connected with something large, vague, and harmless: stars, clouds, the river, shadows—is connected in sum with ο επανερχόμενος ρυθμός της ζωής (life's recurring rhythm; l. 355). It is in this context of the tranquil and eternal rhythm, the silence within the ordered arrangement of seeds and stars (ll. 83-85), that we first encounter the enduring, patient cow (l. 98) whose large eyes help the earth familiarize itself with infinity (l. 94).

When we meet the cow again we realize that it, too, more starkly than any of the preceding figures, incarnates conflicting opposites. For it is no longer associated idyllically, as before, with leaves, blue sky, warm soil, and sturdy farmers (ll. 95-99). Just unyoked from the plow, it is

λαβωμένη
στα πλευρά και στη ράχη, ραβδισμένη στο μέτωπο,
ίσως γνωρίζοντας την άρνηση και την υποταγή,
την αδιαλλαξία και την εχθρότητα μέσα στη συμφωνία

wounded
on its ribs and back, caned across the forehead,
perhaps knowing refusal and submission,
the intransigence and hatred found in agreement. (ll. 411-414)

Thus it partakes in both the creative rhythms of eternity and the destructive suffering of earthly life. This paradox is explored in the following lines as the cow laps up water from a stream:

γλείφοντας με τη ματωμένη γλώσσα της, την άλλη εκείνη
δροσερή γλώσσα του νερένιου ειδώλου της, σα νάγλειφε
...
τη σιωπηλή, μεγάλη, στρογγυλή πληγή του κόσμου...

licking with its bloodied tongue that other
cooling tongue of its liquid image, as though licking

the silent, large, round wound of the world... (ll. 418-419, 422)

We remember that other stream, the dark river flowing toward the sea disturbed by stones that someone perhaps threw in. Now the stones have escalated into blood—which of course connects with the bloody sword (l. 479) that Orestes will use to assassinate Clytemnestra and Aegisthus. But an entirely new factor has been added. In the previous dualities the contrast was between things pure and impure. Now the recurring rhythm of life is no longer pure; on the contrary, it is a universal wound. Paradox is piled upon paradox: what first was paradoxical because it yoked seeming opposites together is now doubly paradoxical because the opposites have nearly become the same. Yet even the impure river of ever-flowing life still retains its healing qualities. In the succeeding lines we read that the blood from the cow's lips gradually disappears within this great wound as though passing

ελευθερωμένο, ανώδυνο,
σε μιαν αόρατη φλέβα του κόσμου...

released, without pain,
through some invisible vein of the world... (ll. 430-431)

This regenerative vein is deliberately contrasted to that other feeble, bloodless vein around Electra's belly (l. 194), and well it might be. Whereas Electra in her imprisoning blindness (l. 225) remains an enemy to paradox, i.e. to everything "unreasonable" (l. 216), the cow in its wisdom seems to have learned—seems able to accept with tranquility

πως το αίμα μας δε χάνεται, πως τίποτα δε χάνεται,
τίποτα, τίποτα δε χάνεται μέσα σ' αυτό το μέγα τίποτα.

that our blood is not lost, that nothing is lost,
absolutely nothing is lost in this great nothing. (ll. 433-434)

This wisdom is now shared by Orestes; it is the fruit of his long meditation in front of the Lion Gate. He realizes that he carries such a cow in his shadow (we are meant to remember the earlier farmer with the cloud's shadow beneath his arm; ll. 438-439); he realizes as well that the soft, immaterial shadows of the cow's two horns may turn into a pair of sharpened wings enabling him to pass through the closed door (we are meant to remember Electra, by contrast, banging against her obdurate bell; ll. 443-445).

To summarize, we may say that Orestes has discovered:

(a) a serene, universal context for turbulent, specific actions;
(b) a context that includes the negation that is a prerequisite for life and that in effect universalizes the paradoxical and unreasonable;
(c) a much fuller understanding of the process formulated incompletely near the beginning of the poem when the cow is first introduced and we are told, Έτσι οικειώνεται η γής με το άπειρο (This is how earth becomes intimate with infinity; l. 94).

Specifically, he has discovered that we first participate in universal truth (the "great nothing") by allowing ourselves, through contemplation, to be taught the paradox that all usurpers are innocent (l. 256). Why are they innocent? Because όλοι μας / σφετεριστές σε κάτι (all of us [are] / usurpers in some respect; ll. 256-257). Next, we participate in universal truth by acting in accord with it. This is our fate. Orestes may seem to act in the name of Electra's insufficient justifications—punishment, justice, revenge, and hate—but these are only a useful mask that he will wear in order to cover his true self: his ashes (l. 472). Being himself a participant in death, he freely chooses τη γνώση και την πράξη του θανάτου που τη ζωή ανεβάζει (the knowledge and the act of death that elevates life; l. 494).

The final paradox, therefore, is that destructive actions by an individual, because such actions participate in a universality that includes destructiveness, are somehow affirmative. Orestes cannot act for the inadequate reasons proposed by Electra; yet perhaps he can act for this unreasonable "yes" that shines vague and incorruptible beyond every individual, or "perhaps for a certain useless victory over our first and last fear" (l. 500).

This is how Ritsos solves the conflict between contemplation and action. On the one hand he refuses to accept unreflective action while on the other he refuses to allow the deep knowledge of moral complexity, a knowledge granted by contemplation, to paralyze his hero. Unlike Hamlet, Orestes overcomes his hesitation. His resolve strengthened rather than weakened by tragic wisdom, he does the deed, whereupon the cries of Clytemnestrta and Aegisthus are immediately absorbed into the recurring rhythm of life, a rhythm that now includes the sounds not only of songbirds but of destructive hunters. How appropriate, therefore, that at the epilogue's very end the poem's major image of resolved paradox, the cow, should place itself in the middle of the Lion Gate and gaze with pitch black eyes into the morning light.[73]

---

73   At one point Orestes suggests that the cow is the "symbol of some ancient religion" (l. 452). This is not pursued further in the poem, but one is encouraged to speculate on which cult is meant. My own guess would be the cult of Hera, which was pre-Mycenaean, i.e., ancient from Orestes' point of view, and was practiced in the Argolid and elsewhere in the Peloponnese— Hera says in *Iliad* 4.51 that the three cities she loves best are Argos, Sparta, and Mycenae. Her most usual epithet is ox-eyed, βοῶπις, and a cow was her most frequent sacrifice. Although worshipped primarily as a marriage goddess and a protectress of feminine fertility, in certain places she was warlike. This evidence would seem to make Orestes' cow an appropriately paradoxical symbol for the ancient religion of paradoxical Hera.

8. Yannis Ritsos (from *Critical Survey of Poetry*)

Mᴏʀᴇ ᴛʜᴏʀᴏᴜɢʜʟʏ ᴛʜᴀɴ ᴀɴʏ ᴏᴛʜᴇʀ Greek writer, Ritsos amalgamates the two ideologies that have divided his country: the Communist and the bourgeois. Though he espoused Marxist Leninism early in his career and remained faithful to the Party ever since, he nevertheless borrowed from Western literary movements, especially Surrealism, and struggled frankly with the Western attractions of individualism and subjectivism. All in all, because he presents a Communist orientation expressed through techniques that have evolved in ways typical of non-Communist authors, he speaks for and to the entire Greek nation.

Ritsos proved himself a virtuoso in technique. His range is enormous: from the tiniest lyric to huge narrative compositions, from impenetrable surrealistic puzzles to occasional verse promulgating blunt political messages, from poetry of almost embarrassing sensuality to rarefied philosophical meditations. He is also greatly esteemed because of his personal integrity, demonstrated over years of persecution, exile, and imprisonment. As he said in 1970 when interrogated by the ruling junta: "A poet is the first citizen of his country and for this very reason it is the duty of the poet to be concerned about the politics of his country."

Although known almost exclusively as a poet, Yannis Ritsos published prolifically as a journalist and translator, less prolifically as a critic and dramatist. His collected criticism is available in *Meletemata* (1974; studies), which includes, in addition to essays on Vladimir Mayakovsky, Nazim Hikmet, Ilya Ehrenburg, and Paul Eluard, two invaluable commentaries on Ritsos's own work. Among his translations are Aleksandr Blok's *Dvendtsat* (1918), anthologies of Romanian, Czech, and Slovak poetry, and selected poems by Mayakovsky, Hikmet, and Ehrenburg.

Ignored or banned for decades by the establishment, he is now published in handsome editions and received many honors, including the International Dimitrov Prize (Bulgaria, 1974), an honorary doctorate from the University of Thessaloniki (1975), the Alfred de Vigny Poetry Prize (France, 1975), the Lenin Prize (1977), and an honorary doctorate from the University of Birmingham, England (1978).

~

Yannis Ritsos was born into a wealthy landowning family of Monemvasia, but he did not have a happy childhood. His father's fortunes declined because of the land reforms under Eleftherios Venizelos in the early 1900's and were obliterated by the Asia Minor campaigns of 1919 to 1922, when labor was unavailable for the harvests. In addition, Ritsos's father gambled compulsively, accelerating the family's decline. As if this were not enough, Ritsos's older brother and his mother died of tuberculosis when Ritsos was only twelve—a prelude to the hardships and suffering that have marked his adult life.

Upon his graduation from high school in the town of Gythion, Ritsos moved to Athens; the year was 1925, a time when that city was desperately trying to assimilate a million and a half refugees from Asia Minor. He managed to find work as a typist and then as a copyist of legal documents, but in 1926 he returned to Monemvasia after coughing blood. There he devoted himself to painting, music, and poetry, completing a group of poems that he called "Sto paleo mas spiti" (in our old house). He returned to Athens in 1927, but a new crisis in his health confined him to a tuberculosis sanatorium for three years, during which, while continuing to write poems, he also began to study Marxism. By 1930, he had committed himself to the Communist cause. Transferred to a sanatorium in Crete, he found conditions there so abominable that he exposed them in a series of newspaper articles; this led to the removal of all the patients to a better facility, where his disease came under temporary control.

Back in Athens, Ritsos directed the artistic activities of the Workers' Club, appearing in in-house theatricals and also on the stage of the Labor Union Theater. Meanwhile, his father was confined to an insane asylum. While eking out a living as actor, dancer, copy editor, and journalist, Ritsos published his first two collections, *Trakter* (Tractor) and *Pyramides* (Pyramids). His career took a leap forward when, in May, 1936, he composed his *Epitaphios* immediately after the slaughter of twelve tobacco workers by Thessaloniki police during a strike. Issued in ten thousand copies, this became the first of Ritsos's poems to be banned. The Metaxas dictatorship, when it came to power in August, publicly burned the 250 unsold copies at the Temple of Olympian Zeus.

In this same year, Ritsos composed *To tragoudi tes adelphes mou* (The song of my sister), after his sister Loula was committed to the same asylum that housed their father. This private dirge, balancing the public one for the slain strikers, so impressed Kostis Palamas, Greece's most influential poet at the time, that he hailed the young author as his own successor. Ritsos suffered a brief recurrence of his tuberculosis, requiring another period in a sanatorium, after which he worked again as an actor, all the while publishing new collections of verse.

During the period of the Albanian Campaign, the German invasion, and the Axis Occupation of Greece (1940-1944), Ritsos—confined to bed almost continuously—wrote without respite but was unable to publish freely. Among the works produced was a long novel burned during the second round of the Civil War (December, 1944) and another prose composition, never published, entitled "Ariostos o prosechtikos aphegeitai stigmes tou biou tou kai tou ypnou tou" (careful Ariostos narrates moments from his life and his sleep).

After the second round of the Civil War, Ritsos fled to northern Greece with the defeated Communist forces. While in Kozani, he wrote plays for the People's Theater of Macedonia. The Varkiza Accord (February 12, 1945) enabled him to return to Athens, where he regularly contributed poems, prose pieces, translations, and dance criticism to the periodical *Elefthera Grammata*, as well as collaborating with the artistic branch of the Communist youth movement. It was at this time that he began to write *Romiosyne* (Greekness) and *The Lady of the Vineyards*, his twin tributes to the Greek Resistance.

In 1948, Ritsos was arrested because of his political activities and sent to various concentration camps on Greek islands. Under the worst of conditions, he nevertheless wrote about his privations, burying manuscripts and notes in bottles to hide them from the guards. Naturally, his work was banned. An international protest by figures such as Pablo Picasso, Louis Aragon, and Pablo Neruda led to his release in August, 1952. Free again in Athens, he joined the newly founded party, the EDA (United Democratic Left), wrote for the left-wing newspaper *Avgi*, married Falitsa Georgiadis in 1954, and became the father of a daughter in 1955. The following year, he visited the Soviet Union, traveling outside Greece for the first time. *Epitaphios* was reissued in a twentieth-anniversary edition, and *The Moonlight Sonata* brought him his first public recognition since Palamas's early enthusiasm, in the form of the State Prize for Poetry. This, in turn, led to international acclaim when Aragon published *The Moonlight Sonata* in *Les Lettres françaises*, accompanied by a flattering notice. In Greece, Kedros Publishers began to bring out all the work that could not be published earlier and planned for a multivolume collection of Ritsos's poems.

In 1960, the popular composer Mikis Theodorakis set eight sections of *Epitaphios* to music, making Ritsos a household name in Greece. In 1962, Ritsos traveled again, this time to Romania, Czechoslovakia, and East Germany, as a result of which he became acquainted with the Turkish poet Hikmet and his anthologies of Balkan poets. Despite a relapse of his tuberculosis, Ritsos composed prolifically during this period. In May, 1963, he journeyed to Thessaloniki to participate in the vigil for the parliamentary deputy Gregory Lambrakis, who had been mortally wounded by right-wing thugs. The following year, Ritsos himself stood for parliament as an EDA candidate. In 1966, he traveled to Cuba. Theodorakis set *Romiosyne* to music, again with immense popular success.

On April 21, 1967, the day of the Colonels' coup, Ritsos was arrested and again sent into exile on various islands, his works once more under ban. Protests poured in from around the world, leading to his transfer to house arrest in his wife's home on Samos. A group of seventy-five French Academicians and other writers, including several Nobel laureates, nominated him for the Nobel Prize. Translations of his poetry multiplied, especially in France.

Offered a passport by the junta to attend a poetry festival in England in 1970—on the condition that he refrain from all criticism of the regime—Ritsos refused, but later in the same year, owing to his health, he was allowed to return to Athens to undergo an operation and to remain there. In 1971, he joined others in publishing in *Ta nea keimena* in defiance of the regime. After the relaxation of censorship in 1972, Ritsos's works written in exile came out in a flood of publication that increased after the junta's fall in 1974.

Ritsos continues to gain worldwide recognition. His poetry has been translated into many languages, and he received numerous honors both in Greece and abroad.

~

Greece produced at least three world-class poets in the mid-twentieth century: George Seferis, Odysseus Elytis, and Yannis Ritsos. The first two received the Nobel Prize and were bourgeois; Ritsos received the Lenin Prize and was a Communist. Yet it would be entirely wrong to call him Greece's leading leftist poet or even a political poet. His range is so immense, his career so diverse, the traditions from which he draws so eclectic that these or any other labels distort his contribution. Though the leftist element is clearly present in Ritsos's work, he shares with bourgeois poets an interest in nature, in personal anguish, even in Christianity, and he participates as fully as they do in pan-European movements such as surrealism and folklorism. In sum, Ritsos speaks not only to one camp but also to all humanity.

On the other hand, it is clear that Ritsos found his first voice only because he had aligned himself with the political Left. It was Communism that transformed him, in the decade 1926 to 1936, from an imitator of others in content and style to a unique singer of revolution. *Epitaphios* provided the breakthrough. A dirge gasped out by a simple mother over the body of her son, slain by police in a labor dispute, this poem modulates from the dirge itself to the mother's thirst for revenge and finally to her solidarity with the oppressed working class. Every aspect of the poem—not merely its content—is intended by the author to make it accessible to the common people and not only about them. Thus, it exploits diverse elements from their cultural storehouse, primarily their Greek Orthodox liturgy and their folk songs, melding a call to revolution with the Christian hope for resurrection, and voicing all of this through the tone, metrics, and imagery of the demotic ballads that were produced by anonymous folk poets throughout the centuries of Turkish rule. Ritsos did not do this self-consciously in order to erect a bulwark of tradition that would fortify national identity, but almost naïvely; the liturgy and the demotic ballads were friends with which he had grown up as a child. What he sought to avoid, and conversely to accomplish, is best expressed by his estimation of Hikmet in *Meletemata*: "His poetry is not just…'folkloristic' (i.e. extremely…'aesthetic' on a so-called 'popular plane'—hence non-popular)… but essentially *popular* because of participation…in popular forces, which it expresses not in their static, standardized forms…but…in their dynamic motion."

It is characteristic of Ritsos's own dynamic motion that the mode of *Epitaphios* was never to be repeated. The poet broadened his range immediately—owing to the external circumstances of Yannis Metaxas's censorship, which confined Ritsos to nonpolitical subjects. But even when he returned to political poetry after the dictator's death early in 1941, Ritsos did so in a different way, if only because he had liberated his technique in the meantime from the constraints of rhyme and strict stanzaic form. *To tragoudi tes adelphes mou* is the chief fruit of the Metaxas period. The first of many extended elegies about family members or others, chiefly women, overcome by misfortune, it matches *Epitaphios* in that it shows how pain can lead to illumination, here the lamenting poet's conviction that poetry itself—the very act of singing of his sister's insanity—will save both him and her: "The poem has subdued me./ The poem has granted me the victory…/ I who could not/ save you from life/ will save you from death." Poetry thus joins revolution as a wonder-working power for Ritsos, who in his espousal of an "aesthetic solution" joined hands with his bourgeois colleagues throughout Europe.

In the many short poems written during this same period, Ritsos learned to escape the stridency still present in both *Epitaphios* and *To tragoudi tes adelphes mou*; he learned to distance himself from his material, to be laconic, to have poems "be," not merely "say." This he achieved chiefly through a painterly technique whereby motion, time, and sound were transfixed into immobility, space, and sight. Consider these lines: "Lone chimes speak silence,/ memories in groups beneath the trees,/ cows sad in the dusk./ Behind the young shepherds a cloud was bleating at the sunset." In this Keatsian cold pastoral, sound is frozen into a composition, time is spatialized. It is no wonder that the poem is entitled 'Engraving.'

Similar techniques are more difficult to apply to longer works, which cannot help but evolve in time. One of Ritsos's most successful works is an extended political poem written in September and October, 1942. Entitled *The*

Burial of Orgaz, it employs El Greco's celebrated painting, *Burial of the Conde de Orgaz* (1586-1588), as a static, two-tiered composition, holding in place the extraordinarily varied figures of the poet's political vision: on the earthly level, mutilated veterans of Albania, resisters executed by the Germans, innocent Athenians dying from famine; on the heavenly, in place of El Greco's John the Baptist kneeling at Christ's feet, robust workers building a new road—a Marxist paradise. Because of the painterly technique, the emotions are frozen into beauty; life is transformed into art. Later in his career—as in *Philoctetes*, for example—Ritsos was to achieve the same control over the mad flow of life's images by superimposing them on a myth rather than on a painting.

The Burial of Orgaz treats war tragically. It is ironic that Ritsos could treat it exultantly only after his side had met defeat in the second round of the Civil War and had then begun to suffer systematic persecution. Mortified at the discrediting of the Resistance by the Greek Right, he determined to apotheosize the heroes (Communist or not) who had opposed the Axis throughout the Occupation period and to insist on their patriotism. In *Romiosyne*, written between 1945 and 1947 but obviously not publishable until much later, he therefore amalgamated his twentieth-century heroes with the historical freedom fighters in the Greek War of Independence and the legendary stalwarts who had harassed the Turks in preceding centuries. Ending as it does with the hope of a peaceful, loving tomorrow, the resulting ode combines visionary transcendentalism, realism, and epic exaggeration into a blend that energetically celebrates—along with *The Lady of the Vineyards*, written at the same time—Greece's most difficult years.

The exultant tone disappeared from Ritsos's poetry during the four years (1948-1952) that he spent once more in internment camps. His aim was no longer either epic or transcendental; it was merely to encourage his fellow prisoners with simple verses that they could understand. There is an entire collection of these poems written in 1949 while he was on the infamous island of Makronesos, the "Makronesiotika," available now in *Ta epikairika*. Many more were composed on Agios Efstratios (Ai-Strati), the most celebrated being the *Letter to Joliot-Curie* of November, 1950, which was smuggled out of Greece at the time. It begins: "Dear Joliot, I'm writing you from AiStrati./ We're about three thousand here,/ simple people.../ with an onion, five olives and a stale crust of light in our sacks/…people who have no other crime to their account/ except that we, like you, love/ freedom and peace." To his credit, Ritsos later realized that the comrades did have other crimes to their account, but the circumstances of imprisonment made such self-criticism inappropriate for the moment. What is remarkable, as Pandelis Prevelakis remarks, is that Ritsos "not only maintained his intellectual identity, but also prodded his sensibility to adjust to the conditions of exile."

More important is the tender poem entitled 'Peace,' written soon after Ritsos's release. Here, the title word is no longer a political slogan; it expresses the poet's genuine sense of tranquillity after four years of terror: "Peace is the evening meal's aroma,/ when a car stopping outside in the street isn't fear,/ when a knock on the door means a friend…"

The years 1956 to 1966 were Ritsos's most remarkable decade of artistic productivity and growth. The great outpouring of this period surely derived in part from unaccustomed happiness—this was the first outwardly untraumatic decade of his life—but also, paradoxically, from a new, disagreeable condition to which his sensibility (along with that of all Communists) had to adjust. Nikita Khrushchev denounced Stalin in 1956, whereupon the Greek Communist Party immediately denounced its Stalinist leader, Nikos Zachariadis. Later in the same year, the Soviet Union—presumably a lover of freedom and peace—invaded Hungary. Ritsos, who had sung hymns to both Stalin and Zachariadis, was forced to step back from his previous commitments and certainties, to view them with doubt or irony. "The first cries of admiration," he wrote in his introduction to Mayakovsky, "have given way to a more silent self-communing… We have learned how difficult it is not to abuse the power entrusted to us in the name of the supreme ideal, liberty…" This new understanding, he continued, has led modern poets to a self-examination that is at the same time self-effacing and hesitant. Elsewhere, he spoke of his growing consciousness of all that is "vague, complicated, incomprehensible, inexplicable and directionless in life."

The first fruit of this new awareness of the complexity of life was *The Moonlight Sonata*, a nonpolitical poem constituting for Ritsos a breakthrough fully as significant as the one achieved precisely twenty years earlier by the quintessentially political *Epitaphios*. The 1956 poem, though once again a kind of elegy for a suffering woman, avoids all stridency and authorial assertion by hiding its tragic elements behind a mask of ironic impassivity. At the same time, however, it allows the woman's anguished emotions to stir the *reader's* emotions. Ritsos accomplishes this by making the major voice not his own but the woman's and then by framing her dramatic monologue inside yet another nonauthorial voice, a narrator's, which questions and neutralizes the emotions of the first voice. As a result, the reader is never quite sure how to feel about the poem or how to interpret it; instead, both emotionally and mentally, the reader is ushered into all that is "vague, complicated, incomprehensible..."

Philoctetes carries this process still further. It retains the technique of dramatic monologue inside a narrative frame but adds to it an all-encompassing myth that fulfills the same kind of "painterly" purpose served earlier by El Greco's *Burial of the Conde de Orgaz*. At the same time, the myth connects Ritsos's version of the Philoctetes story and hence the Greek Civil War (which is clearly suggested) not only with Homer's Achaeans and Trojans but also with the Peloponnesian War, clearly suggested in Sophocles's version. If one notes as well that the poem employs the surrealistic and expressionistic techniques that Ritsos had been perfecting in short poems dating from the same period (collected as *Martyries*; testimonies), it becomes clear that a work of such complexity is deliberately meant to make the reader feel uncomfortably suspended above nothing. That, in turn, is a perfect technical equivalent for the thrust of the poem, which dismisses every justification for Philoctetes's collaboration in the Trojan War yet affirms his need to stand by his comrades even though he knows their perfidy. The poem thus examines Ritsos's own dilemma as a Stalinist betrayed by Stalin, determined to bring his understanding and indulgence to the cause instead of merely defecting. It is a self-examination that is at the same time self-effacing and hesitant.

The poet's new stance was soon put to the test by imprisonment under the Colonels. Despite this provocation, Ritsos did not revert to the optimistic assurance displayed during earlier privations; the new poems of exile are exasperated, sardonic, even sometimes despairing. Bitten (like Philoctetes) by the snake of wisdom, he could never return to the propagandistic verse produced on Agios Efstratios. On the contrary, he felt the need to reaffirm the predominance of mystery. 'The Disjunctive Conjunction *Or*,' written in exile on June 18, 1969, says this loud and clear: "O that *or*," cries the poet, that "equivocal smile of an incommunicable…wisdom/ which…/ [knows] full well that precision/ …does not exist (which is why the pompous style of certainty is so unforgivable…)./ Disjunctive *or*…/ with you we manage the troubles of life and dream,/ the numerous shades and interpretations…"

In his more recent poems, Ritsos continued to grapple with mystery, asking basic questions but realizing that answers do not always follow: "So many dead/ without death/ so many living corpses./ You sit in a chair/ counting your buttons./ Where do you belong?/ What are you?/ What are you doing?" The sardonic element is still present, but so is a certain spirit of indulgence or clemency—precisely what Philoctetes brought to Troy. Furthermore, a parodistic flavor entered many of Ritsos's later poems, a kind of macabre humor that neutralizes the worst that life can offer. Ritsos thus stood above all that his countrymen had done to him, playing with his experience, turning it round beneath his philosophic gaze—a gaze annealed by hardship into resilience.

9. Introduction to *The Wavering Scales*

YANNIS RITSOS (1909-1990) IS INCREASINGLY recognized as the greatest talent of Greece's remarkable twentieth-century literary renaissance. George Seferis and Odysseas Elytis received Nobel prizes; Ritsos surely deserved one. The problems—his steadfast adherence to communism and the huge bulk of his output—have receded because the Cold War ended and because we now understand that his immense productivity derived not from sloppiness or deficient self-criticism but from an unquenchable compulsion to express. "I write a verse, / I write the world," Ritsos affirms. "I exist, the world exists. / A river flows from the tip of my little finger." Perhaps we can best appreciate his productivity if we hail him as the Greek Walt Whitman.

An active communist since his late teens, Ritsos, was born into an aristocratic, landowning family. His earliest poems evoke the decaying family mansion in Monemvasia on the one hand, the promise of socialist revolution on the other. This dual orientation, private and public, continued. The celebrated *Epitaphios* (1936, about a striking worker killed by police) and *The Song of My Sister* (1937, about his sister's insanity) established his voice to such a degree that Kostis Palamas, the leading Greek poet of the time, wrote to him: "Your song is made of the god's divine blood, / ...We step aside, dear poet, for you to pass."

Ritsos's ensuing output includes tiny two-line lyrics like 'April' ("Springtime. Your eyes two drops of sea. / A goldfinch climbs up and down on a wooden cross.") and large, complicated meditations like *Philoctetes* (using Homeric material to consider whether to continue communist allegiance given Stalin's excesses) or *The Moonlight Sonata* (examining an aristocratic woman's sentimentality against the non-sentimentality of Beethoven). A Marxist poet popular with the masses, yet also immensely sophisticated, Ritsos employs mythical materials with no fear of restricting his audience to highbrows or of deserting contemporary reality either for some fantastical vision of the past or some disinterested quiver of aesthetic appreciation.

Owing to his communist allegiance, he spent extended periods in detention and could not publish freely, or at all. But when the Germans occupied Greece in 1941 and a far-left resistance movement developed, he produced a series of poems that circulated clandestinely among the Maquisards and buoyed their spirits. *The Wavering Scales*, dated January 1943, belongs to this period. Parts of the poem are immediately relevant—for example: "carrying in your arms two severed legs / ... / here you'll stop for a night to be tested" (in 'The Obligation to Persevere'). Other parts are perplexing and thus more typical of Ritsos's metaphorical method. Consider "The moon reeks of tar" followed by "sometimes the moon is a spider devouring blue flies" (in 'Insufficiency'). Tar suggests boats, the spider something unpleasantly destructive. It is not until the poem's penultimate stanza that these metaphors connect with the torment of the German occupation, for there we meet a vessel heading in a direction opposite from what is desired, followed (in the final stanza) by anti-aircraft searchlights ready to "snatch away your youth."

The Wavering Scales must be read carefully. We always need to remember Ritsos's metaphorical method as well as his situation in 1942-1943, when he was confined to occupied Athens because his bad health did not allow him to join the resistance fighters in the mountains. Life of course went on in Athens ("we combed our hair in the taverna mirror"), yet violence and loss lurked everywhere ("the ship's cats / ran their claws down our silence"). Ritsos gazed both outward and inward, establishing metaphors that link external material to the innermost psyche of us all but especially of those who have been injured. "Each word," he declares, "is an outlet / for a meeting (often postponed). / The word is real when it insists upon the meeting." In *The Wavering Scales* as elsewhere, the ostensible content exists not for its own sake, but in order to meet with human feeling.

PART TWO: TRANSLATIONS

1. ΦΙΛΟΚΤΗΤΗΣ

(Καλοκαιριάτικο απόγευμα. Σε μιάν ερημική ακρογιαλιά νησιού—ίσως της Λήμνου. Τα χρώματα σβήνουν λίγο-λίγο. Ένα καράβι αραγμένο στο βραχώδη ορμίσκο. Ακούγονται οι φωνές και τα γέλια τών ναυτών που λούζονται, γυμνάζονται, παλεύουν, λίγο πιο κάτω. Εδώ, έξω από μια βραχοσπηλιά, διαμορφωμένη σε κατοικία, κάθονται δυο άντρες—ο ένας ωραίος, γενειοφόρος, ώριμος, με αρρενωπή, πνευματική μορφή· ο άλλος, γεροδεμένος νέος, με φλογερά, ερευνητικά κ' ερωτικά μάτια. Έχει κάτι απ' τα χαρακτηριστικά του Αχιλλέα, μα κάπως πιο εκπνευματωμένα, σα νάναι ο γιός του, ο Νεοπτόλεμος. Ένα φτενό, αφανές φεγγάρι, μετακινείται αόριστα κι αργά κάπου στον ουρανό, ασημί, μέσα στις παρατεταμένες τριανταφυλλιές και μενεξελιές ανταύγειες του ηλιοβασιλέματος. Φαίνεται πως ο ώριμος άντρας, ύστερ' από χρόνια μόνωσης και σιωπής, είχε μιλήσει πολύ στον Νέο, σ' αυτόν τον απροσδόκητο επισκέπτη του, πούχε φτάσει μόλις πριν δυο ώρες, και τώρα σωπαίνει πάλι, βαθύς, κορεσμένος, κουρασμένος από μιάν άλλη, ανώφελη κι αυτήν, μα ανθρώπινη, κούραση και θλίψη. Μια αόριστη τύψη σκιάζει το ευρύ μέτωπό του. Ωστόσο παρατηρεί ακόμη το εξαίσιο πρόσωπο τού Νέου, σαν κάτι να περιμένει. Στο βάθος της σπηλιάς αντιλαμπίζουν πότε-πότε τα όπλα του—η μεγάλη καλοδουλεμένη ασπίδα του με παραστάσεις απ' τους άθλους του Ηρακλή, και τα τρία φημισμένα του δόρατα—μοναδικά στο είδος τους. Ο Νέος, σα να παίρνει μια δύσκολη απόφαση, αρχίζει να μιλάει):

1   Σεβάσμιε φίλε, είμουνα βέβαιος για τη βαθειά σου κατανόηση. Εμείς οι νεότεροι
    που κληθήκαμε, όπως λένε, την ύστατη στιγμή για να δρέψουμε τάχα
    τη δόξα την ετοιμασμένη με τα δικά σας όπλα,
    με τις δικές σας πληγές, με το δικό σας θάνατο,
    γνωρίζουμε κ' εμείς κι αναγνωρίζουμε, κ' έχουμε, ναι, κ' εμείς τις πληγές μας
    σ' άλλο σημείο του σώματος—πληγές αθώρητες,
    χωρίς το αντίβαρο της περηφάνειας και του αξιοσέβαστου αίματος
    του χυμένου ορατά, σε ορατές μάχες, σε ορατά αγωνίσματα.

1. PHILOCTETES: The Ultimate Mask

*(Summertime on the deserted shore of an island—perhaps Lemnos. Early eve-
ning, colors beginning to fade. A boat anchored in the rocky cove. The crew, a little way below, washing, exercising, wrestling, their shouts and laughter audible.
Here above, two men are seated before a stony cavern fitted out as a dwelling-
place. One is handsome, bearded, mature, with a manly, spiritual face, the other
a wiry youth with fervent, inquisitive eyes filled with love. He has something
of Achilles' features, but slightly more spiritualized, as though he were his son
Neoptolemos. Somewhere, a frazzled, indiscernible moon shifts slowly, obscure-
ly, across the sky, silver amid the protracted violet and pink reflections of the
sunset. Apparently the older man, after years of solitude and silence, has been
speaking at length to the youth, that unexpected visitor who arrived scarcely
two hours earlier. But now, silent once again, he is inscrutable and sated, weary
with yet another wearying grief—one of no greater avail than the first, yet understandably human. A vague remorse clouds his broad forehead; nevertheless,
he continues to observe the youth's splendid face, as though expecting something.
Reflections from his weapons gleam from time to time at the back of the cavern:
his huge, well-wrought shield with its depiction of Herakles' labors, and his three
famous, incomparable spears. The young man seems to be making a difficult
decision. He begins to speak…)*

I was sure, my worthy friend, that you would understand profoundly. We of
   the younger generation,
called up at the very last minute, as they say, supposedly to reap
the glory that all of you prepared for us
with your arms, your wounds, your deaths:
we too recognize and know—yes, we too possess our wounds
elsewhere on the body, wounds unseen,
unrecompensed by pride or by respectable blood
shed visibly in the visible battles, visible competitions.

Μια τέτοια δόξα ας μας έλειπε·—ποιός τους την ζήτησε;
10   Μήτε μιάν ώρα δεν είχαμε δική μας, πληρώνοντας
τα χρέη και τις υποθήκες άλλων. Μήτε καν προφτάσαμε
να δούμε μιάν αυγή ένα ήσυχο χέρι ν' ανοίγει το παράθυρο απέναντι
και να κρεμάει απ' έξω, στην πρόκα του τοίχου, ένα κλουβί καναρίνια
με τη σεμνότητα μιάς περιττής κι αναγκαίας χειρονομίας.

Όλες οι ομιλίες τών μεγάλων, για νεκρούς και για ήρωες.
Παράξενες λέξεις, τρομερές, μας κυνηγούσαν ως μέσα στον ύπνο μας
περνώντας κάτω απ' τις κλεισμένες πόρτες, απ' την αίθουσα των συμποσίων
όπου άστραφταν ποτήρια και φωνές, κ' ένας πέπλος
αόρατης χορεύτριας κυμάτιζε αθόρυβα
20   σαν ένα διάφανο, στροβιλιζόμενο χώρισμα
ανάμεσα στη ζωή και στο θάνατο. Αυτή η παλλόμενη
ρυθμική διαφάνεια του πέπλου, παρηγορούσε κάπως
τις παιδικές μας νύχτες, αραιώνοντας τις σκιές τών ασπίδων
που γράφονταν στους άσπρους τοίχους με τ' αργό φεγγαρόφωτο.

Μαζί με τη δική μας την τροφή ετοιμάζανε
και την τροφή τών νεκρών. Την ώρα του γεύματος
έπαιρναν πάνω απ' το τραπέζι υδρίες με μέλι και με λάδι
και τις μετέφεραν σ' άγνωστους τάφους. Δεν ξεχωρίζαμε
τους αμφορείς τού κρασιού απ' τις νεκρικές ληκύθους. Δε γνωρίζαμε
30   ποιό το δικό μας και ποιο των νεκρών. Ένας χτύπος
του κουταλιού μες στο πιάτο, είταν ένα άξαφνο δάχτυλο
επιτιμητικό, που μας χτυπούσε στον ώμο. Στρέφαμε να δούμε. Τίποτα.

Απ' έξω απ' τις κρεββατοκάμαρές μας τύμπανα και σάλπιγγες,
κόκκινες σπίθες και μουγγές σφυριές σε μυστικά σιδηρουργεία
όπου νυχτόημερα σφυρηλατούσαν ασπίδες κι ακόντια,
κι άλλες σφυριές σε υπόγεια εργαστήρια
για προτομές κι ανδριάντες πολεμικών θεών, πολεμικών ανθρώπων, κι όχι
   διόλου
αθλητών και ποιητών· μαζί κ' εκατοντάδες επιτύμβιες στήλες

124

We could have done without such glory! Did we ever ask for it?
Fulfilling others' duties and paying off
their debts, we had not a moment for ourselves, no time even
to observe a tranquil hand unlatch a window across from us at dawn
and suspend a canary cage outside from the bracket on the wall
with the seemliness of a superfluous yet necessary gesture.

Our elders spoke of nothing but dead men and heroes.
Strange words followed us even into sleep, terrible words
that slipped beneath closed doors, out of the banqueting hall
where shouts and goblets flashed, and the veil
of an unseen dancing-girl fluttered soundlessly
like a transparent partition whirling
between life and death. It comforted
our childish nights somehow, that rhythmic,
throbbing transparency of the veil, dispersing the shields' shadows
inscribed on white walls by lingering moonlight.

They prepared food for the dead
together with our own food. Jugs
of honey and oil were taken from table at mealtime
and carried to unknown tombs. We never distinguished
funerary urns from amphorae of wine, never knew
what belonged to us and what to the dead. The tap
of a spoon on a plate became an unexpected finger
tapping our shoulder in rebuke. We turned to look. Nothing.

Drums and bugles outside our bedroom windows;
red sparks and muted hammer-blows in hidden smithies
where shields and javelins were forged day and night;
hammering as well in basement studios
for statues and busts of warring men and warring gods (never poets
or athletes); also tombstones by the hundreds

με ωραίους, γυμνούς εφήβους, πάντοτε όρθιους,
40   μεταμφιέζοντας, με την κάθετη στάση τους,
το αιώνια οριζόντιο της νεκρότητας. Μονάχα, πότε-πότε,
έγερναν το κεφάλι, καμπυλώνοντας ελαφρά τον αυχένα,
σαν άνθος σε χείλος γκρεμού· κι ο γκρεμός δε φαινόταν·—οι τεχνίτες
είχαν μάθει (ή μήπως τάχα τους το επέβαλλαν;)
να παραλείπουν γκρεμούς και κάτι τέτοια.

Είταν ένας μακρύς, λευκός διάδρομος (κι απόμεινε έτσι)
ντυμένος όλος μ' επιτύμβιες στήλες. Κι ούτε επιτρεπόταν
ν' αργοπορήσουμε για λίγο το βλέμμα στα εύγραμμα μέλη τους
η στους μαρμάρινους βοστρύχους που έπεφταν κάποτε στο μέτωπό τους
50   σαν φυσημένοι απ' τα χείλη ενός αιφνίδιου, μυροφόρου ανέμου
σ' ένα πάγχρυσο, θερινό μεσημέρι,—θαρρώ, ναι, πως ευώδιαζε
λεμονανθούς και ζεσταμένη απ' τον ήλιο λυγαριά. Μεγάλα πρότυπα
μας κληροδότησαν·—ποιος τους τα ζήτησε;—ας μας άφηναν
μέσα στο ελάχιστο, στο δικό μας ελάχιστο· δε θέλουμε
να μετρηθούμε μ' αυτά·—τί κερδίσατε άλλωστε; τί κερδίσαμε;

Καταλαβαίνω τη δική σου ευγενική αποχώρηση, σεβάσμιε φίλε,
μ' ένα πρόσχημα κοινά παραδεκτό—πόνος του σώματος,
όχι του πνεύματος η της ψυχής·—καλό πρόσχημα
το δάγκωμα εκείνο του φιδιού (μήπως το φίδι της σοφίας;)
60   να μείνεις μόνος και να υπάρξεις,—εσύ, κι όχι ένας άλλος—
να μην υπάρξεις έστω, κουλουριασμένος σ' έναν κύκλο,
καθώς το φίδι δαγκώνοντας την ουρά του. (Συχνά κ' εγώ το επιθύμησα.)

Κ' ίσως να μελετούσες μες στη μόνωσή σου μιαν εκδίκηση,
μιαν αναγνώριση δική σου ή, τουλάχιστον, την αναγνώριση
της σημασίας των όπλων σου. Και, ιδού που δικαιώθηκες·—
δε θέλω να κρυφτώ—γι' αυτά έχω έλθει, όπως το μάντεψες—
αυτά θα δώσουν επιτέλους τη νίκη στους Έλληνες,
(ρητός ο χρησμός:) αυτά, με το δικό μου χέρι.

with handsome, naked youths standing invariably erect,
masking, with their vertical pose,
death's everlasting horizontal. Sometimes, to be sure,
they drooped their heads and gently arched their necks
like flowers at chasm-edge, but the chasm never showed, the artists
having learned (having been compelled, perhaps?)
to leave out chasms and all things similar.

We had a long, white corridor (and so it remained).
Tombstones lined it everywhere, yet to rest our gaze
upon the youths' well-shaped limbs for even a moment was
forbidden, or upon the marble ringlets which fell across their brow some-
    times
as if tousled by the lips of sudden incense-bearing gusts
on a golden summer's noon—I think sun-warmed willow
perfumed the place, yes, and lemon blossoms. Great models
they bequeathed to us! Did we ever ask for them? If only we'd been left
to our littleness, our own restricted selves! We'd rather not
compete with models. All of you, besides: what have you gained? And what
    have we?

Worthy friend, I understand your dignified withdrawal.
Your excuse (acceptable to all): bodily woe,
not mental pain or spiritual. A fine excuse
that snakebite (the snake of wisdom, maybe?) for you
to stay alone, existing—you, none other,
even if not existing—…existing like a snake
curled into a ball, biting its tail (How often have I yearned for that myself!)

You studied revenge perhaps in your solitude,
recognition for yourself or at least for the importance
of your arms. And now, behold your vindication.
I have come for them (why not admit it frankly?) just as you predicted.
They'll bring victory to the Greeks at last
(on this the oracle is clear): they, in my hands.

Όμως εγώ, ήρθα πρώτα για σένα. Κι ούτε θα τα δεχόμουν τα όπλα σου
70 σαν αντάλλαγμα της αναγνώρισής μου ή σαν αντάλλαγμα
στη σωτηρία που σου προσφέρω: να σε πάρω μαζί μου στα καράβια μου
μ' όλες τις αθεράπευτες πληγές σου, μ' όλη σου τη μοναχικότητα—ποια
σωτηρία;
Πολύ τα συνηθίζουν τώρα κάτι τέτοια λόγια—τα μάθαμε·—
τί να πούμε;—δεν προφταίνει κανένας να δεί και να μιλήσει.

Λαμπαδηδρόμοι τρέχουν μες στη νύχτα. Οι πυρσοί χρυσώνουν τους
δρόμους.
Για μια στιγμή τ' αγάλματα των θεών φωτίζονται πάλλευκα
σαν πόρτες ανοιχτές σε τείχη θεόρατα. Ύστερα
πέφτει η σκιά των πέτρινων χεριών τους σκεπάζοντας το δρόμο.
Κανένας πια δεν ξεχωρίζει τίποτα. Είδα ένα βράδι
80 αλλόφρονα πλήθη να σηκώνουνε κάποιον στους ώμους τους
επευφημώντας τον. Μια δάδα έπεσε πάνω του.
Πήραν φωτιά τα μαλλιά του. Αυτός δε φώναξε.
Είταν απ' ώρα νεκρός. Τα πλήθη σκόρπισαν. Απόμεινε
το βράδι καταμόναχο, δαφνοστεφές, με τα χρυσά φύλλα των άστρων.

Η εκλογή, θαρρώ, ακατόρθωτη—κι ανάμεσα σε τί; Θυμάμαι
όταν είμουν παιδί·—απ' τους ξενώνες του σπιτιού μας μ' έφταναν
οι ωραίες, αρρενωπές φωνές των ξένων,
λίγο πριν απ' τον ύπνο, την ώρα που θα γδύνονταν·—και, βέβαια,
κείνη την ώρα θα ξεχνούσαν σχέδια πολεμικά κι αγώνες και φιλοδοξίες,
90 σάρκινοι μες στη γύμνια τους, ερωτικοί κι αθώοι,
καθώς θ' αγγίζαν, κατά λάθος ίσως, τα ίδια τους τα στήθη,
κι αργοπορούσαν στην άκρη της κλίνης μ' ανοιχτά σκέλη,
ξεχνώντας μες στις ζεσταμένες φούχτες τους τα γόνατά τους,
ώσπου ν' αποτελειώσουν μια μικρή, χαρούμενη ιστορία
διανθισμένη με τα γέλια τους και με των κρεββατιών το τρίξιμο.

Εγώ, τ' άκουγα τότε απ' το διάδρομο, καθώς, κρυφά, περιεργαζόμουνα
τα στίλβοντα σπαθιά και τις ασπίδες τους
ακουμπισμένες στον τοίχο, αντανακλώντας μυστικά το φεγγαρόφωτο

But first of all I've come for you. I would never accept your arms
in exchange for recognition of myself, or for the "deliverance"
I offer you. What deliverance to take you with me in my ships
with all your incurable wounds and all your loneliness?
Such words are quite the fashion now. We've learned them—
what more can we say? No chance to see or speak.

Runners hurry through the night: their torches gild the streets.
Whiter than white, the statues of the gods shine a moment
like open gateways in giant walls; then
shadows fall again from their stony hands and overcast the road.
No one distinguishes clearly after that. I beheld
a frenzied mob one night raise a person to their shoulders
in acclamation. A torch fell on him.
His hair caught fire. *He* did not shout.
He was long since dead. The mob dispersed. The night
was left in solitude, garlanded with the golden leaves of the stars.

Impossible to choose, I think. And what alternatives were given us? I recall
my childhood: from the visitors' quarters of our house,
the manly, resonant voices of our guests would reach me
just before bedtime. Most likely they were undressing then, and surely
must have forgotten struggles, battle plans, and ambitions for a time—
sensual in their nudity; aroused and innocent; while
(most likely) they fondled their own chests as though by chance,
and dawdled at their bedsides with thighs spread wide,
knees forgotten beneath heated palms,
until they finished a brief, happy tale
embellished by laughter and the creaking of beds.

I heard this from the corridor as I perused
in stealth their polished swords and shields
which, propped against the wall, reflected mystically the moonlight striking
    them

πούπεφτε απ' την τζαμόπορτα·—κ' ένιωθα τόσο μόνος κι αμήχανος
100   σα νάταν κείνη τη στιγμή να διαλέξω για πάντα
ανάμεσα στο γέλιο τους και στα όπλα τους (που είταν δικά τους και τα δυό).
    Φοβόμουνα κιόλας
μη σηκωθεί τη νύχτα ο πατέρας και με βρεί στο διάδρομο
ν' αγγίζω κείνα τα περίεργα όπλα—προπάντων
μην καταλάβει πως άκουσα το γέλιο τους, μην καταλάβει
το μυστικό μου δίλημμα. Καθόλου δεν πλησίαζα τους ξενώνες·
άκουγα μόνο τις φωνές των ξένων
σα να περνούσαν διαδοχικές στοές—μια στο σκοτάδι
και μια στο φώς—συχνά πνιγμένες στους θορύβους
απ' τις οπλές των αλόγων, έξω, στο προαύλιο·—κάποτε μάλιστα τρόμαξα
110   απόναν ίσκιο μεγάλο πούπεσε μπρος στα πόδια μου,—ένα άλογο
στεκόταν στην τζαμόπορτα και κοίταζε μέσα
ισκιώνοντας τις σφυρήλατες παραστάσεις των ασπίδων.

Έτσι μεγάλος είταν κι ο ίσκιος του πατέρα· σκίαζε ολόκληρο το σπίτι,
έκλεινε πόρτες και παράθυρα από πάνω ως κάτω,
και κάποτε θαρρούσα πως για να δω τη μέρα
θάπρεπε να περάσω το κεφάλι μου κάτω απ' τα σκέλη του·—
αυτό με τρόμαζε ιδιαίτερα—τ' άγγιγμα των μηρών του στον αυχένα μου.
    Προτιμούσα
να μένω μες στο σπίτι, στο αγαθό μισόφωτο των δωματίων,
ανάμεσα στα υπάκουα έπιπλα, με την πειθήνια αφή των παραπετασμάτων,
120   κι άλλοτε μες στην έρημη αίθουσα των αγαλμάτων,—αγαπούσα τους
    κούρους.

Κει μέσα βασίλευε δροσιά και σιωπή, την ώρα που έξω
στους ελαιώνες και στ' αμπέλια, φρενιάζαν τα τζιτζίκια
μες στο καυτό, μαλαματένιο μεσημέρι. Στο δάπεδο
διασταυρώνονταν πράες, συμφωνημένες, οι σκιές των αγαλμάτων
σχηματίζοντας διάφανους, γαλάζιους ρόμβους· και κάποτε
ένα μικρό ποντίκι, ξεθαρρεμένο απο την ησυχία,
περνούσε αργά πάνω στα πόδια των κούρων, σταματούσε,
παρατηρούσε με δυο σταγόνες λάδι, όλο υποψία, τα στενόμακρα παράθυρα

through glazed doors. I felt so lonely then, so perplexed,
as though that very instant I was forced to choose for ever
between their laughter and their weapons. (Both belonged to them.) My
    father
made me tremble even more, lest he wake and find me in the corridor
touching those curious arms, but chiefly lest he realize
I had overheard their laughter and apprehend
my secret dilemma. I never dared approach the visitors' domain
but only heard their voices cross successive galleries
—or so it seemed—of alternating light
and dark. The din of horses' hoofbeats, outside in the courtyard, often
drowned them; indeed, a giant shadow
fell before my feet one time and startled me—at the glazed doors
a horse stood looking in, obscuring with its shade
the images hammered on the shields.

My father's shadow was just as large. He cast his gloom
throughout the house, shutting doors and windows from top to bottom.
I felt as though constrained sometimes to place my head
between his legs should I wish to see the sun.
That's what unnerved me most: the sensation of his thighs against my neck. I
    preferred
to stay indoors in the kindly semidarkness of the rooms,
with docile furniture surrounding me and curtains so yielding to the touch,
or else within the deserted sculpture hall. I loved the kouroi.

Quiet ruled in there, and coolness, while out-of-doors
in olive grove and vineyard cicadas raged
in noontime's golden swelter. Statues' shadows
intersected tranquilly in concord upon the tiles,
shaping parallelograms of transparent blue. Emboldened by the calm,
a tiny mouse strolled leisurely
now and then across a kouros's foot, halted with suspicion
to contemplate the oblong windows with its pair of oil-drop eyes,

στυλώνοντας το οξύ του ρύγχος, σα μαλακό βέλος, προς το απόλυτο,
130 εξ ονόματος όλων των μαρμαρωμένων—ο μικρός συνεταίρος τους.

Ο πατέρας δεν αγαπούσε τ' αγάλματα. Ποτέ δεν τον είδα
να στέκεται μπροστά σε κάποιο·—ίσως κιόλας ο ίδιος
νάτανε τ' άγαλμα του εαυτού του, ένα άγαλμα χάλκινο
αγέρωχου, απλησίαστου ιππέα. Και μόνον
η φιλία του εκείνη με τον Πάτροκλο
τον έφερνε κάπως κοντά μου, σα να κατέβαινε
με φαρδειές δρασκελιές απ' το βάθρο του
και να χάνονταν κάτω απ' τα δέντρα. Μου φαινόνταν παράξενο
πώς δεν ακούγονταν καθόλου τρίξιμο
140 απ' τις κλειδώσεις των χάλκινων γονάτων του.

Κ' η μητέρα, ένας ίσκιος κι αυτή, διάφανος ίσκιος,
ανάλαφρος και μακρινός—μια τρυφερότητα παρούσα
μέσα στη διαρκή απουσία της. Οι άντρες,
γυρίζοντας απ' το κυνήγι, λίγο πριν φτάσουν στο σπίτι,
βλέπαν, πίσω απ' τα δέντρα, το δυτικό παράθυρο
σαν κρεμασμένο απ' τα κλαδιά, μετέωρο, μόνο του,
κ' εκεί, μέσα στη σκοτεινή κορνίζα του, η μητέρα,
σαν κρεμασμένη κι αυτή, να κοιτάζει
μακριά, το λιόγερμα, σα φλωροκαπνισμένη. Οι άντρες νόμιζαν
150 πως τους περίμενε, πως έτρωγε το δρόμο. Πολύ αργότερα
το νιώσαμε πως έλειπε, πως είταν στ' αλήθεια κρεμασμένη.

Στο πρόσωπό της, ο ίσκιος του σκοινιού διακρίνονταν αδιόρατα,
καθώς, μόλις ακούγονταν οι κυνηγοί κάτω στο δρόμο,
διόρθωνε την έκφρασή της, διώχνοντας με το χέρι της
έναν κατάμαυρο βόστρυχο που τής έπεφτε τάχα στα μάτια·—
τον ίσκιο εκείνου του σκοινιού παραμέριζε·—αργότερα το μάθαμε,
όταν ακούγονταν πάνω απ' τη λίμνη το τελευταίο κέρας, μέσα στο
    λυκόφως,
όταν έπεφτε λίγος σουβάς απ' την πρόσοψη του σπιτιού εντελώς αθόρυβα
κι άχνιζε ολόκληρος ο κάμπος ρόδινος και χρυσός με τα γαλάζια φάσματα
    των δέντρων,

and on behalf of all the enmarbled—as their tiny partner—
fixed its pointed snout, like a flaccid arrow, upon the absolute.

My father hated statues. I never saw him
stand before one: he had turned perhaps
into the statue of himself already—a monument in bronze
of a horseman arrogant and unapproachable. Only
his friendship with Patroklos
brought him somewhat close to me, as though with massive strides
he had stepped off his pedestal
and vanished beneath the trees. How strange
to hear no creaking
from his knee-joints of bronze.

Mother—one more shadow, transparent too,
weightless and remote: a tenderness present
in her constant absence. Just before they reached the house,
returning from the hunt, the men would glimpse
the west window behind the trees, hanging
all alone in mid-air from a branch, it seemed,
and inside its sombre frame my mother
hanging too (it seemed) and powdered all with gold-dust,
as she peered far off into the sunset. They thought
she'd been awaiting them, devouring the road with expectation.
We understood much later: she was never there at all, but actually hanged.

Her face betrayed the noose's shadow imperceptibly as she corrected
her expression, once the hunters could be heard
along the road. Banishing with her hand
a coal-black curl on pretext it blocked her vision,
that noose's shade is what she pushed aside. We learned this later,
as horns blared out their last above the lake in twilight,
and stucco from our home's facade peeled off in noiseless bits,
as trees' blue phantoms joined pink and golden mists rising everywhere

160 και τα σκυλιά, παρ' ότι κουρασμένα, με τις γλώσσες τους έξω,
ελαφροπάταγαν σα ν' ανηφόριζαν στον ουρανό, μέσα σ' έκσταση.

Σε λίγο, γέμιζε η εσπέρα από στιλπνές, πολύχρωμες φτερούγες
σκοτωμένων πουλιών, εκεί στο πέτρινο υπαίθριο τραπέζι,
με τις πιατέλες γεμάτες μαβιά, κεχριμπαρένια, κόκκινα σταφύλια
και δροσερό νερό του πηγαδιού. Κ' η μητέρα χαμογελούσε περίλυπη:
«Είδες που μου ήθελες νάσαι πουλί;» μου έλεγε,
κ' έδινε εντολή στις υπηρέτριες να μαδήσουν τα πουλιά για το δείπνο
στην πίσω αυλή, εκεί που κιόλας η σκιά του βουνού
έπεφτε σα λιωμένο, σπιθόβολο σίδερο, και τα πελώρια κυπαρίσσια,
170 αυστηρά, σκοτεινά και φιλέρημα,
έπαιρναν μια βουβή, ανεξήγητη πρωτοβουλία.

Κείνη την ώρα, οι άντρες, ιδρωμένοι απ' το κυνήγι,
με κάτι χνούδια αγκαθιών στα μαλλιά τους,
με λεκέδες απ' τη γύρη των πεύκων στους ώμους τους,
είχαν μπει στους λουτρώνες, κι ακουγόταν ως έξω
το πέσιμο του νερού κ' η μυρωδιά του σαπουνιού, ανακατεμένη
με τα μύρα του κήπου—ζεσταμένο ρετσίνι, αρμπαρόριζα, δυόσμος,
    δεντρολίβανο—
δροσερές ευωδιές, βαθιανασαίνουσες. Κι ο κηπουρός ακουμπούσε
πάνω στον πέτρινο πάγκο το μεγάλο ποτιστήρι του, βρίσκοντας ευκαιρία
180 να πει μια ταπεινόφρονη, γελαστή «καλησπέρα» στη σεβάσμια δέσποινα
ανάμεσα σε ονόματα λουλουδιών, συνήθειες σπόρων, και κάτι
για αρρώστιες φύλλων και καρπών, για κάμπιες και έντομα.

Επάνω στους ευκάλυπτους, χιλιάδες πουλιά ξελαρυγγιάζονταν
δοξαστικά, παράφρονα, σάμπως διαλαλητάδες σ' εμποροπανήγυρη· ενώ
    κάτω τους
οι υπηρέτριες μαδούσαν τ' άλλα πουλιά. Κ' ερχόταν το βράδι
ήρεμο, αργό, τελεσίδικο, γεμάτο ανάλαφρα, πρασινόχρυσα πούπουλα
μ' ένα αδιόρατο κόκκινο στίγμα στη ρίζα τους. Κάποτε,
είχε σταθεί ένα τέτοιο πούπουλο στα μαλλιά της μητέρας
και τη σκίαζε ολόκληρη. Εγώ, τότε, με τρόπο,

above the plain, and exhausted dogs, despite their hanging tongues,
trod lightly, as though climbing in ecstasy to heaven.

Brilliant plumage quickly filled the evening; colorful feathers
of slaughtered birds lay there upon the tabletop of stone, outdoors,
with purple, red and amber grapes on overflowing platters,
and cooling water from the well. Mother always smiled with sorrow then;
"And to think you wanted to be a bird!" she'd say to me,
directing the servant-girls to pluck the fowl for dinner
in the yard behind the house, where mountain-shade already
fell like scintillating molten iron, and giant cypresses,
austere, reclusive, dark,
assumed a mute, inexplicable initiative.

The men, all this time—begrimed and sweaty from the hunt,
fuzzy burrs in their hair,
shoulders blotched with pollen from the pines—
were in the baths. The sound
of falling water reached outside, the smell of soap
mixed with garden scents: geranium and heated resin, rosemary and mint—
full, refreshing exhalations. Having placed his ample watering-pot
upon the stone settee, the gardener would seize the chance
to say a humble, bright "Good evening" to his worthy mistress,
blended with names of flowers, habits of seeds, and something else
concerning grubs and caterpillars, and the blights of leaves and fruit.

Thousands of songbirds atop the eucalyptus trees strained their throats like
    hawkers
at a market fair, madly giving praise while servants
beneath them plucked those other birds. Night came on,
tranquil, slow, irreversible, filled with fluffy green and golden down.
At its root each feather bore an imperceptible red blot.
Such a plume had settled once on mother's hair;
it shaded her completely. I approached her then a moment, slyly,

190 πλησιάζοντάς την μια στιγμή, τής το αφαίρεσα·—δεν άντεχα
να βλέπω τη μητέρα σκιασμένη από ξένες αμαρτίς. Ένα μικρό επιφώνημα
τής ξέφυγε άθελα σα να της έβγαλαν ένα μαχαίρι απ' το στήθος.

Ένα άλλο βράδι—θυμάμαι—είχε βάλει τα χέρια της γύρω στη λυχνία
να προστατεύσει τη φλόγα απ' τον άνεμο· τα χέρια της
έγιναν διάφανα, τριανταφυλλένια, σα δυο μεγάλα ροδοπέταλα—
ένα περίεργο άνθος, κ' η φλόγα της λυχνίας
ένας απίθανος ύπερος. Τότε, είδα
τα κλειδιά της αφημένα στην πέτρινη σκάλα,
πλάι στα σακκίδια και στα τόξα των κυνηγών·—κατάλαβα:
200 αυτά τα χέρια τίποτα δε θα μπορούσαν πια να ξεκλειδώσουν,
τόσο μοναχικά, τόσο περίβλεπτα, κλειδωμένα για πάντα
μέσα στην ίδια τους διαφάνεια. Όταν μιλούσε
είταν σα ν' αποσιωπούσε το κυριότερο· και τα χείλη της πρόβαιναν μόλις
μες απ' τον ίσκιο που έρριχναν τα μακριά της ματόκλαδα.

Θυμάμαι ακόμη κάποιο μεσημέρι: καθώς έπινε νερό κάτω απ' τα δέντρα,
πρόσεξα πάλι τα χέρια της—πιο διάφανα
απ' το ποτήρι που κρατούσε· η σκιά του ποτηριού της
έπεσε πάνω στο χορτάρι—ένας κύκλος φωτεινός, ανεπαίσθητος· τότε
μια μέλισσα κάθησε στο κέντρο του κύκλου, με τα φτερά της ελαφρά
 φωτισμένα,
210 σαν πολιορκημένη απ' το συναίσθημα μιας ανεξήγητης ευτυχίας.
Είταν το τελευταίο καλοκαίρι, πριν κληθώ κ' εγώ με τη σειρά μου.

Σού μίλησα πολύ για τη μητέρα,—ίσως να διέκρινα στα χέρια σου, φίλε μου,
κάτι απ' το φέγγος των χεριών της. Ό,τι άγγιζε
γινόταν άξαφνα μακρινή μουσική—δεν αγγιζόταν,
μόνο ακουγόταν πια μήτε κι αυτό. Δεν απόμεινε τίποτα—
λησμονημένος ήχος, αίσθηση αόριστη—όχι γνώση.

Άλλαξε ο φωτισμός μετά—φωτιές καταυλισμών, τα γυμνά σώματα
κόκκινα, κατακόκκινα απ' τις φλόγες, σα ματωμένα,

and removed it—to see her shaded by the sins of others
was more than I could bear. Despite herself she voiced
a tiny exclamation: you'd think a dagger had been taken from her breast.

Another evening, I remember, she curled her palms around the lamp
to guard the flame against a breeze. Her hands
became transparent and pink, like two enormous rose-petals—
a peculiar blossom, with the lamp-flame
an unlikely pistil. I saw
her keys abandoned then on the stone steps,
beside the hunters' satchels and their bows. I understood:
those hands—so set apart, so visible from every vantage point,
locked forever inside their very own transparency—could never
unlock anything again. When she spoke,
she always seemed to withhold the crucial point, and her lips protruded
scarcely beyond her long eyelashes' shadow.

I recall a certain afternoon as well. She was drinking water beneath the trees;
I noticed her hands again—more transparent than the glass
she held. That glass's shadow
struck the lawn—a circle of light, barely visible. Then a bee
alighted at the center of this circle and remained with wings illumined
    faintly—
beleaguered, so it seemed, by sensations of inexplicable bliss.
That was the final summer, before I too was called up, in my turn.

I have told you very much about my mother. Perhaps, my friend, in your
    hands I've discerned
a little of the luster found in hers. Everything she touched
was suddenly transformed to distant music; it could be touched no longer
but only heard—not even heard. Nothing at all was left:
unremembered sound, a vague sense…; no knowledge.

After that the lighting changed: fires at the bivouac, naked bodies
ruddy and scarlet from the flames: blood-smeared, so you'd think,

σα γδαρμένα απ' το δέρμα τους—πιο σάρκινα και ζωώδη,
220 πιο αδιάντροπα κ' ερωτικά, σαν ένα μεγάλο σφαγείο
που άντερα κι αμελέτητα κρέμονταν στα τσιγγέλια μες στη νύχτα,
ανάμεσα στ' αστέρια, που η φωτιά τα ξεθώριαζε,
ενώ, στ' αυλάκια δίπλα, κύλαγαν
αίματα, σπέρματα, ούρα, περιττώματα, βρωμόνερα,
κ' οι σκιές καλπάζανε μακριά μες στην κόκκινη λάμψη,
ώσπου έβγαινε η σελήνη μαλακιά και υγρή σαν ένα αιδοίο
κι άρχιζε η τύψη κ' η μετάνοια κ' η δημιουργία.

Τότε ακουγόταν ο θόρυβος του ποταμού κάτω απ' τα δέντρα—
μια ηχητική δροσιά—χωρίς να ρωτάς πού πηγαίνει.
230 Οι φωτιές σβήναν λίγο-λίγο. Μεγάλα πουλιά, κοιμισμένα
επάνω στα κλαδιά, μισάνοιγαν πότε-πότε τα μάτια τους
κ' ένα ελάχιστο φέγγος περνούσε στα φύλλα.

Οι άντρες ψειρίζανε τα στήθεια και τα σκέλια τους·
οι έφηβοι, άτριχοι σχεδόν, σεμνοί σαν προσβλημένοι,
ένιωθαν κάθε τόσο δυο ισχυρά τινάγματα στις ρώγες του στήθους τους
σα να τους κάρφωναν δυο ηδονικές σαΐτες πάνω στη νύχτα
κ' οι μυώνες της κοιλιάς τους σαν σκοινιά τους έσφιγγαν τη μέση. Οι
  φρουροί
έβγαζαν τα σαντάλια τους και τρίβανε τα δάχτυλά τους
φτιάχνοντας κάτι μαύρα, λιπαρά σβωλάκια, που τα ζύμωναν ώρες,
240 εύπλαστα κι αναπαυτικά, σα μυστικά αγαλμάτια,
και τα σφεντόνιζαν αθόρυβα στη νύχτα. Ύστερα,
μυρίζοντας τα δυο τους δάχτυλα, ρουθούνιζαν για ώρα,
ωραίοι, κτηνώδεις, ναρκωμένοι, ως να τους πάρει ο ύπνος.

Οι μεγάλες ασπίδες, αφημένες στο χώμα,
άφηναν έναν ήχο αργό, μεταλλικό, καθώς χτυπούσαν πάνω τους
οι μακρινές αιχμές των άστρων. Μες στο κοίλωμά τους
πήζαν κρυμμένες εντολές στρατηγών. Πάνω απ' τ' αντίσκηνα
σπίθιζε το τεράστιο γυμνό ψαροκόκκαλο του γαλαξία. Κ' είταν πάλι,

or flayed of all their skin; more sensual and beastly,
more shamelessly erotic, like a giant slaughterhouse
with guts and testicles suspended in the night from meat hooks
between stars made dim by our fires
while urine, semen, excrement, slops and blood
surged in ditches near us,
and shadows galloped far in glaring redness
until the moon appeared, soft and moist like a vagina,
and remorse commenced, repentance too, and creation.

The river's din beneath the trees refreshed
our hearing then, though no one asked about its course.
Campfires died slowly into embers; large birds, asleep
on branches, half-opened their eyes from time to time;
a feeble glimmer slipped between the leaves.

The men deloused their chests and inner thighs;
the lads, with scarce a body-hair upon them, so retiring you'd think they'd
    been offended,
often felt two potent twinges at the nipples of their chests
as though a pair of passion's darts had been nailed in them at midnight.
The muscles of their bellies tautened then around their waists, like ropes.
    The sentries,
removing both their sandals, rubbed two fingers between their toes
to make some greasy, blackish clods. These they kneaded endlessly
like mystic statuettes, pliant, comforting,
then slung them noiselessly into the night. Afterwards
—handsome, brutish, torpid—they smelled their fingers,
sniffed at them for hours, until they fell asleep.

On the ground where they'd been left, the massive shields
gave forth metallic, sluggish rumbles as the stars' far-off lances
battered them. Commands by generals
lay hidden and congealing in their hollows. The huge bare fishbone
of the Milky Way was sparkling above the tents. Again,

όπως τότε σχεδόν, στα παλιά καλοκαίρια, ένας φόβος
250   για κάποιον κλέφτη αόρατο, αόριστο, ή και για τους συνηθισμένους
    κλέφτες,
μην πηδήσουν στις κάμαρες απ' τ' ανοιχτά παράθυρα κι απ' τα μπαλκόνια·—
δεν ξέραμε πριν να φυλαχτούμε, (ούτε τώρα)—αφαιρενόμαστε
με το ζουζούνισμα ενός κουνουπιού, με το βόμβο του φεγγαρόφωτου,
με τους αντίλαλους των αψίδων απο λαθραία φιλήματα—
μια γυναίκα, εμπιστευμένη στην ερημιά, αποπατούσε γαλήνια στο χωράφι,
νιώθοντας στους γοφούς της τα έντονα τσιμπήματα των χόρτων και των
    άστρων.

Αυτή η συναίσθηση μιας αιώνιας κλοπής—μάλλον λεηλασία
βουβή, κρυφή και σταθερή. Και ξαφνικά η κουρτίνα της κρεββατοκάμαρας
έκανε τρία χορευτικά πηδήματα πάνω απ' τη ζέστη
260   με πρόθεση ολοφάνερη να μεταθέσει την προσοχή μας
σε χρυσοκέντητα κράσπεδα μιας γυναικείας εσθήτας· κ' ύστερα
ακινητούσε θαμπογάλανη στη νηνεμία, καλύπτοντας ένα άγαλμα,
ίσως της νύχτας απο γρανίτη, η της κλοπής απο κόκκινη πέτρα,—
και πάλι εκείνο το παραπλανητικό πριόνισμα των γρύλλων
κ' εκείνες οι καθησυχαστικές φωνές των βατράχων
ή ο ξερός κρότος απ' το κυκλικό περπάτημα μιας κατσαρίδας μέσα σ' ένα
    κράνος.

Δεν είχαμε καιρό να εξακριβώσουμε. Προτού τελειώσουμε
το πρώτο μέτρημα των άστρων, αποκοιμιόμαστε. Τα ξημερώματα
μια τυφλή κουκουβάγια χαρχάλευε πεσμένη στα χαμόκλαδα
270   ενώ τα γαλατώδη μάτια της διερευνούσαν έναν άλλο χώρο
κι ο ίσκιος της Οίτης αποσύρονταν απ' την πεδιάδα
σα μια πελώρια χελώνα που μαζεύει τα πόδια της.

Τότε αντηχούσε στον ορίζοντα ο ήλιος. Ψηλά στον αέρα
αστράφτανε οι εξηντατέσσερις οπλές των αλόγων του
και κάτω αντιφεγγίζαν οι βοϊδάμαξες. Οι πύλες άνοιγαν.
Συνωστισμός στην αγορά—οι οπωροπώλες, οι έμποροι—
βουνά οι καρποί και τα λαχανικά, κ' οι αγρότες με τα γαϊδούρια τους.

almost as in summers past, we feared
some thief unseen and undefined, if not the customary thieves
that might vault into our rooms from balconies or open windows.
We knew nothing then (or now) about self-protection. A mosquito's buzz
distracted us, as did the moonlight's hum
or stolen kisses resounding in the archways—
a woman, sure she would not be seen, defecated tranquilly in the meadow,
feeling sharp pinches on her haunches from the grass and from the stars.

Oh, that sense of perpetual thievery—pillage rather:
secret, mute and steadfast pillage! In mid-heat
the bedroom curtain suddenly would leap in dance-step, thrice,
intending clearly to draw our attention
to gold-embodied hems on a woman's gown. Then it stood stockstill;
pale blue in the dead calm, and veiled a sculpture
—a granite one perhaps of Night, or one depicting Thievery in red stone—
and again we heard that seductive sawing of the crickets
and those reassuring croakings of the frogs
or sharp clacks from a cockroach circling inside a helmet.

We lacked the time to verify: before we'd counted
the constellations even once, we fell asleep. At dawn
an owl rummaged blindly, having fallen in the undergrowth
while its milky eyes sought another place;
and Oeta's shadow receded from the plain
like a monstrous tortoise drawing in its legs.

The sun resounded then on the horizon. The sixty-four hoofs
of its horses flashed high in the air
while oxcarts below reflected the rays. The gates swung open.
Hubbub in the marketplace—fruit sellers, merchants,
mountains of lemons, greens; farmers with their donkeys.

Κάποις φιλόσοφος αγουροξυπνημένος περπατούσε αμίλητος
ανάμεσα σε δυο σειρές σφαγμένα βόδια. Οι αγγειοπλάστες
280   βάζανε σε παράταξη τις στάμνες τους δίπλα στο δρόμο
σαν ένα αλλόκοσμο πήλινο στράτευμα. Στα γυμναστήρια,
ακόμη δροσερά απ' την αυγινή υγρασία, φωτισμένα διαγώνια,
έβγαιναν απ' τ' αποδυτήρια οι πρώτοι δρομείς και δοκίμαζαν
μικρούς γύρους, όπως περίπου τα πουλιά στον αέρα. Στρατιώτες
έπλεναν στις αυλές των στρατώνων μεγάλα καζάνια εκστρατείας.

Κάποιες ξεχτένιστες γυναίκες τίναζαν απ' τα παράθυρα
απίθανα κάτασπρα σεντόνια. Λαμποκοπούσαν
μετόπες ναών κ' οι πάνω κερκίδες των σταδίων. Τούτη η λαμπρότητα,
τυφλή, εκτυφλωτική, σ' αυτή της ακριβώς την επίδειξη,
290   σαν κάτι να μας έκρυβε—κι αλήθεια μας έκρυβε·—
μήπως εκείνη την κλοπή; Κ' είταν ακόμη
τα πελώρια πιθάρια στους κήπους και στα υπόγεια
κ' οι χρυσές προσωπίδες με τα κενά, ερευνητικά τους μάτια.
Μια στιγμιαία σιωπή· το ίδιο αόριστο νόημα· κοινή συνωμοσία.

Μεγάλωναν τα γένεια, τα μαλλιά, τα νύχια, τα όργανα·
και πάντα ειδήσεις για νεκρούς και για ήρωες, και πάλι για ήρωες·
μεγάλα κόκκαλα αλόγων στις πλαγιές με τις ξερές αφάνες·
πυκνώνανε οι αναπνοές των άπλυτων σωμάτων. Μια γυναίκα, κάποτε,
περνούσε απόμακρα μες στην εσπέρα με μια υδρία στον ώμο της.
300   Πίσω της έκλεινε ο αέρας το πέρασμα. Η βραδιά
διπλωνόταν στην άκρη μιας σημαίας. Κάποιο αστέρι
φώναζε ξαφνικά ένα ακατανόητο «όχι», κ' ύστερα
έσβηνε ο καλπασμός των αλόγων κατά μήκος της νύχτας
αφήνοντας πιο σιωπηλά τ' αστέρια πάνω απ' το ποτάμι.

Κανείς δεν πρόφταινε πια να θυμηθεί, να σκεφτεί, να ρωτήσει—
μια διαρκής μετακίνηση· όλα σύντομα, κομμένα, ασυμπλήρωτα.
Οι θρήνοι κ' οι ζητωκραυγές, έπαιρναν λίγο-λίγο
τον ίδιο τόνο· επίσης κ' οι μορφές εχθρών και φίλων—δεν ξεχώριζες.

Awakened before his hour, a philosopher sauntered mutely
between two rows of slaughtered cattle. Potters
arranged their jugs in ranks along the road
like earthenware troops from another planet. In the gymnasiums,
cooled as yet by morning damp and lighted with slanting rays,
the earliest runners were emerging from the dressing-rooms and sprinting
short trial-laps—almost like birds in the air. Soldiers
in barracks courtyards scrubbed enormous cauldrons.

At their windows, some unkempt women shook out
bedsheets of startling whiteness. Temple metopes and the upper
tiers of stadiums glistened. This blind and blinding
luster seemed—precisely in its ostentation—
to be holding something back from us (which truly was the case).
That thievery perhaps? The massive jars
were in the gardens still and in the cellars,
as were the golden masks with their vacuous, searching eyes.
A moment's silence; the same ill-defined significance; a general conspiracy.

Beards, hair, fingernails and penises grew longer.
The news: forever concerning heroes and the dead, then still more concern-
    ing heroes.
Large horse-bones on the hillsides with the dry twigs.
Increasing stench from unwashed bodies. Far away, a woman
passed from time to time at close of day, a water jug upon her shoulder;
the breeze filled in the space where she had been. Sundown
was enfolded in a banner's tip. A certain star would cry
an incomprehensible "No!"—abruptly—whereupon
the horses' gallop vanished along the length of the night,
leaving the stars more silent above the river.

No one managed to remember any more, to think or question.
Constant shifting about. Everything curt, abortive, incomplete.
Wails and cheers acquired an increasingly similar tone.
Indistinguishable too the faces of friend and foe.

Μόνο τις νύχτες που έπεφτε η σιωπή οριζόντια—σαν κόπαζε η μάχη—
310 ακούγονταν ανάμεσα στις πέτρες μακρυσμένοι βόγγοι πληγωμένων
και το φεγγάρι είταν σα μάτι διεσταλμένο σκοτωμένου αλόγου·—τότε
    μόνον
γνωρίζαμε πως δεν έχουμε ακόμη πεθάνει.

Τότε, μια πονηρία χιλιοόμματη σπίθιζε σ' όλες τις γωνιές της νύχτας:
να πάρουμε πίσω όσα μας έκλεψαν, να τα υποκλέψουμε έστω. Εκεί, κάτω,
στο φεγγερό ακρογιάλι, σκοτεινά τα καράβια μας,
ασάλευτα, μαρμαρωμένα, μελετούσαν ένα άλλο ταξίδι—
κι αν κάποτε άστραφτε για λίγο ένα βρεγμένο κουπί, αντιχτυπούσε αιφνίδια
στο σφυγμό του χεριού μας. Ελαφροπάτητοι αγγελιαφόροι
πηγαινορχόνταν με το γλύστρημα της νυχτερίδας, κ' ίσως νάμενε
320 προδοτικό σημάδι στ' άσπρα βότσαλα ή ανάμεσα στ' αγκάθια,
ένα μαύρο φτερό, ένα κομμάτι από λουρί σανδάλου, μια ασημένια πόρπη,
και θάπρεπε την άλλη μέρα, με τον όρθρο, να τα εξαφανίσουμε.

Κ' είτανε κιόλας σα ν' ακούγαμε τα μυστικά πελέκια μες στο δάσος
να κόβουν ξύλα. Ακούγαμε το μέγα γδούπο, όταν σωριάζονταν
ένα δέντρο στο χώμα, και τη σιωπή τρομαγμένη
να κρύβεται πίσω απ' τους ώμους μας. Κ' είταν σα νάβλεπα κιόλας
τον Δούρειο Ίππο, κούφιον, θεόρατο, να λάμπει επικίνδυνος
μες στην αστροφεγγιά, θρησκευτικός σχεδόν, ενώ η σκιά του
εκτεινόταν μυθική πάνω στα τείχη. Κ' ένιωθα κιόλας
330 σα να βρισκόμουν μες στο κούφωμα του αλόγου, μαζί με τους άλλους,
ολομόναχος, σε άβολη στάση, μέσα στο λαιμό του αλόγου,
και να κοιτάζω με τ' άδεια του μάτια τη γυάλινη νύχτα,
σαν κρεμασμένος μες στο χάος, γνωρίζοντας
πως η χαίτη που ανέμιζε πάνω απ' τον αυχένα μου
δεν είταν δική μου,—ούτε κ' η νίκη, φυσικά. Ωστόσο ετοιμαζόμουνα
για το τεράστιο, μάταιο άλμα μέσα στο άγνωστο.

Έτσι, σ' αυτή τη στάση, εκεί ψηλά, μέσα στο σανιδένιο λαρύγγι του αλόγου,
θάνιωθα καταβροχθισμένος, κι όμως ζωντανός, να εποπτεύω

Only at night when battle ceased, when silence came flatly down,
the wounded's protracted groans were heard among the rocks
and the moon was like a slaughtered mare's dilated eyes:
only then did we realize that we still had not died.

Machination next sparked its myriad eyes in nighttime's every corner:
"Whatever they stole from us we should now take back—even comman-
    deer!" Down below
on the bright seashore, our vessels—dark,
unmoving, turned to stone—were planning yet another voyage,
and if a wet oar briefly flashed at times, the pulses on our wrists
throbbed unexpectedly in response. Tiptoeing messengers
darted back and forth like slippery bats, and when by chance
a compromising trace remained upon the milk-white pebbles or among the
    thorns
—a black feather, bit of sandal-thong, a silver buckle—
at dawn we'd make sure that it had vanished.

We seemed to hear the secret axes already in the forest
cutting wood. We heard the giant thump when a tree
subsided to the ground; we heard the silence
hide in fright behind our backs. Already I seemed to view
the Trojan Horse gleaming in the starlight—hollow and huge,
dangerous, almost religious—while its shadow
spread fablelike across the walls. Already I sensed
myself inside the horse's cavity together with the others,
positioned awkwardly within its neck, alone,
watching through its vacant eyes the crystal night
as though I were suspended over chaos, and knowing that
the mane which waved above my nape
was not my own—nor the victory, of course. Nonetheless, I prepared myself
for the enormous, futile leap into the unknown.

High above, in this position inside the horse's plank-lined throat,
I must have felt swallowed; swallowed alive, however, in order to observe

τ' αντίπαλα στρατόπεδα, τις φωτιές, τα καράβια, τ' αστέρια,
340 όλο το οικείο, το τρομερό, τ' αναρίθμητο θαύμα—όπως λένε—του κόσμου,
σα νάμαι μια μπουκιά σταματημένη στο λαρύγγι του απείρου και
   ταυτόχρονα μια γέφυρα
πάνω από δυο, το ίδιο απόκρημνες κι άγνωστες, όχθες—
μια γέφυρα ψεύτικη, βέβαια, από ξύλο και πικρή πανουργία.
(Απο κεί πάνω, θαρρώ, μες σ' έναν τέτοιο εφιάλτη,
αγνάντεψα πρώτη φορά την πραϋντική λάμψη των όπλων σου).

Άλλοτε πάλι, τα μεγάλα μεσημέρια, σ' ένα διάλειμμα της μάχης,
ή σ' ώρα πορείας, σ' ένα σταμάτημα, νιώθαμε μονομιάς πως διψούσαμε—
τίποτ' άλλο: διψούσαμε. Δεν ονομάζαμε το νερό και τη δίψα μας·
σκύβαμε μόνο αμήχανοι να δέσουμε τάχα τα σαντάλια μας,
350 κ' έτσι, σκυμμένοι, κοιτούσαμε πέρα, κρατώντας
μια εικόνα αντεστραμμένη απο τοπία, ανθρώπους κι από μας τους ίδιους,
μια εικόνα απατηλή, συγγνωστική, διαυγή, τεθλασμένη,
σάμπως καθρεφτισμένη σε νερό. Και νερό δεν υπήρχε. Διψούσαμε.

Κείνος ο δρόμος ερημώθη ως το βάθος. Απ' τις δυο πλευρές του
πηγάδια σκεπασμένα, μολυσμένα απ' τους νεκρούς. Ράγιζε η πέτρα
απ' τη μεγάλη ζέστη. Τα τζιτζίκια ξεφώνιζαν. Ο ορίζοντας
είταν ασβέστης και γλώσσες φωτιάς. Μέσα στην ανελέητη λιακάδα
σπίθιζαν στα σαμάρια των τειχών, όρθια, σπασμένα τζάμια,
χωρίζοντας συντρόφους, φίλους, συμπολεμιστές. Πάρ' όλη
360 την αιχμηρή, δοξαστική ακτινοβολία, δεν κρυβόταν τίποτα. Είδα άντρες
   γενναίους
να ρίχνουν στάχτη στα μαλλιά τους· κ' είδα τη στάχτη
ν' ανακατεύεται με τα δάκρυά τους· μαύρα αυλάκια
χώνονταν μες στα γένεια τους, ως κάτω στα σαγόνια τους.

Αυτοί που πλέναν τ' άλογά τους άλλοτε στ' ακροθαλάσσι ολόγυμνοι
κι αλείβανε τις χαίτες με λάδι ξανθό, λάμποντας όλοι

the enemy camp, the fires, ships and stars,
the entire miracle (as it's called), the familiar, dread, incalculable miracle of
    the world,
as though I were a morsel stuck in the infinite's gullet, and concurrently a
    bridge
above two embankments equally precipitous and unknown—
a jerry-built bridge, to be sure, of wood and bitter scheming.
(From there on high, I think, in such a nightmare,
I first espied the soothing brilliance of your weapons.)

At various other times—during the long middays, an interval in the fighting,
while on march, or halting for rest—suddenly we felt that we were thirsty.
Nothing more—: only thirsty. We did not call the water or our thirst by
    name,
but just bent down in confusion, feigning to tie our sandal thongs.
In this position, bending down, we gazed out into the distance and retained
    a topsy-turvy
view of landscapes, people and ourselves,
a view fallacious, forgiving, pellucid, diffracted,
as though mirrored in some water. There was no water. We were thirsty.

That road was ravaged along its entire length. Its wells on either side
were covered over, polluted by cadavers. The cobbles were splitting
from so much heat, the cicadas shouting. Seething lime
on the horizon; tongues of fire. Atop the coping of the walls
stood bits of broken glass that sparked in unrelenting sunlight as they di-
    vided
comrades, friends and fellow-fighters. Despite
the glorious, piercing brilliance, nothing was concealed: I saw courageous
    men
throw ashes in their hair and saw the ashes
mingle with their tears. Black furrows
dug into their beards, down to the chin.

Those who, naked on the seashore, used to wash their horses
and grease their manes with yellow oil, men and beasts alike resplendent

άνθρωποι κι άλογα σε μεγαλόφωτα πρωϊνά: αυτοί οι ίδιοι
που χόρευαν τα βράδια πάνω απ' τις φωτιές κι αστράφτανε
τα γυμνά πέλματά τους ολοπόρφυρα,—τώρα ζαρώνουνε
ανάμεσα στα βράχια, χολώνουν, γκρινιάζουν, βάζουν την παλάμη
370 μπροστά στα σκέλια τους, ντρέπονται, κρύβονται,
σα νάχουν φταίξει, σα να τους έχουν όλοι φταίξει. Κ' ίσως να φθονούν
τους νέους πολεμιστές για την ωραία ανυποψία τους, για την τόλμη τους,
για την ενθουσιαστική, αποστηθισμένη ευφράδειά τους, κ' ίσως πιότερο απ'
        όλα
για τα βαριά, στιλπνά μαλλιά τους, τα ογκωμένα απο υγεία και έρωτα.

Κι όμως κι αυτοί ξεκίνησαν κάποτε με τη χαριτωμένη αφέλεια
και την κρυφή ματαιοδοξία ν' αναμορφώσουν τον κόσμο. Ξεκίνησαν
όλοι μαζί, καθένας χώρια, και τόδαν και τόβλεπαν: καθένας
για ένα δικό του λόγο, μια ξεχωριστή φιλοδοξία, στεγασμένη
κάτω από μια μεγάλη ιδέα, έναν κοινό σκοπό,—διάφανη στέγη
380 που κάτω της διακρίνονταν καλύτερα του καθενός το κομμάτιασμα,
η δυστυχία κ' η μικροπρέπεια όλων. Πώς νάβαζες, φίλε μου, τάξη
σ' αυτό το χάος; Πώς να σταθείς κοντά τους; Τώρα καταλαβαίνω.

Τις νύχτες, μες στα πλοία, όταν οι απλοί, κουρασμένοι στρατιώτες
κοιμόνταν σωριασμένοι σαν τσουβάλια στο κατάστρωμα,
αξιολάτρευτοι στην ευπιστία της νεότητάς τους,
μέσα στην άγνοια, τη ζωώδη αγνότητα, στο σαρκικό τους κάλλος,
εύρωστοι από την άσκηση της χρήσιμης δουλειάς, στους αγρούς, στα
        εργαστήρια, στους δρόμους,
υποταγμένοι στην ανάγκη και στην εύκολη ελπίδα,
με την πηγαία γενίκευση της δικής τους αθωότητας, σαν πρόβατα
390 που τα οδηγούν στη σφαγή για τα συμφέροντα άλλων, κι όμως
χαμογελώντας μες στον ύπνο τους, παραμιλώντας, ροχαλίζοντας,
βλαστημώντας μια ονειρική αγελάδα ή μουμουρίζοντας πάλι και πάλι
ένα όνομα γυναικείο, ημίγυμνοι, σε νύχτια στύση,

on brilliant mornings, those same who
danced at night vaulting campfire flame, their bare soles
flashing vermilion—they cower now
amid the crags, they sulk and whine, they place their palms
over their thighs, they hide in shame as though they'd done some wrong
to others and all the others had done some wrong to them. Perhaps they also
   begrudge
the young recruits their lovely absence of suspicion, their pluck,
their enthusiastic, rote grandiloquence, and most of all perhaps
their hair so thick and glossy, swollen out with health and sex.

Yet those too set forth one day to reform the world.
Charmingly naive, secretly vainglorious, they set forth together,
each one individually, and saw and looked, each for
a private reason, a distinct ambition sheltered
underneath a single great idea, a common purpose whose transparency
made that much clearer every man's fragmented self,
the wretchedness and contemptibility of the lot. How, my friend, could you
   have brought
some order to that chaos? How could you stand by them? Now I see.

During the night on the boats when the common soldiers, exhausted,
slept on deck like sacks heaped together,
so admirable for their youthful good faith,
asleep in their ignorance, their animalistic innocence and their fleshly
   beauty,
robust from the pursuit of useful employment in the fields, in workshops, on
   the roads,
subject to necessity and to facile hopes,
effortlessly universalizing their own guilelessness, like lambs
being led to slaughter for others' profit, yet
smiling in their sleep and babbling, snoring,
cursing a dream-born cow, or—half naked, with nocturnal erections—
whispering again and again a woman's name

149

περιχυμένοι τη μυστική αιωνιότητα της ωκεάνειας αστροφεγγιάς· —αυτές
  τις νύχτες,
άκουσα, ανάμεσα στους παφλασμούς των κουπιών, τις φωνές, τους
  καυγάδες
των αρχηγών, για λάφυρα που δεν είχαν ακόμη συναχτεί, για τίτλους
που δεν είχαν ακόμη θεσπιστεί. Κ' είδα στα μάτια τους
το μίσος για όλους, τ' άγριο πάθος των πρωτείων,
και μέσα-μέσα, όπως στο βάθος σκοτεινής σπηλιάς ανίσχυρη πυγολαμπίδα,
400 είδα και τη δική τους μοναξιά. Πίσω απ' τα γένεια τους
σπίθιζε ολόγυμνη η μοίρα τους, σαν πίσω απ' τα γυμνά κλαδιά ενός δάσους
μια στεγνή πεδιάδα στο φεγγαρόφωτο, σπαρμένη μ' άσπρα κόκκαλα.

Κ' είταν σα μια ευτυχία η γνώση αυτή· —μια άφεση,
μια κατευναστική παραδοχή, μια αδρανής ευφροσύνη
απ' την αφή του αιώνιου και του τίποτα. Λίγες στιγμές,
παρ' όλ' αυτά, μπορούσα ακόμη νάχω το προνόμιο:
να διακρίνω πίσω η ανάμεσα από τις ασπίδες και τα δόρατα
ένα κομμάτι θάλασσα, λίγο λυκόφως, ένα ωραίο γόνατο,
και να μ' αρέσει, —ναί, παρ' όλα αυτά· —μια ελάχιστη δικαίωση,
410 κι όλος ο φόβος, αναρίθμητος κι άγνωστος, διαλύονταν πέρα,
ένα βαθύ, ιλαρό σύννεφο στη μυθική απεραντοσύνη.

Θυμάμαι μια νύχτα, που πλέαμε με πανσέληνο. Το φεγγαρόφωτο
απόθετε μια εντάφια, χρυσή προσωπίδα σ' όλα τα πρόσωπα·
οι σταριώτες, μια στιγμή, σταθήκαν και κοιτάχτηκαν
σα να μη γνώριζε ο ένας τον άλλον η σα να γνωρίζονταν
για πρώτη τους φορά· καί, μεμιάς, όλοι στράφηκαν
και κοίταξαν ψηλά το φεγγάρι,
ακίνητοι όλοι, πάνω στο αεικίνητο πέλαγος,
σιωπηλοί, μαγεμένοι, σαν πεθαμένοι κιόλας κι αθάνατοι.

420 Τότε, σα νάνιωσαν αόριστα ένοχοι, σα να μην άντεχαν
αυτό το απέραντο, ανάλαφρο βάρος, άρχισαν να φωνάζουν,

while laved in the mystic sempiternity of ocean starlight—during those
      nights,
I heard, amid the splashing of the oars, our leaders'
shouts and squabbles over booty still to be acquired, titles
still to be decreed. And in their eyes I saw
hatred toward all, the savage passion for preeminence,
and deep deep within, like a fragile glowworm at the farthest end of a dark
      cave,
I saw their loneliness as well. Behind their beards
their fate was glinting in its nakedness, as, behind the leafless branches of a
      forest,
an arid plain sown with white bones sparkles in the moonlight.

This knowledge was a kind of happiness: a release,
a mitigating acceptance, an inert delight
from the touch of everlastingness and nothingness. Despite all that,
I managed still to have the privilege now and then
of discerning behind the shields and spears, or between them,
a bit of sea, a little twilight, a well-shaped knee,
and of liking this—yes, despite all the rest. A remission, though scant;
and all the countless, unknown fears were dispelled into the distance:
a dense and cheery cloud in fabulous infinitude.

I remember one night when we sailed beneath a full moon. On every face
the moonlight fixed a burial mask of gold.
The soldiers stood in place a moment and exchanged looks
as though they did not recognize each other or were meeting
for the very first time, then abruptly turned
and gazed up high at the moon,
immobile one and all upon the ever-mobile sea,
not speaking, in a spell, as though dead already and immortal.

Afterwards, as if they vaguely felt some guilt and could not bear
this huge, imponderous weight, they began to shout,

151

να χωρατεύουν, να χειρονομούν χυδαία, να συγκρίνουν τα όργανά τους,
ν' αλείφονται με το λίπος των ψητών, να πηδούν, να χορεύουν, να παλεύουν,
να κάνουν πως διαβάζουν στις γυμνές πλάτες των κριών εύθυμους οιωνούς
   κ' αισχρές ιστορίες,
ίσως για να ξεχάσουν κείνη τη στιγμή, κείνη τη νόηση, κείνη την απουσία.

Ίσως κ' εσύ, μια τέτοια νύχτα, μέσα στις αντίρροπες
φωνές των συμπολεμιστών σου, ν' άκουσες ολοκάθαρα
την απουσία της δικής σου φωνής—όπως εγώ, τότε με την πανσέληνο·
τ' άκουσα, ναί, πως εγώ δεν εφώναζα· κ' έμεινα εκεί
430 καθηλωμένος ανάμεσα σ' όλους, ολομόναχος
ανάμεσα και στους πιο αγαπημένους μου, ολομόναχος
σ' έναν μεγάλο κύκλο ερημικόν, σ' ένα πανύψηλο αλώνι,
ν' ακούω με τρομερή διαύγεια τις φωνές των άλλων, και ταυτόχρονα
ν' ακούω τη σιωπή μου. Από κεί πάνω
αγνάντεψα για δεύτερη φορά τη λάμψη των όπλων σου. Κ' εννόησα.

Ίσως κ' εσύ, μια ανάλογη στιγμή, σεβάσμιε φίλε, θ' αποφάσισες
ν' αποσυρθείς. Τότε, θαρρώ, θ' αφέθηκες να σε δαγκώσει
το φίδι του βωμού. Γνώριζες, άλλωστε, πως μόνον
τα όπλα μας χρειάζονται, κι όχι τους ίδιους εμάς (όπως είπες).
440 Όμως εσύ είσαι τα όπλα σου, τα τίμια κερδισμένα
με τη δουλειά, τη φιλία και τη θυσία, δοσμένα απ' το χέρι
εκείνου που στραγγάλισε την Επτακέφαλον, εκείνου που σκότωσε
τον φύλακα του Άδη. Και τόδες
με τα ίδια σου τα μάτια· και τόζησες: κληρονομιά σου
και τέλειο όπλο σου. Αυτό νικάει μονάχα. Τώρα,
παρακαλώ σε να μου δείξεις τη χρήση. Η ώρα έφτασε.

Ίσως θα πούνε πως η νίκη είναι μονάχα δική μου, κ' ίσως θα ξεχάσουν
τον κάτοχο και τον τεχνίτη·—αυτό κανένας δε θα τόθελε·
μα τί σημαίνει αυτό για σένα;—εσύ θα κρατήσεις

to joke, to gesticulate obscenely, to compare their penises,
to coat themselves with drippings from the roasts, to jump, dance, wrestle,
pretend to read amusing fortunes and dirty stories on the exposed shoulder
    blades of rams—
in order to forget, perhaps, that moment, that comprehension, that absence.

Perhaps you as well, on such a night, clearly heard
among the countervailing voices of your fellow combatants
the absence of your own voice—just as I did then, beneath the full moon.
Yes, I heard myself not shouting, and I remained
transfixed there among them all, companionless
even among my closest friends, companionless
in a giant circle of desolation, an alpine threshing-floor,
overhearing the others' voices with terrifying clarity and simultaneously
hearing my own silence. From there on high
I espied a second time the brilliance of your weapons. And I comprehended.

Perhaps you as well, my worthy friend, decided at some corresponding mo-
    ment
to withdraw. I imagine you must have let yourself be bitten then
by the serpent at the shrine. Besides, you realized that our weapons alone
are needed and not (as you said) we ourselves.
You, however, *are* your weapons. Honorably earned
through labor, sacrifice and friendship, they were given you by the hand
that choked the seven-headed Hydra, that killed
the guardian of Hades. With your own two eyes
you have seen, you have experienced: that is your inheritance
and your consummate weapon. That alone gains victories.
Now please show me how to use them. The time has come.

It will be said perhaps that the triumph is mine alone; people will forget,
    perhaps,
who took possession of the arms and who first fashioned them. That no one
    would desire.
But what difference will this make to you? Reserved for you will be

450 την ύστατη νίκη, και τη μόνη (όπως είπες),
τη γνώση αυτή τη μελιχρή και τρομερή: πως δεν υπάρχει καμμιά νίκη.

Εσύ μονάχος κρέμασες στο δέντρο το άδειο σου πουκάμισο
για να παραπλανήσεις τους περαστικούς, να πούνε: «πέθανε»·
κ' εσύ κρυμμένος πίσω απ' τους θάμνους, ακούγοντας
πως νεκρόν πια σε θεωρούσαν, να ζήσεις
σ' όλο το μήκος της δικής σου αίσθησης· και τότε θα μπορούσες
να φορέσεις ξανά το πουκάμισο του εικονικού θανάτου σου
ώσπου να γίνεις (όπως έγινες) η μεγάλη σιωπή της ύπαρξής σου.

Ένα δόρυ παλιό, βαμμένο στο αίμα, αποσυρμένο απ' τη μάχη,
460 μοναχικό, γαλήνιο, ανώφελο,
ακουμπισμένο ορθό στα βράχια, με τη χάλκινη αιχμή του
γραμμέμη στο φεγγάρι, τεθλασμένη απ' τις αχτίνες,
θα καμπυλώνεται σα δάχτυλο ανεξίθρησκο
επάνω σε μια λύρα—στην αιώνια λύρα, που είπες. Τούτη την ώρα,
θαρρώ πως νιώθω κατά που κοιτά η ευγνωμοσύνη σου.

Τώρα θυμήθηκα ένα ένδοξο λυκόφως στον ωκεανό—μια νηνεμία
λησμονημένη, απίστευτη,—η ακάλυπτη απεραντοσύνη
των ουρανών και των νερών· κανένα ακρωτήριο η νησίδα,
μόνο οι τριήρεις σκιώδεις, πετώντας η λάμνοντας
470 σ' ένα βαθύ, μυθικό τριανταφυλλώνα· τα κουπιά
αθόρυβα, ομοιόμορφα, σα φαρδειές, διαγώνιες, νοτισμένες αχτίνες. Ένας
   ναύτης
δοκίμασε να τραγουδήσει, κ' έμεινε έτσι
με το στόμα ανοιχτό σα μια τρύπα,
κι ανάμεσά της φάνηκε ξανά το φέγγος της θάλασσας.

Τότε έλυσα κ' εγω τη ζώνη μου κ' αισθάνθηκα
την ίδια μου την κίνηση ήρεμη, αναπότρεπτη, ανεξήγητη,
μ' εκείνη την αυθεντικότητα της μεταφυσικής. Κ' είταν σα νάλυνα
μια προαιώνια θηλειά απ' το λαιμό μου. Κράτησα τη ζώνη μου για λίγο

the ultimate and only victory (as you said):
this knowledge—so sweet, so terrible—that victories do not exist.

You and no one but you hung your vacant shirt upon a tree
to misdirect those who passed, to make them say "He's dead!"
so that—concealed behind the bushes, hearing
yourself considered dead—you might experience
the fullness of your sensibility, and afterwards might
don again the shirt of your make-believe demise
until you became (as you have become) the great silence of your own being.

An old spear stained with blood—retired from the fray,
left standing by itself, tranquil, useless,
propped against a boulder with its bronze head
imprinted on the moon and diffracted in the rays—
will slowly crook itself like a compliant finger
on a lyre: the eternal lyre that you mentioned. Right now
I can sense, I think, precisely where your gratitude is directed.

I've just recalled a glorious dusk on the open sea, an astonishing dead calm
that I'd forgotten: the exposed infinitude
of sky and water; not a single islet or promontory;
the shadowy triremes only, soaring or gliding
in a dense and fabulous rose-garden, the noiseless oars
identical in shape, broad, oblique, like moistened sunbeams. A sailor
tried to sing; he remained that way,
his mouth spread open like a hole
in which the ocean's glitter reappeared.

I, in turn, removed my belt then; I felt
my movement placid, inescapable, inexplicable,
possessing the authenticity of metaphysics—as though I were removing
a primeval noose from round my neck. I held my belt a little,

κ' ύστερ' ακούμπησα τη μιά της άκρη στο νερό, βλέποντας να χαράζει
480   μια γαλήνια γραμμή μέσα στο απέραντο, ενώ, ταυτόχρονα,
στα δάχτυλά μου αντιχτυπούσε ο ακίνητος σφυγμός
μιας σπάνιας ελαφρότητας. Τότε,
τράβηξα απ' το νερό τη ζώνη μου, κ' έτσι βρεγμένη
την έσφιξα και πάλι δυνατά στη μέση μου.

Καμμιά φορά, το φώς του λυκόφωτος είναι μια φώτιση—δεν είναι;—
έτσι άπλετα καθρεφτισμένο στο νερό, ενωμένο
με το ίδιο το είδωλό του, αυτόνομο
απέναντι της νύχτας και της μέρας—μια ολότελα ανεξάρτητη σύνθεση
της νύχτας και της μέρας. Το φέγγος εκείνο,
490   τόσο σύντομο, κι αθάνατο ωστόσο,—ένας ολόχρυσος θώρακας
ασφαλής τριγύρω στο στήθος μας· προπάντων
εκείνο το άτρωτο, λεπτότατο στρώμα του αέρα
ανάμεσα στο θώρακα και στη σάρκα μας, που επιστρέφει ξανά προς τα μέσα
την κίνηση της αναπνοής μας προς τα έξω. Κάποτε,
σε μια βαθύτατη εισπνοή, νιώθουμε τις αιχμές του στήθους μας
ν' αγγίζουν μυστικά το μέταλλο του θώρακα, δροσισμένο απ' το δείλι,
με την υπέρτατη ηδονή του ανύπαρκτου, σ' ερωτικήν απτότητα.

Μπορώ να σού δείξω το σημάδι της ζώνης πάνω στο σώμα μου—
σφραγίδα ενός μικρού τροχού—το χαραγμένο αποτύπωμα της πόρτας.
500   Ώ, ναι, η ελευθερία είναι πάντα κλειστή, περισφίγγει
ολόκληρο το σώμα—και τη φτέρνα οπωσδήποτε.
Το σφίξιμο, άλλωστε, της ζώνης, υποχρεώνει το στήθος να φαρδαίνει.
Αυτή η βαθειά κι οδυνηρή απομάκρυνση, που λίγο-λίγο ημερεύει.

Όμως, ας μας φυλάξουν οι θεοί να μη γίνουμε αιχμάλωτοι
έστω και της πιο ωραίας ακόμη αποκάλυψης, μη χάσουμε για πάντα
την τρυφερήν αφέλεια των μεταμορφώσεων
και την έσχατη πράξη του λόγου. Ίσως αυτό να σε φόβιζε μόνον
μέσα στην πλήρη μοναξιά σου,—κ' η έλλειψη των αντικειμένων, λέω,

then rested one end upon the water and watched it etch
a peaceful track within the infinite, while simultaneously
a motionless pulsation of uncommon buoyancy
resounded in my fingers. Afterwards,
I hauled my belt out of the water and secured it
tightly again, wet as it was, around my waist.

On occasion the light of twilight is enlightening, is it not?—
mirrored so dazzlingly in the water, united
with its own image, autonomous
in relation to night and day, a completely independent synthesis
of night and day. This glimmer
so brief and yet immortal is a cuirass of pure gold
secured around our breasts, and most of all
it's that thinmost layer of invulnerable air,
between the cuirass and our flesh, that turns inward again
the outward motion of our breath. Sometimes,
during the deepest inhalations, we feel the tips of our chest
covertly graze the cuirass's evening-cooled metal, feel them
contact non-existence with the extreme delight of tactile sensuality.

I can show you the belt's mark upon my body,
a small wheel stamped there, the engraving of the clasp.
Freedom—O, yes—is always buckled and taut
round the entire body, including without fail the heel.
The belt's tight embrace, in addition, obliges the chest to expand.
It's that deep and painful estrangement which grows tractable in time.

May the gods, however, keep us from falling prisoner
to even the most beautiful of revelations, lest we lose forever
the tender ingenuousness that transforms actuality,
and the ultimate action: speech. Perhaps this alone dismayed you
in your thoroughgoing isolation; also, I'd say, the lack of objects,

όχι για χρήση σου, μα για επαφή, για σύγκριση και για παράσταση,
510 για αδελφική παρομοίωση του απέραντου και στάθμηση του αστάθμητου.

Γι' αυτό, τουλάχιστον, γύρνα μαζί μας. Τον περήφανο πόνο
της ασυντρόφιαστης αγιοσύνης σου, δε θα τον μαρτυρήσω σε κανέναν.
Κανένας δε θα καταλάβει ούτε κανένας ποτέ θα τρομάξει
απ' την ανέγγιχτη ευφροσύνη της ελευθερίας σου. Το προσωπείο της
    δράσης,
που σούχω φέρει κρυφά μες στο γυλιό μου, θα καλύψει
το διάφανο, μακρινό πρόσωπό σου. Φόρεσέ το. Πάμε.

Όταν θα φτάσουμε στην Τροία, το ξύλινο άλογο, που σούλεγα,
θάναι έτοιμο πιά. Εκεί μέσα θα κρυφτώ μαζί με τα όπλα σου. Αυτό θάναι
το προσωπείο το δικό μου, και των όπλων σου άλλωστε. Έτσι μόνο
520 τη νίκη θα κερδίσουμε. Αυτό θάναι
η νίκη μου,—κ' η νίκη σου θέλω να πώ. Θάναι η νίκη
όλων μαζί των Ελλήνων και των Θεών τους.—Τί να γίνει;
μονάχα τέτοιες νίκες υπάρχουν. Ας πηγαίνουμε.

Πέρασαν πια τα δέκα χρόνια. Πλησιάζει το τέλος.
Έλα να δεις ό,τι πρόβλεψες. Να δεις με τι λάφυρα
ανταλλάξαμε τόσους νεκρούς μας· με τι δικές μας εχθρότητες
ανταλλάξαμε τους παλιούς μας εχθρούς. Μέσα στα ερείπια,
που οι στήλες των καπνών θα υψώνονται κάθετα προς τον ήλιο,
ανάμεσα στους σκοτωμένους, τις πεσμένες ασπίδες, τους τροχούς των
    δίφρων,
530 ανάμεσα στους γόους των νικημένων και των νικητών, το δικό σου
νοητικό, μειλίχιο χαμόγελο θα μας είναι ένα φέγγος,
η δική σου επιείκεια και σιωπή, μια πυξίδα.

Έλα· σε χρειαζόμαστε όχι μόνο για τη νίκη, μά, προπάντων,
μετά τη νίκη·—όταν θα μπούμε, όσοι απομείνουμε, ξανά στα καράβια,
    γυρίζοντας
μαζί με την Ελένη, γερασμένη κατά δέκα χρόνια,

not for you to use but rather for coming into contact; for comparisons and
   representations;
for brotherly images of the illimitable and calculations of the incalculable.

Return with us, if only because of this. I shall betray to no one
the dignified sufferings of your uncompanioned saintliness.
No one will comprehend your freedom's unmarred joy
or be frightened by it ever. The mask of action,
which I have brought you hidden in my pack, will conceal
your remote, transparent face. Put it on. Let's be going.

When we get to Troy, the wooden horse I described to you
will be ready. I shall hide in it, together with your weapons. Such will be
my own disguise, my mask, and your weapons' mask as well. In this way
   only
shall we gain the victory. This subterfuge will be
my triumph—yours too, I mean to say. It will be the victory
of all the Greeks together and of their gods. What did you expect?
Such victories are the only ones. Let's be on our way.

The ten years are over now. The end is near.
Come to see what you foresaw. See for what variety of plunder
we exchanged so many of our dead, for what internal hatreds
we exchanged our former enemies. Amid the debris
whose smoke will rise in upright columns toward the sun,
amid the slain, the fallen shields, the chariot-wheels,
amid the groans of vanquisher and vanquished,
your affable, intelligent smile will be a light for us,
your clemency and silence a compass.

Come. We need you not just for the victory but after it especially,
when we board the ships again (those who have survived) to return
with Helen—a Helen ten years older,

με αλλοιωμένη προφορά, με παραστάσεις άλλες μες στα μάτια της,
κρύβοντας σε μακριά, χρυσοποίκιλτα πέπλα
την ξενητειά της και τα γηρατειά της, κρύβοντας
μες στα δικά της πέπλα και τη δική μας ξενητειά, την τύψη, την απελπισία
540 και τον μεγάλο, αφυγάδευτο τρόμο της ερώτησης:
γιατί ήρθαμε, γιατί πολεμήσαμε, γιατί και πού επιστρέφουμε;

Θαρρώ πως κ' οι πιο ωραίες γυναίκες, σαν γεράσουνε,
γίνονται κάτι σα μητέρες, όλο συγκατάβαση και πικρή καρτερία,
όλο στοργή και τρυφερότητα, κι αυτή μεταμφιεσμένη
σε ρητή τάχα δικαιοσύνη των αναγκαίων σφαλμάτων,
των αναγκαίων απωλειών, των αναγκαίων δέκα χρόνια. Τότε, οι γυναίκες
φουχτώνουν τα κλειδιά της ζώνης τους και με τις δυο παλάμες τους,
με μια κοινότατη χειρονομία σα να τις έπιασε σφάχτης στη μέση—
ωραίες γυναίκες, γερασμένες, μυθικές μητέρες,
550 σε μια ύστατη χειρονομία απλής αγιότητας:
μη δούμε πως εκείνα τα κλειδιά τίποτε πια δεν ξεκλειδώνουν.

Πώς θα το αντέξουμε το βλέμμα της Ελένης,
πίσω απ' τα σκοτεινά, σπιθίζοντα πέπλα της,
μέσα στο μελιχρό φέγγος των άστρων, στην ανερεύνητη νύχτα,
ενώ οι κωπηλάτες θα σιωπούν και τα κουπιά θα χτυπάνε
τα μυστικά, ωκεάνεια τύμπανα της επιστροφής, στο ρυθμό του
    ανεπίστρεπτου;

Γι' αυτή την ώρα, τουλάχιστον, μείνε κοντά μας. Αυτό μάς χρειάζεται
περισσότερο ακόμη κι απ' τα όπλα σου. Και το γνωρίζεις.
Ιδού το προσωπείο που σού έφερα. Φόρεσέ το. Πηγαίνουμε.

*(Ο ήρεμος γενειοφόρος, πήρε το πορσωπείο και το ακούμπησε χάμω. Δεν
το φόρεσε. Το πρόσωπό του λίγο-λίγο μεταμορφώνεται. Γίνεται πιο νέο, πιο
θετικό, πιο παρόν. Σα ν' αντιγράφει το προσωπείο. Μεγάλη παύση κι αναμονή.
Ένα άστρο έπεσε. Ο Νέος ένιωσε ένα ελάχιστο φύσημα, στο πρόσωπό του και
τα μαλλιά του χώρισαν στρωτά στη μέση απο μόνα τους, σαν από μια λεπτή,*

160

her accent altered, different scenes in her vision,
concealing her exile and old age behind
long, gold-embroidered veils, concealing
our own exile too behind her veils, our remorse, despair,
and the huge inescapable fear of asking
why we went, why we fought, why we are going home—and where.

Even the most beautiful women become something like mothers, I suppose,
when they grow old, full of self-abasement and sorrowful persistence,
full of tenderness and parental affection—and that disguised
as the supposedly strict justice of unavoidable error,
unavoidable loss, the unavoidable ten years. Women
clutch the key-ring at their belts with both their palms then
in a gesture wholly common, as though racked by abdominal pangs—
beautiful women grown old, mythical mothers
in an ultimate gesture of unaffected saintliness,
lest we realize that those keys can never unlock anything again.

Helen's gaze: how shall we endure it
behind her sombre, sparkling veils,
amid the honeyed brightness of the stars in unfathomable night,
while the rowers hold their silence and the oars are beating
ocean's secret timbrels of return in the tempo of all things that do not re-
    turn?

Remain with us, at least for now. This we need
even more than we need your weapons—as you yourself well know.
Here is the mask I've brought for you. Put it on. We're leaving.

(The serene man with the beard takes the mask and rests it on the ground. He does not put it on. Little by little his face is transformed. It becomes younger, more positive, more present—it seems to duplicate the mask. A long pause. Great expectation. A star shoots across the sky. The youth feels a scant breeze on his face, and his hair is parted neatly in the middle, spontaneously, as if by a fine

χρυσή χτένα. Κάτω, στ' ακρογιάλι, ακούγεται το τραγούδι των ναυτών—ένα απροσποίητο, λαϊκό τραγούδι, περικλείνοντας σκοινιά, κατάρτια, κωπηλάτες, άστρα, πίκρα πολλή και λεβεντιά και καρτερία—όλη τη σκοτεινή, σπιθόβολη θάλασσα, όλη την απεραντοσύνη, σε ανθρώπινα μέτρα. Ίσως νάταν το ίδιο τραγούδι, που, από άλλο δρόμο, είχε γνωρίσει κι ο Ερημίτης. Κ' ίσως γι' αυτό να πήρε την απόφασή του. Σηκώθηκε ήσυχα, έφερε απ' τη σπηλιά τα όπλα του, τα παρέδωσε στον Νέο, τον άφησε να περάσει μπροστά,και τον ακολούθησε προς το ακρογιάλι. Καθώς προχωρούσε ανάμεσα στις πέτρες και στα ξεράγκαθα, έβλεπε τα όπλα του που προπορεύονταν, να λαμπυρίζουν στην αστροφεγγιά κι άκουγε ν' αντηχεί στο μέταλλό τους το τραγούδι των ναυτών. Κ' είταν έτσι σα ν' ακολουθούσε όχι τον Νέο, αλλά τα ίδια του τα όπλα, βαδίζοντας προς τα εκεί που έδειχναν πάντα οι στιλπνές, καλοακονισμένες αιχμές τους—εναντίον του θανάτου. Κ' εκείνο το προσωπείο είχε απομείνει εκεί πάνω, στα βράχια, έξω απ' τη σπηλιά, λαμπυρίζοντας κι αυτό μες στη μυστηριώδη μακαριότητα της νύχτας, με μια παράξενη, ακατανόητη κατάφαση).

ΑΘΗΝΑ, ΣΑΜΟΣ, Μάης 1963 – Οχτώβρης 1965

162

golden comb. The crew's song is audible from the shore below: an unassuming folksong which encompasses hawsers, masts, rowers, stars, abundant sorrow, gallantry and persistence, the whole murky sparkling sea, the whole of infinity, in human dimensions. Perhaps it is the same song that the anchorite came to know by other means. And perhaps this is why he made his decision. He rises calmly, fetches his weapons from the cave, hands them over to the youth, allows him to go out in front, and follows him toward the shore. While advancing between stones and thistles, he sees his weapons glitter in the starlight as they precede him, and he hears the crew's folksong reverberate against their metal. Thus it seems that he is following not the youth but his weapons themselves, heading in the direction that their burnished, well-honed tips ceaselessly indicate: against death. The mask has remained up above on the stones, outside the cave. It too glitters in the mysterious nocturnal beatitude—with a curious, incomprehensible affirmation.)

Athens, Samos, May 1963 – October 1965

2. Η ΣΟΝΑΤΑ ΤΟΥ ΣΕΛΗΝΟΦΩΤΟΣ

(Ανοιξιάτικο βράδι. Μεγάλο δωμάτιο παλιού σπιτιού. Μία ηλικιωμένη γυναίκα
ντυμένη στα μαύρα μιλάει σ' έναν νέο. Δεν έχουν ανάψει φως. Απ' τα δυο
παράθυρα μπαίνει ένα αμείλικτο φεγγαρόφωτο. Ξέχασα να πω ότι η Γυναίκα
με τα Μαύρα έχει εκδώσει δυο-τρεις ενδιαφέρουσες ποιητικές συλλογές
θρησκευτικής πνοής. Λοιπόν, η Γυναίκα με τα Μαύρα μιλάει στον νέο.)

1   Άφησέ με νάρθω μαζί σου. Τι φεγγάρι απόψε!
    Είναι καλό το φεγγάρι,—δε θα φαίνεται
    που άσπρισαν τα μαλλιά μου. Το φεγγάρι
    θα κάνει πάλι χρυσά τα μαλλιά μου. Δε θα καταλάβεις.
    Άφησέ με νάρθω μαζί σου.

    Όταν έχει φεγγάρι, μεγαλώνουν οι σκιές μες στο σπίτι,
    αόρατα χέρια τραβούν τις κουρτίνες,
    ένα δάχτυλο αχνό γράφει στη σκόνη του πιάνου
    λησμονημένα λόγια—δε θέλω να τ' ακούσω. Σώπα.

10 Άφησέ με νάρθω μαζί σου
    λίγο πιο κάτου, ως τη μάντρα του τουβλάδικου,
    ως εκεί που στρίβει ο δρόμος και φαίνεται
    η πολιτεία τσιμεντένια κι αέρινη, ασβεστωμένη με φεγγαρόφωτο,
    τόσο αδιάφορη κι άυλη,
    τόσο θετική σαν μεταφυσική
    που μπορείς επιτέλους να πιστέψεις πως υπάρχεις και δεν υπάρχεις
    πως ποτέ δεν υπήρξες, δεν υπήρξε ο χρόνος κ' η φθορά του.
    Άφησέ με νάρθω μαζί σου.

2. THE MOONLIGHT SONATA

(An evening in springtime. A large room in an old house. A woman advanced in years is speaking to a young man. She is dressed entirely in black. They have not turned on the lights. Pitiless moonlight enters through the two windows. Oh, I forgot to mention that the woman in black has published two or three collections of verse—interesting volumes, religious in spirit.... As I was saying, the woman in black is addressing the young man.)

Let me come with you. What a moon tonight!
The moon is kind—no one will sense
my hair's turned gray. The moon
will make it blond again. You will not notice.
Let me come with you.

Moonlight lengthens shadows inside the house,
unseen hands draw aside the drapes,
a sallow finger writes long-forgotten words
in the piano's dust—I refuse to hear them. Quiet!

Let me come with you
a little way, as far as the brickyard wall,
where the road turns and downtown
slips into view, all concrete and thin air, stuccoed white with moonlight,
so unconcerned and immaterial
so positively real (as though metaphysical)
you can believe at last that you exist and do not exist,
that you never did exist, nor did time exist, nor time's ruins.
Let me come with you.

Θα καθήσουμε λίγο στο πεζούλι, πάνω στο ύψωμα,
20   κι όπως θα μας φυσάει ο ανοιξιάτικος αέρας
μπορεί να φαντάζουμε κιόλας πως θα πετάξουμε,
γιατί, πολλές φορές, και τώρα ακόμη, ακούω το θόρυβο του φουστανιού
    μου,
σαν το θόρυβο δυο δυνατών φτερών που ανοιγοκλείνουν,
κι όταν κλείνεσαι μέσα σ' αυτόν τον ήχο του πετάγματος
νιώθεις κρουστό το λαιμό σου, τα πλευρά σου, τη σάρκα σου,
κι έτσι σφιγμένος μες στους μυώνες του γαλάζιου αγέρα,
μέσα στα ρωμαλέα νεύρα του ύψους,
δεν έχει σημασία αν φεύγεις ή αν γυρίζεις
κι ούτε έχει σημασία που άσπρισαν τα μαλλιά μου,
30   (δεν είναι τούτο η λύπη μου—η λύπη μου
είναι που δεν ασπρίζει κι ούτε η καρδιά μου).
Άφησέ με νάρθω μαζί σου.

Το ξέρω πως καθένας μονάχος πορεύεται στον έρωτα,
μονάχος στη δόξα και στο θάνατο.
Το ξέρω. Το δοκίμασα. Δεν ωφελεί.
Άφησέ με νάρθω μαζί σου.

Τούτο το σπίτι στοίχειωσε, με διώχνει—
θέλω να πω έχει παλιώσει πολύ, τα καρφιά ξεκολλάνε,
τα κάδρα ρίχνονται σα να βουτάνε στο κενό,
40   οι σουβάδες πέφτουν αθόρυβα
όπως πέφτει το καπέλο του πεθαμένου απ' την κρεμάστρα στο σκοτεινό
    διάδρομο
όπως πέφτει το μάλλινο τριμμένο γάντι της σιωπής απ' τα γόνατά της
ή όπως πέφτει μια λουρίδα φεγγάρι στην παλιά, ξεκοιλιασμένη πολυθρόνα.

Κάποτε υπήρξε νέα κι αυτή,—όχι η φωτογραφία που κοιτάς με τόση
    δυσπιστία—
λέω για την πολυθρόνα, πολύ αναπαυτική, μπορούσες ώρες ολόκληρες να
    κάθεσαι

We'll sit a while on the wall at the vantage point
and spring winds will blow on us in such a way
we might even imagine we'll take flight,
since often (and now as well) the swish of my skirt
sounds to me like the swish of two strong, flapping wings,
and when one is shut inside that sound of flight
one feels throat, ribs, flesh all packed together—
cramped like that between the blue wind's muscles,
between the sky's robust sinews,
who cares if you go away or return,
who cares if my hair's turned gray,
(what I regret is something else: I regret
my heart's not turning gray as well).
Let me come with you.

I know that everyone makes do—alone—with love,
alone with fame and death.
I know; I've had my try. It doesn't help.
Let me come with you.

This house is haunted now; it's evicting me.
I mean it's grown so very old the picture hooks work loose,
the paintings drop as though diving into a void,
plaster falls without a sound,
as a dead man's hat falls from the peg in the darkened hallway,
as silence's frayed woolen glove falls from her knees
or a ribbon of moonlight falls on the old, disemboweled armchair.

That was young, too, once upon a time. Not the photograph
    your viewing with such disbelief—
I mean the armchair; very comfortable, you could lounge in it for hours at a
    stretch,

και με κλεισμένα μάτια να ονειρεύεσαι ό,τι τύχει
—μιαν αμμουδιά στρωτή, νοτισμένη, στιλβωμένη από φεγγάρι,
πιο στιλβωμένη απ' τα παλιά λουστρίνια μου που κάθε μήνα τα δίνω στο
στιλβωτήριο της γωνιάς,
ή ένα πανί ψαρόβαρκας που χάνεται στο βάθος λικνισμένο απ' την ίδια του
ανάσα,
50 τριγωνικό πανί σα μαντίλι διπλωμένο λοξά μόνο στα δυο
σα να μην είχε τίποτα να κλείσει ή να κρατήσει
ή ν' ανεμίσει διάπλατο σε αποχαιρετισμό. Πάντα μου είχα μανία με τα
μαντίλια,
όχι για να κρατήσω τίποτα δεμένο,
τίποτα σπόρους λουλουδιών ή χαμομήλι μαζεμένο στους αγρούς με το
λιόγερμα
ή να το δέσω τέσσερις κόμπους σαν το σκουφί που φοράνε οι εργάτες στο
αντικρινό γιαπί
ή να σκουπίσω τα μάτια μου,—διατήρησα καλή την όρασή μου·
ποτέ μου δεν φόρεσα γυαλιά. Μια απλή ιδιοτροπία τα μαντίλια.

Τώρα τα διπλώνω στα τέσσερα, στα οχτώ, στα δεκάξι
ν' απασχολώ τα δάχτυλά μου. Και τώρα θυμήθηκα
60 πως έτσι μετρούσα τη μουσική σαν πήγαινα στο Ωδείο
με μπλε ποδιά κι άσπρο γιακά, με δυο ξανθές πλεξούδες
—8, 16, 32, 64—
κρατημένη απ' το χέρι μιάς μικρής φίλης μου ροδακινιάς όλο φως και ροζ
λουλούδια,
(συχώρεσέ μου αυτά τα λόγια—κακή συνήθεια)—32, 64,—κ' οι δικοί μου
στήριζαν
μεγάλες ελπίδες στο μουσικό μου τάλαντο. Λοιπόν, σούλεγα για την
πολυθρόνα—
ξεκοιλιασμένη—φαίνονται οι σκουριασμένες σούστες, τα άχερα—
έλεγα να την πάω δίπλα στο επιπλοποιείο,
μα που καιρός και λεφτά και διάθεση—τι να πρωτοδιορθώσεις;—
έλεγα να ρίξω ένα σεντόνι πάνω της,—φοβήθηκα
70 τ' άσπρο σεντόνι σε τέτοιο φεγγαρόφωτο. Εδώ κάθησαν

168

your eyes shut tight, and dream of whatever comes to mind
— of a sandy stretch of wetted shoreline polished by the moon,
more highly polished than my ancient patent-leather boots I
    bring each month to the shoe-black's on the corner,
or of a fisherman's sail that fades in the offing, rocked by breaths its very
    own,
a three-cornered sail like a pocket handkerchief folded only once, diagonally,
as if lacking some object to enclose or hold,
or any need to wave farewell, opened wide.... I've always had a craze for
    handkerchiefs,
not to bind things up and hold them
— some flower seeds or camomile picked in fields at sundown—
or to knot four times, like those head-cloths worn by laborers on
    the construction job across the street,
or to wipe my eyes—my sight continues strong,
I never have worn glasses. Handkerchiefs with me are merely an eccentricity.

I fold them now in fourths, in eighths, sixteenths
to occupy my fingers. Ah, now I remember:
I counted music just like that when I went to the Conservatory
in my blue pinafore and white collar, with my two blond braids
— 8, 16, 32, 64—
holding hands with my beloved little peachtree, all sunlight and rose-red
    blossoms
(forgive such language; an unfortunate habit)—32, 64—my parents
had high hopes for my musical talent. But I was telling you about the arm-
    chair—
disemboweled—the rusty springs hang out, the stuffing too—
I thought to take it to the upholsterer's nearby,
but where's the time and money, or the proper frame of mind—what to fix
    first?—
I thought to throw a sheet over it—I dreaded
the white sheet in such moonlight. In that chair people

άνθρωποι που ονειρεύτηκαν μεγάλα όνειρα, όπως κι εσύ κι όπως κ' εγώ άλλωστε,
και τώρα ξεκουράζονται κάτω απ' το χώμα δίχως να ενοχλούνται απ' τη βροχή ή το φεγγάρι.
Άφησέ με νάρθω μαζί σου.

Θα σταθούμε λιγάκι στην κορφή της μαρμάρινης σκάλας του Άη-Νικόλα,
ύστερα εσύ θα κατηφορίσεις κι εγώ θα γυρίσω πίσω
έχοντας στ' αριστερό πλευρό μου τη ζέστα απ' το τυχαίο άγγιγμα του σακακιού σου
κι ακόμη μερικά τετράγωνα φώτα από μικρά συνοικιακά παράθυρα
κι αυτή την πάλλευκη άχνα απ' το φεγγάρι πούναι σα μια μεγάλη συνοδεία ασημένιων κύκνων—
και δε φοβάμαι αυτή την έκφραση, γιατί εγώ
80   πολλές ανοιξιάτικες νύχτες συνομίλησα άλλοτε με το Θεό που μου εμφανίστηκε
ντυμένος την αχλύ και τη δόξα ενός τέτοιου σεληνόφωτος,
και πολλούς νέους, πιο ωραίος κι από σένα ακόμη, του εθυσίασα,
έτσι λευκή κι απρόσιτη ν' ατμίζομαι μες στη λευκή μου φλόγα, στη λευκότητα του σεληνόφωτος,
πυρπολημένη απ' τ' αδηφάγα μάτια των αντρών κι απ' τη δισταχτικήν έκσταση των εφήβων,
πολιορκημένη από εξαίσια, ηλιοκαμένα σώματα,
άλκιμα μέλη γυμνασμένα στο κολύμπι, στο κουπί, στο στίβο, στο ποδόσφαιρο (που έκανα πως δεν τάβλεπα)
μέτωπα, χείλη και λαιμοί, γόνατα, δάχτυλα και μάτια,
στέρνα και μπράτσα και μηροί (κι αλήθεια δεν τάβλεπα)
—ξέρεις, καμμιά φορά, θαυμάζοντας, ξεχνάς ό,τι θαυμάζεις, σου φθάνει ο θαυμασμός σου,—
90   θέ μου, τι μάτια πάναστρα, κι ανυψωνόμουν σε μιαν αποθέωση αρνημένων άστρων
γιατί, έτσι πολιορκημένη απ' έξω κι από μέσα,
άλλος δρόμος δε μούμενε παρά μονάχα προς τα πάνω ή προς τα κάτω.
    —Όχι, δε φτάνει.
Άφησέ με νάρθω μαζί σου.

170

sat who dreamt great dreams, just as you have and I have too;
they're at rest now beneath the sod, untroubled by rain or moonlight.
Let me come with you.

We'll pause at the top of Saint Nicholas's marble steps;
then you'll go down and I'll go home again,
having on my left some warmth from the chance brush of your jacket
and a few squares of light still, from our neighborhood's tiny windows,
and that pearl-white vapor from the moon, like a grand escort of silvery
    swans—
the expression does not frighten me, since in the past
on many a spring night I conversed with God, who revealed himself to me
dressed in the haze and splendor of such moonlight,
and I sacrificed to him scads of young men even handsomer than yourself,
so that, white and inaccessible, I keep turning to vapor inside my
    snow-white passion, inside the moonlight's whiteness,
kindled by men's voracious looks and youngsters' hesitating ecstasies,
besieged by exquisite sun-tanned bodies,
sturdy limbs trained at swimming, soccer, crew and track (I pretended not to
    stare at them),
brows, lips and throats, knees, fingers and eyes,
chests and arms and thighs (really, I did not stare at them)
— you know, occasionally in your admiration you forget what you admire;
    your admiration itself suffices—
good Lord, what star-filled eyes! Up I flew to those repudiated stars in their
    glorification,
for, besieged like that from outside and within,
the only course left to me was toward the heights—or depths. No, that won't
    do.
Let me come with you.

Το ξέρω η ώρα είναι πια περασμένη. Άφησέ με,
γιατί τόσα χρόνια, μέρες και νύχτες και πορφυρά μεσημέρια, έμεινα μόνη,
ανένδοτη, μόνη και πάναγνη,
ακόμη στη συζυγική μου κλίνη πάναγνη και μόνη,
γράφοντας ένδοξους στίχους στα γόνατα του Θεού,
στίχους που, σε διαβεβαιώ, θα μείνουνε σα λαξευμένοι σε άμεμπτο μάρμαρο
100 πέρα απ' τη ζωή μου και τη ζωή σου, πέρα πολύ. Δε φτάνει.
Άφησέ με νάρθω μαζί σου.

Τούτο το σπίτι δε με σηκώνει πια.
Δεν αντέχω να το σηκώνω στη ράχη μου.
Πρέπει πάντα να προσέχεις, να προσέχεις,
να στεριώνεις τον τοίχο με το μεγάλο μπουφέ
να στεριώνεις τον μπουφέ με το πανάρχαιο σκαλιστό τραπέζι
να στεριώνεις το τραπέζι με τις καρέκλες
να στεριώνεις τις καρέκλες με τα χέρια σου
να βάζεις τον ώμο σου κάτω απ' το δοκάρι που κρέμασε.
110 Και το πιάνο, σα μαύρο φέρετρο κλεισμένο. Δεν τολμάς να τ' ανοίξεις.
Όλο να προσέχεις, να προσέχεις, μην πέσουν, μην πέσεις. Δεν αντέχω.
Άφησέ με νάρθω μαζί σου.

Τούτο το σπίτι, παρ' όλους τους νεκρούς του, δεν εννοεί να πεθάνει.
Επιμένει να ζει με τους νεκρούς του
να ζει απ' τους νεκρούς του
να ζει απ' τη βεβαιότητα του θανάτου του
και να νοικοκυρεύει ακόμη τους νεκρούς του σ' ετοιμόρροπα κρεββάτια και
    ράφια.
Άφησέ με νάρθω μαζί σου.

Εδώ, όσο σιγά κι αν περπατήσω μες στην άχνα της βραδιάς,
120 είτε με τις παντούφλες, είτε ξυπόλητη,
κάτι θα τρίξει,—ένα τζάμι ραγίζει ή κάποιος καθρέφτης,

I know the time is late. Let me,
since so very many years, days and nights, crimson afternoons, I've re-
    mained alone,
unyielding, alone and oh! so chaste,
alone and chaste even in my marriage bed,
composing on God's lap illustrious poems,
poems that shall remain, I assure you,
well beyond my lifetime and yours, as though
carved into unblemished marble—well beyond. That won't do.
Let me come with you.

I cannot stand this house an instant longer,
cannot bear to carry it on my back.
You must always take care, take care,
to steady the wall with the large buffet,
to steady the buffet with the antique, carved table,
to steady the table with the chairs,
to steady the chairs with your hands,
to place your shoulder beneath the sagging beam.
And the piano: like a black coffin, nailed shut. You dare not open it.
Nothing but taking care, taking care, lest they collapse, lest you collapse. I
    cannot bear it.
Let me come with you.

This house, despite its many dead, does not plan to die.
It persists in living with its dead,
living off its dead,
living off the certainty of its own death
and arranging even its corpses tidily on dilapidated beds and shelves.
Let me come with you.

However lightly I tread in here, in the haze of evening,
whether barefooted or with slippers,
something is bound to creak—a windowpane or mirror cracks,

κάποια βήματα ακούγονται,—δεν είναι δικά μου.
Έξω, στο δρόμο μπορεί να μην ακούγονται τούτα τα βήματα,—
η μεταμέλεια, λένε, φοράει ξυλοπάπουτσα,—
κι αν κάνεις αν κοιτάξεις σ' αυτόν ή στον άλλον καθρέφτη,
πίσω απ' τη σκόνη και τις ραγισματιές,
διακρίνεις πιο θαμπό και πιο τεμαχισμένο το πρόσωπό σου,
το πρόσωπο σου που άλλο δε ζήτησες στη ζωή παρά να το κρατήσεις
    καθάριο κι αδιαίρετο.

Τα χείλη του ποτηριού γυαλίζουν στο φεγγαρόφωτο
130 σαν κυκλικό ξυράφι—πώς να το φέρω στα χείλη μου;
όσο κι αν διψώ,—πώς να το φέρω;—Βλέπεις;
έχω ακόμη διάθεση για παρομοιώσεις,—αυτό μου απόμεινε,
αυτό με βεβαιώνει ακόμη πως δε λείπω.
Άφησέ με νάρθω μαζί σου.

Φορές-φορές, την ώρα πού βραδιάζει, έχω την αίσθηση
πως έξω άπ' τα παράθυρα περνάει ο αρκουδιάρης με την γριά βαριά του
    αρκούδα
με το μαλλί της όλο αγκάθια και τριβόλια
σηκώνοντας σκόνη στο συνοικιακό δρόμο
ένα ερημικό σύννεφο σκόνη που θυμιάζει το σούρουπο
140 και τα παιδιά έχουν γυρίσει σπίτια τους για το δείπνο και δεν τ' αφήνουν
    πια να βγουν έξω
μ' όλο που πίσω απ' τους τοίχους μαντεύουν το περπάτημα της γριάς
    αρκούδας—
κ' η αρκούδα κουρασμένη πορεύεται μες στη σοφία της μοναξιάς της, μην
    ξέροντας για που και γιατί—
έχει βαρύνει, δεν μπορεί πια να χορεύει στα πισινά της πόδια
δεν μπορεί να φοράει τη δαντελένια σκουφίτσα της να διασκεδάζει τα
    παιδιά, τούς αργόσχολους τους απαιτητικούς
και το μόνο που θέλει είναι να πλαγιάσει στο χώμα
αφήνοντας να την πατάνε στην κοιλιά, παίζοντας έτσι το τελευταίο παιχνίδι
    της,
δείχνοντας την τρομερή της δύναμη για παραίτηση,

174

some footsteps sound: not mine.
Outside in the street perhaps those footsteps are not heard
—regret, they say, wears wooden clogs—
and if you chance to gaze into that mirror or the other one,
behind the dust and cracks you'll view your face
still dimmer and more shattered,
your face which all your life you sought simply to preserve clear and whole.

The rim of the drinking glass sparkles in the moonlight
like a circular razor-edge. How can I lift that glass to my lips?
Whatever my thirst, how can I? You see?
My penchant for similitudes remains—that's been left to me,
that assures me still I have not slipped away.
Let me come with you.

Every now and then as evening falls I sense
the trainer passing outside my window with his aged, plodding bear,
her fur all thorns and thistles,
stirring up the dust in our neighborhood street,
a solitary dust-cloud misting the sundown with incense.
The children have gone inside for supper and cannot come out again,
even though from behind the walls they surmise the old bear's footsteps.
And the bear: wearily she carries on inside the wisdom of her solitude, not
    knowing wither or why.
She's overweight and cannot dance upon her two hind legs anymore,
cannot wear her petite lace bonnet to entertain children, idlers, or those who
    importune,
and all she wants is to stretch out on the ground
and let them step upon her belly, playing thus her final game,
showing her grim capacity for renunciation,

την ανυπακοή της στα συμφέροντα των άλλων, στους κρίκους των χειλιών
  της, στην ανάγκη των δοντιών της,
την ανυπακοή της στον πόνο και στη ζωή
150 με τη σίγουρη συμμαχία του θανάτου—έστω κ' ενός αργού θανάτου—
την τελική της ανυπακοή στο θάνατο με τη συνέχεια και τη γνώση της ζωής
που ανηφοράει με γνώση και με πράξη πάνω απ' τη σκλαβιά της.

Μα ποιος μπορεί να παίξει ως το τέλος αυτό το παιχνίδι;
Κ' η αρκούδα σηκώνεται πάλι και πορεύεται
υπακούοντας στο λουρί της, στους κρίκους της, στα δόντια της,
χαμογελώντας με τα σκισμένα χείλη της στις πενταροδεκάρες που τις
  ρίχνουνε τα ωραία και ανυποψίαστα παιδιά
(ωραία ακριβώς γιατί είναι ανυποψίαστα)
και λέγοντας ευχαριστώ. Γιατί οι αρκούδες που γεράσανε
το μόνο που έμαθαν να λένε είναι: ευχαριστώ, ευχαριστώ.
160 Άφησέ με νάρθω μαζί σου.

Τούτο το σπίτι με πνίγει. Μάλιστα η κουζίνα
είναι σαν το βυθό της θάλασσας. Τα μπρίκια κρεμασμένα γυαλίζουν
σα στρογγυλά, μεγάλα μάτια απίθανων ψαριών,
τα πιάτα σαλεύουν αργά σαν τις μέδουσες,
φύκια και όστρακα πιάνονται στα μαλλιά μου—δεν μπορώ να τα ξεκολλήσω
  ύστερα,
δεν μπορώ ν' ανέβω πάλι στην επιφάνεια—
ο δίσκος μου πέφτει απ' τα χέρια άηχος,—σωριάζομαι
και βλέπω τις φυσαλίδες απ' την ανάσα μου ν' ανεβαίνουν, ν' ανεβαίνουν
και προσπαθώ να διασκεδάσω κοιτάζοντάς τες
170 κι αναρωτιέμαι τι θα λέει αν κάποιος βρίσκεται από πάνω και βλέπει αυτές
  τις φυσαλίδες,
τάχα πως πνίγεται κάποιος ή πως ένας δύτης ανιχνεύει τους βυθούς;

Κι αλήθεια δεν είναι λίγες οι φορές που ανακαλύπτω εκεί, στο βάθος του
  πνιγμού,
κοράλλια και μαργαριτάρια και θησαυρούς ναυαγισμένων πλοίων,

her defiance of others' profit, the rings through her lips, her teeth's require-
    ments,
her defiance of pain and life
through firm alliance with death, even a lingering death,
her ultimate defiance of death through life's continuity and awareness:
life that, through awareness and deed, transcends its own enslavement.

But who can play that game out to its end?
The bear gets up again and moves on,
obeying her leash, her rings, her teeth,
smiling with torn lips at the pennies tossed her by lovely unsuspecting chil-
    dren
(lovely precisely because unsuspecting)
and saying "Thanks." Because bears grown old
have learned to utter one thing only: "Thanks." "Thanks."
Let me come with you.

This house is drowning me. Indeed the kitchen
seems like an ocean floor. The hanging saucepans gleam
like huge round eyes of improbable fish,
the plates sway slowly back and forth like jellyfish,
seaweed and shells get tangled in my hair—I can't dislodge them afterwards,
I can't float up again to the surface—
the serving tray slips from my hands and drops without a sound. I sink
    downward in a heap
and watch the bubbles from my breath rise up, rise up,
and try to enjoy the sight of them,
wondering, If someone were above and saw those bubbles, what would he
    say?
That a person was drowning, I suppose, or that some diver was probing the
    deep.

Indeed, I often discover pearls and coral and sunken treasure there at the
    depths of drowning,
unforeseen encounters, pearls from past, present and future,

απρόοπτες συναντήσεις, και χτεσινά και σημερινά και μελλούμενα,
μιαν επαλήθευση σχεδόν αιωνιότητας,
κάποιο ξανάσασμα, κάποιο χαμόγελο αθανασίας, όπως λένε,
μιαν ευτυχία, μια μέθη, κι ενθουσιασμόν ακόμη,
κοράλλια και μαργαριτάρια και ζαφείρια·
μονάχα που δεν ξέρω να τα δώσω—όχι, τα δίνω·
180 μονάχα που δεν ξέρω αν μπορούν να τα πάρουν—πάντως εγώ τα δίνω.
Άφησέ με νάρθω μαζί σου.

Μια στιγμή, να πάρω τη ζακέτα μου.
Τούτο τον άστατο καιρό, όσο νάναι, πρέπει να φυλαγόμαστε.
Έχει υγρασία τα βράδια, και το φεγγάρι
δε σου φαίνεται, αλήθεια, πως επιτείνει την ψύχρα;

Άσε να σου κουμπώσω το πουκάμισο—τι δυνατό το στήθος σου,
—τί δυνατό φεγγάρι,—η πολυθρόνα, λέω—κι όταν σηκώνω το φλιτζάνι απ᾽
   το τραπέζι
μένει από κάτω μια τρύπα σιωπή, βάζω αμέσως την παλάμη μου επάνω
να μην κοιτάξω μέσα,—αφήνω πάλι το φλιτζάνι στη θέση του·
190 και το φεγγάρι μια τρύπα στο κρανίο του κόσμου—μην κοιτάξεις μέσα,
είναι μια δύναμη μαγνητική που σε τραβάει—μην κοιτάξεις, μην κοιτάχτε,
ακούστε με που σας μιλάω—θα πέσετε μέσα. Τούτος ο ίλιγγος
ωραίος, ανάλαφρος—θα πέσεις,—
ένα μαρμάρινο πηγάδι το φεγγάρι,
ίσκιοι σαλεύουν και βουβά φτερά, μυστηριακές φωνές—δεν τις ακούτε;

Βαθύ-βαθύ το πέσιμο,
βαθύ-βαθύ το ανέβασμα,
το αέρινο άγαλμα κρουστό μες στ᾽ ανοιχτά φτερά του,
βαθειά βαθειά η αμείλικτη ευεργεσία της σιωπής,—
200 τρέμουσες φωταψίες της άλλης όχθης, όπως ταλαντεύεσαι μες στο ίδιο σου
   το κύμα,
ανάσα ωκεανού. Ωραίος ανάλαφρος
ο ίλιγγος τούτος,—πρόσεξε, θα πέσεις. Μην κοιτάς εμένα,

178

confirmations, almost, of eternal life,
a bit of relief, a certain smile (as they say) of immortality,
some happiness, intoxication, even enthusiasm…,
pearls and coral and sapphires;
only I'm ignorant of how to give them away—no, I do give them away;
only I'm ignorant of whether they can be received—in any case, I give them,
    I do.
Let me come with you.

Just a moment, I'll get my wrap.
One cannot be too careful while this shifting weather lasts.
The evenings are damp, and the moon
really does increase the chill, wouldn't you say?

Let me button up your shirt for you. What a strong chest you have,
— what a strong moon—the armchair. I mean—and when I clear the cof-
    feecup from the table,
a hole-full of silence remains beneath. I lay my palm on top at once
so as not to look inside. The cup I restore to its place again.
The moon: that too a hole in the skull of the universe. Do not look inside.
A magnetic force attracts us—do not look, do not look, dear sir—
listen, sir, to what I'm saying—you'll fall. This swoon,
so lovely, so light—you'll fall—
the moon's a cistern lined with marble,
shadows sway, and soundless wings, mysterious voices—can't you hear
    them, sir?

Deep, deep the fall,
deep, deep the rise,
the airy statue packed firm between outstretched wings;
deep, deep the harsh benevolence of silence;
brilliant flickerings from the other shore, as when you're rocking in your
    personal wake;
ocean air. So lovely and so light
this swoon—look out, you'll fall! Pay no attention to me;

εμένα η θέση μου είναι το ταλάντευμα—ο εξαίσιος ίλιγγος. Έτσι κάθε
   απόβραδο
έχω λιγάκι πονοκέφαλο, κάτι ζαλάδες.

Συχνά πετάγομαι στο φαρμακείο απέναντι για καμιάν ασπιρίνη
άλλοτε πάλι βαριέμαι και μένω με τον πονοκέφαλό μου
ν' ακούω μες στους τοίχους τον κούφιο θόρυβο που κάνουν οι σωλήνες του
   νερού,
ή ψήνω έναν καφέ, και, πάντα αφηρημένη,
ξεχνιέμαι κ' ετοιμάζω δυο—ποιος να τον πιει τον άλλον;—
210   αστείο αλήθεια, τον αφήνω στο περβάζι να κρυώνει
ή κάποτε πίνω και τον δεύτερο, κοιτάζοντας απ' το παράθυρο τον πράσινο
   γλόμπο του φαρμακείου
σαν το πράσινο φως ενός αθόρυβου τραίνου που έρχεται να με πάρει
με τα μαντίλια μου, τα σταβοπατημένα μου παπούτσια, τη μαύρη τσάντα
   μου, τα ποιήματά μου,
χωρίς καθόλου βαλίτσες—τί να τις κάνεις;—
Άφησέ με νάρθω μαζί σου.

Ά, φεύγεις; Καληνύχτα. Όχι, δε θάρθω. Καληνύχτα.
Εγώ θα βγω σε λίγο. Ευχαριστώ. Γιατί επιτέλους, πρέπει
να βγω απ' αυτό το τσακισμένο σπίτι.
Πρέπει να δω λιγάκι πολιτεία,—όχι, όχι το φεγγάρι—
220   την πολιτεία με τα ροζιασμένα χέρια της, την πολιτεία του μεροκάματου,
την πολιτεία που ορκίζεται στο ψωμί και στη γροθιά της
την πολιτεία που όλους μας αντέχει στην ράχη της
με τις μικρότητές μας, τις κακίες, τις έχτρες μας,
με τις φιλοδοξίες, την άγνοιά μας και τα γερατειά μας,—
ν' ακούσω τα μεγάλα βήματα της πολιτείας,
να μην ακούω πια τα βήματά σου
μήτε τα βήματα του Θεού, μήτε και τα δικά μου βήματα. Καληνύχτα.

(Το δωμάτιο σκοτεινιάζει. Φαίνεται πως κάποιο σύννεφο θάκρυψε το φεγγάρι.
Μονομιάς, σαν κάποιο χέρι να δυνάμωσε το ραδιόφωνο του γειτονικού μπαρ,

my place is in the rocking—the superb swoon. Thus every evening
I have a slight headache, a touch of vertigo.

Often I pop over to the drugstore across the street for aspirin,
but sometimes I could not care less, and stay here with my headache
to listen to the water pipes making hollow noises in the walls,
or brew some coffee and, absentmindedly as usual,
forget myself and prepare a second cup—who will drink it?
A joke, to be sure. I leave it on the windowsill to get cold
or sometimes I drink that second cup as well, gazing through the
    panes at the green globe of the drugstore's lamp—
as at the green light of a noiseless train arriving to take me away
with my handkerchiefs, my shoes all down-at-heel, my black purse, my
    poems,
without a single valise— what use are valises?
Let me come with you.

Oh, you're leaving? Good night. No, I won't be coming. Good night.
I'll go out in a little while. Thank you. Because I really must
escape this dilapidated house at long last.
I must see a bit of the city—no, not the moon—
the city with its calloused hands, the city of day laborers,
the city that swears upon bread and its fists,
the city that carries us all on its back
together with our pettiness, our malice, our enmity,
together with our ambition, our ignorance and our aging—
I must hear the city's giant footsteps
so I will not hear your footsteps any longer,
or God's, or my own. Good night.

(*The room grows dark. It seems that some cloud must have covered the moon.
Suddenly, as if a hand had turned up the radio in the neighborhood bar, an extremely familiar musical motif can be heard. I realized then that this entire scene*

ακούστηκε μία πολύ γνώστη μουσική φράση. Και τότε κατάλαβα πως όλη τούτη τη σκηνή τη συνόδευε χαμηλόφωνα η «Σονάτα του Σεληνόφωτος», μόνο το πρώτο μέρος. Ο Νέος θα κατηφορίζει τώρα μ' ένα ειρωνικό κ' ίσως συμπονετικό χαμόγελο στα καλογραμμένα χείλη του και μ' ένα συναίσθημα απελευθέρωσης. Όταν θα φτάσει ακριβώς στον Άη-Νικόλα, πριν κατέβει τη μαρμάρινη σκάλα, θα γελάσει,—ένα γέλιο δυνατό, ασυγκράτητο. Το γέλιο του δε θ' ακουστεί καθόλου ανάρμοστα κάτω απ' το φεγγάρι. Ίσως το μόνο ανάρμοστο νάναι το ότι δεν είναι καθόλου ανάρμοστο. Σε λίγο, ο Νέος θα σωπάσει, θα σοβαρευτεί και θα πει «η παρακμή μιάς εποχής». Έτσι, ολότελα ήσυχος πια, θα ξεκουμπώσει πάλι το πουκάμισό του και θα τραβήξει το δρόμο του. Όσο για τη γυναίκα με τα μαύρα, δεν ξέρω αν βγήκε τελικά απ' το σπίτι. Το φεγγαρόφωτο λάμπει ξανά. Και στις γωνιές του δωματίου οι σκιές σφίγγονται από μιαν αβάσταχτη μετάνοια, σχεδόν οργή, όχι τόσο για τη ζωή, όσο για την άχρηστη εξομολόγηση. Ακούτε; Το ραδιόφωνο συνεχίζει) :

Αθήνα, Ιούνιος 1956

had been accompanied pianissimo by *The Moonlight Sonata*, the first movement only. *The young man must be going down the slope now, with an ironic and perhaps compassionate smile on his well-shaped lips, and with a sense of liberation. As soon as he reaches Saint Nicholas's, there precisely, before he descends the marble steps, he will laugh—loudly, without restraint. His laughter will sound not the least bit improper beneath the moon—the only improper part being perhaps that it is not the least bit improper. Soon the young man, falling silent, will turn serious and say: "The decline of an era." Thus entirely at ease again, he will undo the buttons of his shirt, as before, and continue on his way. As for the woman in black, I do not know if she finally did go out. The moonlight is shining once more, and the shadows in the corners of her room are huddling together out of unbearable remorse, rage almost, directed not so much at life as at the futility of confession. Do you hear? The radio plays on . . .*) :

Athens, June 1956

3. ΕΙΡΗΝΗ

1   Τ' όνειρο του παιδιού είναι η ειρήνη,
Τ' όνειρο της μάνας είναι η ειρήνη.
Τα λόγια της αγάπης κάτω απ' τα δέντρα,
είναι η ειρήνη.

Ο πατέρας που γυρνάει τ' απόβραδο μ' ένα φαρδύ χαμόγελο στα μάτια
μ' ένα ζεμπίλι στα χέρια του γεμάτο φρούτα
κ' οι σταγόνες του ιδρώτα στο μέτωπό του
είναι όπως οι σταγόνες του σταμνιού που παγώνει το νερό στο παράθυρο,
είναι η ειρήνη.

10   Όταν οι ουλές απ' τις λαβωματιές κλείνουν στο πρόσωπο του κόσμου
και μες στους λάκκους πούσκαψαν οι οβίδες φυτεύουμε δέντρα
και στις καρδιές πούκαψε η πυρκαϊά δένει τα πρώτα της μπουμπούκια η
    ελπίδα
κ' οι νεκροί μπορούν να γείρουν στο πλευρό τους και να κοιμηθούν δίχως
    παράπονο
ξέροντας πως δεν πήγε το αίμα τους του κάκου,
είναι η ειρήνη.

Ειρήνη είναι η μυρωδιά του φαγητού το βράδι,
τότε που το σταμάτημα του αυτοκινήτου στο δρόμο δεν είναι φόβος,
τότε που το χτύπημα στην πόρτα σημαίνει φίλος,
και το άνοιγμα του παράθυρου κάθε ώρα σημαίνει ουρανός
20   γιορτάζοντας τα μάτια μας με τις μακρινές καμπάνες των χρωμάτων του,
είναι η ειρήνη.

3. PEACE

The child's dream is peace
The mother's dream is peace
Words of love beneath trees—
is peace

The father coming home at night with a broad smile in his eyes,
with a shopping bag full of fruit in his hands,
and the sweat-drops on his brow
are like the drop on a jug that's just cooling water on the window-sill—
is peace,

When the scars and wounds heal on everyone's
face and we plant trees in bomb craters
and hope forms its first buds in hearts scorched by wildfire
and corpses can turn on their sides and sleep without complaint
knowing their blood did not spill in vain—
is peace.

Peace is the smell of supper in the evening.
When a car stopping in the street is not fear,
when a knock on the door means a friend,
and to open the window at any time means sky
regaling our eyes with its colors' distant chimes—
is peace.

Ειρήνη είναι ένα ποτήρι ζεστό γάλα κ' ένα βιβλίο μπροστά στο παιδί που
    ξυπνάει.
Τότε που τα στάχυα γέρνουν τόνα στ' άλλο λέγοντας: το φως το φως, το
    φως,
και ξεχειλάει η στεφάνη του ορίζοντα φως
είναι η ειρήνη.

Τότε που οι φυλακές επισκευάζονται να γίνουν βιβλιοθήκες,
τότε που ένά τραγούδι ανεβαίνει από κατώφλι σε κατώφλι τη νύχτα
τότε που τ' ανοιξιάτικο φεγγάρι βγαίνει απ' το σύγνεφο
όπως βγαίνει απ' το κουρείο της συνοικίας φρεσκοξυρισμένος ο εργάτης το
    Σαββατόβραδο
30 είναι η ειρήνη.

Τότε που η μέρα που πέρασε
δεν είναι μια μέρα που χάθηκε
μα είναι η ρίζα που ανεβάζει τα φύλλα της χαράς μέσα στο βράδι
κ' είναι μια κερδισμένη μέρα κ' ένας δίκαιος ύπνος
τότε που νιώθεις πάλι ο ήλιος να δένει βιαστικά τα κορδόνια του
να κυνηγήσει τη λύπη απ' τις γωνιές του χρόνου
είναι η ειρήνη.

Ειρήνη είναι οι θημωνιές των αχτίνων στους κάμπους του καλοκαιριού
είναι τ' αλφαβητάρι της καλοσύνης στα γόνατα της αυγής.
40 Όταν λες: αδελφέ μου—όταν λέμε: αύριο θα χτίσουμε
όταν χτίζουμε και τραγουδάμε
είναι η ειρήνη.

Τότε που ο θάνατος πιάνει λίγο τόπο στην καρδιά
κ' οι καμινάδες δείχνουν με σίγουρα δάχτυλα την ευτυχία,
τότε που το μεγάλο γαρύφαλλο του δειλινού
το ίδιο μπορεί νά το μυρίσει ο ποιητής κι ο προλετάριος
είναι η ειρήνη.

Peace is a glass of warm milk and a book in front of the waking child.
When ears of wheat lean to one another saying Light light light
and the horizon's garland brims with light—
is peace.

When they renovate prisons to make them libraries,
when nighttime songs float from doorway to doorway,
when the spring moon steps out of its clouds
like a freshly shaven worker stepping out of the barber's on Saturday night—
is peace.

When the day gone by
is not a lost day
but a seedling that lifts leaves of joy into the twilight,
a day saved and a well-earned sleep,
when you sense the sun tying its shoelaces again
to chase gloom out of time's corners—
is peace.

Peace is bundles of summer sunbeams on the plains,
is decency's primer on the lap of dawn.
When you say Brother, when we all say Tomorrow we shall build,
when we build and sing—
is peace.

When death claims little space in the heart
and chimneys point out happiness with assured fingers,
when poet and proletarian may smell
dusk's great carnation equally—
is peace.

Η ειρήνη είναι τα σφιγμένα χέρια των ανθρώπων
είναι το ζεστό ψωμί στο τραπέζι του κόσμου
50 είναι το χαμόγελο της μάνας.
Μονάχο αυτό.
Τίποτ' άλλο δεν είναι η ειρήνη.

Και τ' αλέτρια που χαράζουν βαθειές αυλακιές σ' όλη τη γης
ένα όνομα μονάχα γράφουν:
Ειρήνη. Τίποτ' άλλο. Ειρήνη.

Πάνω στις ράγες των στίχων μου
το τραίνο που προχωρεί στο μέλλον
φορτωμένο στάρι και τριαντάφυλλα
είναι η ειρήνη.

60 Αδέρφια μου,
μες στήν ειρήνη διάπλατα ανασαίνει
όλος ο κόσμος με όλα τα όνειρά του.
Δόστε τα χέρια, αδέρφια μου,
αυτό 'ναι η ειρήνη.

Αθήνα, Γενάρης 1953

(*Ποιήματα Β'*, Εκδόσεις Κέδρος)

Peace is mankind's linked hands,
oven-fresh bread on the whole world's table,
a mother's smile.
Only that.
Nothing else is peace.

Plows carving deep furrows everywhere on earth
write one name only:
Peace. Nothing else. Peace.

The train that heads for the future
on my poetry's rails
loaded with wheat and roses—
is peace.

Brothers,
in peacetime the whole world swells
its lungs with all its dreams.
Join hands, brothers—
that is peace.

Athens, January, 1953

Publications Record

The author wishes to thank those who have previously published sections of this work.

"Introduction to *Yannis Ritsos: Selected Poems*" — *Yannis Ritsos: Selected Poems*, tr. Nikos Stangos (Penguin, 1974).

"Myth in Modern Greek Literature, with Special Attention to Ritsos's *Philoctetes*" — *Books Abroad* 48 (1974), pp. 15-19.

"Yannis Ritsos's *Philoctetes*: Approaching a Modern Poem through its Ancient Prototype—A Methodology and a Demonstration" — *Classical and Modern Literature*, vol. 9, no. 4 (July 1989), pp. 299-313. An earlier version printed in Peter Bien, *Αντίθεση και σύνθεση στην ποίηση του Γιάννη Ρίτσου* (Athens: Kedros, 1980), 77-109.

"Antithesis and Synthesis in Yannis Ritsos's *Philoctetes*" — In Peter Bien, *Αντίθεση και σύνθεση στην ποίηση του Γιάννη Ρίτσου* (Athens: Kedros, 1980), 111-146. [Published here, in English, for the first time.]

"Ritsos's Painterly Technique in Long and Short Poems" — *Το Γιοφύρι* (Sydney, Australia) no. 11 (1990-91), pp. 5-11.

"A Ritualistic View of Ritsos's *The Moonlight Sonata*" — *Journal of Modern Hellenism*, no. 19/20 (Winter 2002-2003), pp. 29-46.

"Orestes' Cow" — *The Charioteer*, no. 29/30 (1987-1988), pp. 126-132. An earlier version printed in Peter Bien, *Αντίθεση και σύνθεση στην ποίηση του Γιάννη Ρίτσου* (Athens: Kedros, 1980), 147-156.

"Ritsos" — *Critical Survey of Poetry*: Foreign Language Series. (La Canada, California: Salem Press, 1984), pp. 1344-1352.

"Introduction to *The Wavering Scales*" — *The Wavering Scales* (Red Dragonfly Press, 2006).

'Philoctetes' — *Shenandoah* (Fall 1975), pp. 68-87. Reprinted in Yannis Ritsos: *Selected Poems 1938 – 1988* (Brockport, NY: BOA Editions, 1989), pp. 149-169.

'The Moonlight Sonata' — *New England Review* (Spring 1979), pp. 301-309. Reprinted in A Century of Greek Poetry 1900 – 2000 (Cosmos Publishing, 2004), pp. 282-301.

'Peace' — *Greece in Print*, no. 145 (May 2000), pp. 19-20.

Bibliography

The Collected Works of Yannis Ritsos are published by Kedros, Athens (in Greek): Currently at 15 Volumes and 6,254 pages:

Ποιήματα Α' (Kedros, 1961) 528 σελ.

Ποιήματα Β' (Kedros, 1961) 480 σελ.

Ποιήματα Γ' (Kedros, 1964) 528 σελ.

Τέταρτη Διάσταση (Kedros, 1972) 320 σελ.

Τα Επικαιρικά (Kedros, 1975) 468 σελ.

Ποιήματα Δ' (Kedros, 1975) 500 σελ.

Γίγνεσθαι (Kedros, 1977) 380 σελ.

Επινίκια (Kedros, 1984) 248 σελ.

Ποιήματα Θ' (Kedros, 1989) 352 σελ.

Ποιήματα Ι' (Kedros, 1989) 480 σελ.

Αργά, πολύ αργά μέσα στή νύχτα (Kedros, 1991) 264 σελ.

Ποιήματα ΙΑ' (Kedros, 1993) 436 σελ.

Ποιήματα ΙΒ' (Kedros, 1997) 480 σελ.

Ποιήματα ΙΓ' (Kedros, 1999) 368 σελ.

Ποιήματα ΙΔ' (Kedros, 2007) 422 σελ.